KU-094-771

irreverent guides

London

other irreverent guides: Amsterdam • Boston • Chicago
Manhattan • Miami • New Orleans • Paris • San Francisco
Santa Fe • Virgin Islands • Washington, D.C.

guides

ndon

BY

KATE SEKULES

A BALLIETT & FITZGERALD BOOK

MACMILLAN • USA

Where to bathe like a Lady...

Portobello, see Accommodations

Dine like a Lord...

Simpson's in the Strand Restaurant, see Dining

Wander lonely as a cloud...

Hyde Park, see Getting Outside

Watch the sun set on the Empire...

London Central Mosque, see Getting Outside

Shop in the most fabulous way...

Selfridges, see Shopping

Go cruising on a barge...

Regent's Canal, see Diversions

Dance in the street...

Notting Hill Carnival, see Diversions

Make fun of busbies...

Changing of the Guard, see Diversions

Talk with the animals...

London Zoo, see Diversions

Look for the *Toilet of Venus...*

The National Gallery, see Diversions

Meet the real East Enders.

Pearlies, see Diversions

what's so irreverent?

It's up to you.

You can buy a traditional guidebook with its fluff, its promotional hype, its let's-find-something-nice-to-say-about-everything point of view. Or you can buy an Irreverent guide.

What the Irreverents give you is the lowdown, the inside story. They have nothing to sell but the truth, which includes a balance of good and bad. They praise, they trash, they weigh, and leave the final decisions up to you. No tourist board, no chamber of commerce will ever recommend them.

Our writers are insiders, who feel passionate about the cities they live in, and have strong opinions they want to share with you. They take a special pleasure leading you where other guides fear to tread.

How irreverent are they? One of our authors insisted on writing under a pseudonym. "I couldn't show my face in town again if I used my own name," she told me. "My friends would never speak to me." Such is the price of honesty. She, like you, should know she'll always have a friend at Frommer's.

Warm regards,

Michael Spring

Michael Spring
Publisher

a disclaimer

Prices fluctuate in the course of time, and travel information changes under the impact of the varied and volatile factors that influence the travel industry. Neither the author nor the publisher can be held responsible for the experiences of readers while traveling. Readers are invited to write to the publisher with ideas, comments, and suggestions for future editions.

about the author

Native Londoner **Kate Sekules** writes about travel, food, and fitness for magazines, including *The New Yorker, Travel and Leisure, Health and Fitness, Time Out,* and *Vogue,* and for the *Condé Nast* Web site *Epicurious.*

photo credits

Page 1: © Bo Zaunders; Page 2: courtesy of the British Tourist Authority; Page 4, top: courtesy of The Portobello, bottom: courtesy of The British Tourist Authority; Page 5, top: courtesy of The British Tourist Authority, middle: © 1995 Judith Langley, bottom: courtesy of The British Tourist Authority; Page 6, top: courtesy of the British Tourist Authority, bottom: © David Corio; Page 7, top and bottom: © 1995 Judith Langley; Page 8, top: courtesy of The British Tourist Authority, bottom: © David Corio.

Balliett & Fitzgerald, Inc.
Series editor: Holly Hughes / Executive editor: Tom Dyja / Managing editor: Duncan Bock / Production editor: Howard Slatkin / Photo editors: Rachel Florman, Sue Canavan / Assistant editor: Maria Fernandez / Editorial assistants: Sam Weinman, Jennifer Leben

Design by Tsang Seymour Design Studio
All maps © Simon & Schuster, Inc.

Air travel assistance courtesy of Continental Airlines

MACMILLAN TRAVEL
A Simon & Schuster Macmillan Company
1633 Broadway
New York, NY 10019

ISBN 0-02-860654-X
ISSN 1085-4789

special sales

Bulk purchase (10+ copies) of Frommer's Travel Guides are available to corporations at special discounts. The Special Sales Department can produce custom editions to be used as premiums and/or for sales promotions to suit individual needs. Existing editions can be produced with custom cover imprints such as corporate logos. For more information write to: Special Sales, Simon & Schuster, 1633 Broadway, New York, NY 10019.

Manufactured in the United States of America

contents

introduction

The only thing about London that everybody knows is that there's a royal family here. Londoners tend to be blasé about the queen, but she raises a dilemma for the visitor: whether to do the royal thing or ignore it. Do you, as you secretly are dying to, visit Buckingham Palace, Kensington Palace, Kew Palace, Hampton Court Palace, the Crown Jewels, the Queen's Gallery, the Queen's Mews, St. James's Palace, and take a day trip to Windsor Castle, or do you grit your teeth and pretend you're not interested? Oh, the hell with it, you do the royals—with the proviso that you let go your preconceptions first. Because the pomp and circumstance of royal London today is as hollow as St. Paul's dome, and everyone knows the royal family is on its last legs. However, the history is still fascinating (if you choose, say, Hampton Court when it's not busy, over boring old Buck House) and the riches are impressive (if you don't think too hard about how they were amassed, or to whom they should belong).

Releasing preconceptions before you get to London is a good idea all round. If you arrive all hyped up with a headful of Big Ben in the mist and jolly rollicking pub singalongs, or gritty all-night illegal warehouse raves, or of whatever your ideal London consists, you'll be disappointed. To avoid further disappointment, you should also release another common misconception: that London is a beautiful city. Of course, there are many parts that are, but great chunks of England's capital are quite hideous. Tottenham Court Road—where Londoners buy electronic, hi-fi, and computer goods, and you'll almost certainly exit the tube there at some stage—is one of the ugliest streets in Europe. Oxford Street is no great shakes either, and all over the place, including most of the city, there is plenty of uninspired architecture that got hurled up after the World War II Blitz, plus acres of projects (called council housing here), awful Sixties blocks, and just tatty, shabby mush. There's a certain urban *jolie-laide* style about this real London, however, unlike the charmless reality of another misconception that should be corrected early on—that all the theater here is great. If you believe that, you may as well just tear up a dozen ten-pound notes now for practice. Anyway, you get the picture—London has a whole lot in it that guide books don't like.

Guide books—and many of the first-time visitors who are their consumers—would prefer it if London would stick to its old image, the one that left after the Fifties, when the "Great" in Great Britain still seemed an appropriate qualifier, and ladies wore white gloves to tea. That city of polite rituals, colonial hauteur, and gracious monuments was demolished once and for all by the Swinging Sixties—which in turn also left its handprint on London's image. That—plus the punky Seventies, and the money-mad Eighties—rendered London a much more complicated place, harder to grasp and still harder to penetrate.

For a concrete symbol of this city's image crisis, and a signifier of the complexity of modern London, take the Royal Festival Hall. This South Bank concert hall was built in the Fifties for the Festival of Britain—a public-relations scheme to swell the native breast with post-war hope and pride. It retains its original function as home of the London Philharmonic, but it also stages, say, the environmental flick *Koyaanisqatsi*, with Philip Glass conducting his score to it, while installed in the foyer are exhibits like the recent pair entitled "After Auschwitz" and "Homeworks," in which soon-to-be-lost crafts of the British Isles (blacksmithery, thatching, etc.) were demonstrated by their final practitioners. Upstairs, the masses are fed in The People's Palace, new (too new for our listings) restaurant of buzz-cut, cockney superchef Gary Rhodes, well known for extolling on TV the virtues of almost-lost British dishes like faggots and spotted dick. The entire building, along with its South Bank Centre neighbors, is meanwhile due to be enshrined in a post-post-Postmodern, National Lottery-funded crystal canopy (echoes of the Victorian Crystal Palace built for the Great Exhibition), designed by Sir Richard Rogers, who is most famous for the Centre Georges Pompidou in Paris. (Rogers' wife, Ruthie, is known for launching London's rustic Tuscan cuisine craze in his firm's staff canteen, which long ago metamorphosed into the River Café—the priciest Italian restaurant in town.) It's easy to relate to the visitor's bewilderment at this spaghetti of cultural crossed wires—especially when you've been expecting Beefeaters and roast beef.

Another preconception is ready to bite the dust—the roast beef of England—dried up meat and leathery Yorkshire pudding and sad vegetables with the color boiled out. In the demolition of this old saw, Gary Rhodes and Ruthie Rogers are a mere two players in a cast of thousands, improvising a riveting kitchen drama. Neophytes are astonished to find London in its gastronomic early twenties, with childhood tantrums and teenage rebellions already past, and a glorious culinary confidence set in, influenced by every cuisine of the world. The high-octane dining scene is a measure of this once xenophobic city's looser relationship with Europe, and the world. England is, of course, officially part of Europe now, and boundary-free work permits mean more cross-fertilization with continental neighbors. The concrete link with France via the Channel tunnel has underlined that connection—even though the poor tunnel is economically ailing. London is also every bit as much a melting pot as New York, with West Indian, Bangladeshi, and Pakistani culture particularly firmly integrated—and not only in the outer boroughs. Look at Soho. Quite unlike its New York namesake, this square mile or so of the deepest West End, having hosted successive immigrant waves (French Huguenots in the late 17th century, then Italians, Germans, Russians, Poles, Greeks, Chinese), and gone through a protracted red-light and sleaze period, never lost its cosmopolitan, bohemian spiciness, and has settled in as London's playground of clubs and restaurants and a jumping gay scene. When you decide where to have your first dinner in London, perhaps you could bear this in mind. Too many tourists look only for fake Londons—the Ealing Studios *Passport to Pimlico* "cor blimey luv-a-duck guvnor" version, or some Dickensian, Jack the Ripper, pea-souper-over-the-Thames fantasy.

Of course, it's not wrong to seek auld London towne—and efforts to do so are amply supported by the tourist industry—but that is not the focus of this guide. The London that can't be packaged is harder to find, but more rewarding because it's personal. How to get personal with people who stay inside by the fire, throw dinner parties for each other, and belong to exclusive clubs you're not allowed to join is a challenge, but not a hopeless enterprise. To begin a relationship with London, it's best to dilute, or eschew, the tourist trail. See all the big sights on one visit, and you'll come away with your stiff-upper-lipped British bulldog prejudices reinforced—because it's relentless, hard work. Westminster Abbey, St. Paul's, the Houses of Parliament, Tower of London, and Buckingham Palace are heavy dough. Even when you add the leavening of art (the National, the Tate, the Hayward Galleries, and the Royal Academy), and include the amazing museums (the British, the Natural History, the Victoria & Albert, and the London), you're cramming for an exam, not living the good life. And you won't meet a soul who isn't a fellow tourist.

If you'd rather befriend the Londoner, there's no foolproof method. For every American who visits twice a year with their adopted London family whom they met in the line at the National Theatre, there's a sad story of a lonely week being snubbed in the pub and dining in Siberia. Since knowing people is the best route to some version of the real London, though, you should reach out, regardless of the British reputation. It's only habit that keeps us from talking to strangers, and the worst you'll have to deal with is a withering glance or a muttered reply. Pubs—those communal sitting rooms with large drinks cabinets—sometimes offer the perfect environment to get chatting, though they do revolve around alcohol (as do their "regulars"), and aren't the most comfortable environments for lone women. But alcohol sure does loosen the British tongue. Failing that, ask questions—we love trying to explain our culture. Ask about the rules of cricket; the class system; the difference between a *Guardian* and a *Telegraph* reader; whether anyone has heard of John Grisham and who's Jeffrey Archer anyway; what led *The Archers* to this crisis (that's a Radio 4 thing); what's with Brits and toilet humor; and, by all means, ask about the weather, which remains a popular and safe topic. At the bottom of the opening gambit hit-parade, you might find money, personal questions, the royals (too much cliché), American politics, and Hugh Grant.

Where to go to meet the candidates for your friendly overtures depends on where you're coming from. Midwesterners, suburbanites, and professionals won't bond with youth-culture-oriented neighborhoods, like Notting Hill and Camden Town. Perhaps only New Yorkers, San Franciscans, Angelenos, and other big city babes, who speak the language of street style, will. On the other hand, Chelsea—the swinging King's Road of the Sixties, and the Sex Pistols punk life of the Seventies—is now full of the scenes made by models and trust funders, Eurotrash and bankers, and is (along with neighboring Knightsbridge) quite the place to which Elvis Costello didn't want to go. For Chelsea's diametric opposite, you might want to go to Brixton, a 'hood far more West Indian than white-guys-with-dreadlocks Notting Hill, and which is also home to dyke chic, to bike messengers, and to young families restoring Georgian houses. It also has a reputation for being unsafe, and all of that makes it a draw for the hip and intrepid city anthropogist. College professors and free-lance creatives may find soulmates in Islington, where Camden kids go when they grow up. Islingtonians work in television or the print media, or act, and never leave their borough of restaurants, pubs, bookshops, boutiques, and the Almeida—London's best Off-West End theater.

But since you're not moving here forever, and your exploring time is limited, even the Almeida may be further off the West End than you have time to wander. Perhaps, like the priciest hotels on the British Monopoly board, you'll just keep landing on Mayfair and St. James's, following the royal path from Kensington to Belgravia, and merely grazing the green and pleasant surface of the city. But that's OK. Whatever you do in London, you'll be left to get on with it. Let's hope you feel at home here too.

London Neighborhoods

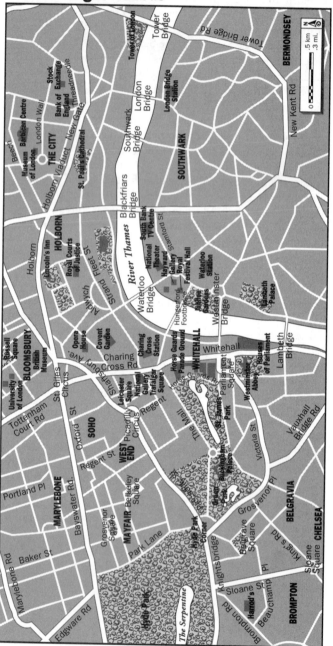

you probably didn't know

How to get London smarts... You can't. You have to live here at least two years to qualify for your provisional license as a Londoner, and that's just for tourist rights. Sure, London's a great city, but it inspires affection without trying at all. Its reputation for impenetrability is no myth. Londoners are friendly underneath, though. Swallow your pride and be persistent.

Where to get a drink after hours... English licensing laws forbid the selling of alcohol after 11pm. Since everybody, incuding those responsible for enforcing them, thinks these laws are stupid, laxity has been creeping nearer the West End. You used to have to pay club cover, eat, or be present at a "lock-in" in a neighborhood "local" to continue abusing your liver into the small hours. Then **The Atlantic** (tel. 0171/493–6150, 1 Shepherd Market, W1) got a pioneer 3am license in late 1993 and was followed by other late drinking arenas (**Bar Solona, Riki-Tik, The Edge, Brixtonian Backayard, Cuba**... see the Nightlife chapter), but none so big, so initially hip.

Where are the insomniacs?... **Bar Italia**, on **Frith Street** in Soho. The tiny, echt-Italian, stand-up espresso bar with a Rocky Marciano altar and stale panettone contains London's only life after 4am.

Where's the hot neighborhood?... There are two. For going out of an evening, Soho's still the place, as it has been since the 1950s, when bohemian friends of painter Francis Bacon colonized the **Colony Club** (an illicit drinking den—there is a pattern here). Now licit drinking dens—membership-only **Groucho**, **Fred's**, and **Soho House**—harbor hordes of media types, PR flacks, hacks, publishers, actors, and their ilk, while a fab gay ghetto has grown up around the main drag, Old Compton Street. Soho is also restaurant land. **Notting Hill**—the West London neighborhood around famous **Portobello Road**—is another restaurant land, but it's also got bars, galleries, markets, West Indian culture, even its own Carnival. Native Notting Hillbillies look cool and deconstructed, so you can't tell if they're slackers or trust-funders with a bestseller under their belt.

Where's the beach?... In Hyde Park, on the south side of the Serpentine. Don't believe it? Go look when the sun's out, and you'll realize that Londoners aren't scared of skin cancer. Or go at 6am on a midwinter's morning and see the **Serpentine Swimming Club** break the ice before diving in.

Where do you park?... You shouldn't have rented a car, but since you did, don't park beside a broken parking meter, a double yellow line, a single yellow line before 6pm, a red line, or a resident's parking bay. You may think you can ignore a parking ticket, but nobody escapes the immobilizing yellow wheel clamp. It'll cost you an entire day and about £120; the same goes if you're towed. Now that London has no centralized government, boroughs have taken it upon themselves to "clamp" down on parking cowboys and rake in a bit of cash. Really, park in an NCP multistory car park (they're all over town), despite the rip-off prices, because you'll never find a legal spot on the street.

When to be somewhere else... Christmas. The streets are deserted, and not a single cinema, theater, gallery, museum, or shop is open. The only places that will feed you are hotels, and they only have turkey.

Where are the top chefs?... Many are in hotels, especially since hotel mogul **Rocco Forte** went shopping for them. Some weren't for sale, though, like former Four Seasons' **Bruno Loubet** (Mr. Cuisine du Terroir), who has his own place, **Bistro Bruno**; like Simon Hopkinson

(Mr. God Chef), formerly at **Bibendum**, who has traded his toque for a newspaper column; like Fergus Henderson (Mr. Trendy Dishes), who owns St. John. And like Pierre Koffman (Mr. Gascon Genius), who's still at **La Tante Claire** after all these years. See the Dining chapter for the complete run-down.

How can we afford to sample their cooking?...
Lunch, prix fixe. The three-hour lunch never did die here, so you'll be in good company. Also, every February, the *Financial Times* does a promotion where top tables go for a ridiculously cheap amount, for five or ten pounds— entrance ticket is a copy of *FT*, printed on its distinctive pink paper, and booking is essential.

How to save buckets of cash on museums...
Obviously, you can go to the free ones, like the **British Museum**, and you could even be cheap and ignore the suggested voluntary donation at some others (a backhand fashion of charging admission). But once you've exhausted those possibilities, you'll have to buy a White Card, a relatively new cultural discount card that, having not been heavily promoted, has passed most Londoners by. This is a three- or seven-day passport ticket to 13 museums and galleries, including the **V&A** (which is apparently confused about how voluntary its voluntary donation is), its South Kensington neighbors the **Natural History** and **Science Museums**, the **Courtauld Institute Galleries**, and the **Hayward** and **Barbican Galleries**. See the Diversions chapter for full details.

Children's Hour
Some of our favorite characters in children's literature are Londoners. Mr. and Mrs. Dearly, who owned Pongo, Perdita and the 99 other dalmations, lived on the Outer Circle of Regent's Park while Wendy and Michael Darling left their Victorian house on the north side of Kensington Gardens for NeverNeverLand. As for bears, Paddington had a station named after him from which British Rail trains still depart for the West Country, and a certain bear named Winnie had residence for a time in the Polar Bear pit at the London Zoo.

How to stay with London friends when you haven't any... Upscale B&Bs are a new thing in a country where a B&B sign normally heralds a depressing room with no matching furniture. Unlike American B&Bs, which are often small inns, these London digs are truly private homes with rooms to let to an exclusive few. The **Bulldog Club** agency (tel 0171/622–6935) is top drawer—Amanda St. George practically runs a credit check on you before you're allowed into her friends' tony houses—and **Gail O'Farrell**'s got some gorgeous cottagey places in Hampstead and Highgate (phone her at 0171/722–6869). The **English Speaking Union** has a hosting scheme (tel 212/879-6800), though the standard of decor is not guaranteed, and there's always home-swapping. This works like it sounds: trading places with your counterparts in London. Although nearly all participants describe their abode accurately in the home-swap organizations' catalogs, Americans often experience an unexpected degree of culture shock when staying in an English home, running into privations like snowed-up iceboxes, lack of central heat, doormanless walk-ups (a normal London flat), and stick-shift cars with the wheel on the wrong side. If you're persnickety and inflexible, or if you're Martha Stewart and believe God is in the details, don't swap your home. Otherwise, get registered with Intervac (tel 0133/255–8931, 6 Siddals Lane, Allestree, Derby DE3 2DY); Homelink International (tel 01628/31951, 84 Lees Gardens, Maidenhead, Berks SL6 4NT); Home Base Holidays (tel 0181/886–8752, 7 Park Avenue, London N13 5PG); or the Worldwide Home Exchange Club (0171/589–6055, 45 Hans Place, London SW1X 0JZ), and start house-hunting.

Where does the Queen get her groceries?... Fortnum & Mason.

What is a Prom?... No, it's not a high school dance–this is the familiar name for the Henry Wood Promenade Concerts at the Royal Albert Hall, an incredibly popular annual summer series of concerts that don't cost much, especially if you "promenade," or BYO cushion and sit on the floor in front of the orchestra pit. All the big names of classical music appear at the Proms, and they're broadcast live on Radio 3. You know it's summer when it's Prom season.

How to order Indian food... With 1,500-odd Indian restaurants in London alone, curry is England's unofficial national cuisine. Everyone orders the following: onion bhajia (onion fritters), murgh tikka masala (yogurt-spice-marinated chicken breast, baked in the tandoor oven, and served with thick sauce), sag ghosh (lamb with spinach), mattar paneer (peas with cubes of Indian curd cheese), tarka dahl (garlic lentil sauce), and pulau rice (cooked in ghee and stock). If you want heat, order vindaloo; for extra mild and creamy, have korma. Beware of young men in packs on Saturday nights ordering chicken biriani and buckets of lager.

How to get designer labels cheap... Yes, shop the sales in January and June, when all the stores slash prices on the previous season's stuff. Visit consignment shops, too. But the best sources are "warehouse sales," where a single designer or a group of them offload samples and surplus to the cognoscenti. Look in the *Evening Standard*'s Tuesday fashion section, and in *Time Out*'s "Buys and Bargains" section for notices. Or call the office of your favorite London designer (Katharine Hamnett, Jasper Conran, Nicole Farhi) and ask about the next sample sale. See the Shopping chapter for more.

How to hear Queen Victoria... The **National Sound Archive** (tel 0171/589–6603, 29 Exhibition Rd., London) has a recording of Her Majesty made around 1880. Hear it (and about a million more historic sound bytes) by appointment.

How to get theater tickets when they're sold out... From the theater. Every theater holds at least one row of "house seats," which the management holds for their own use. If no one fabulously important wants to see the show that night, or the theater didn't overbook, the tickets are sold at the last possible moment, along with the "returns"—unpicked-up bookings. Some theaters want you to queue up that morning, others an hour or two before curtain. Call ahead to each theater for the policy. The better hotel concierges—usually the ones at posh hotels—are good at getting ahold of these in their special way.

What to do on Sunday... Sunday can be a really dead day in London, especially when you don't have a home to lounge around in. Sunday trading laws, which are based on the Christian Sabbath notion, lie behind this official enforcement of a day of rest, though they are fast being eroded. The other reason Sunday is sleepy is that Londoners are wading through a huge stack of Sunday papers—look on the newsagent's shelf that day and you'll see what we mean. But more active things you can do include: Go to market (especially the East End ones— Brick Lane, Petticoat Lane, Spitalfields); have an old-fashioned Sunday lunch; stroll in the park; play softball; see a movie. Some theaters are experimenting with performances on this traditionally "dark" day, too.

What not to do on Sunday... Don't go to the South Ken museums, or see the show at the Tate or the Royal Academy, unless you like crowds. Don't plan a fancy dinner, since most of the best restaurants are closed Sunday night (except for the hotel ones, that is).

What's the weather like?... This wouldn't be the number-one topic of conversation in London if anyone understood the British climate. Guidebooks tell you stories about 40-degree winters and 70-degree summers, but literally anything could happen. There was a hurricane in 1987, a 97-degree heatwave in 1989, long hot summers in 1976 and 1995, and nearly always a fortnight in April when temperatures hit the upper 80s—which sometimes gives way to frost in May. Sometimes the rain sets in for a week, but not in dramatic downpours or picturesque thunderstorms—just relentless soaking drizzle. The local light is flat and diffuse, which is sheer misery on those endless wet days, but absolute perfection on a sunny day in a park.

Do we need a gun?... No. The police increasingly carry firearms, it's true, but London is still a relatively safe city. Relative to where? Well, according to 1994 statistics on the past decade's crime rates, it's safer than Los Angeles, New York, and Rio de Janeiro, but more dangerous than Miami, Toronto, and Paris. London's average annual murder rate in the 1980s was one-tenth that of New York (183:1,859)—which must be largely a result of the fact that personal firearms are not yet an issue in the UK. Still, the usual city precautions for taking care of your property and your person apply. Just use common sense. More distressing is the rise in the number of homeless people you'll see wherever you go. At some point you will almost certainly be offered a copy of *The Big Issue*, the newspaper produced by and for the homeless, which can actually be worth reading.

How can I tell where I am?... Take a look at a map of London. See how big it is? London, which originally grew out of a pack of once-separate villages, is still divided into 32 boroughs—plus the City of London—each separately governed by its own council. Every corner street sign (big white rectangles, mounted on walls at about knee level) tells you which borough you're in, in smaller letters above the street name. But the borough system doesn't really tell you where you are; postcodes are marginally better, once you've deciphered them. The letters simply refer to compass points, with the *C* of "EC1" and "WC2" and so on denoting "central." The numbers seem helpful at first: "West Central One" is indeed sandwiched between "West One," "West Central Two," and "East Central One," with "North One" and "North West One" to the (that's right) north. However, travel a tiny bit farther, and you find that W2 segues into W11, that W8 lies next to SW7, and W9 is NW6's neighbor.

Why did the Londoner cross the river?... To get back to the other side. South Londoners hate the snobbish attitude of the majority that lives on the north side and thinks it needs a passport to cross a bridge. South London highlights include the National Theatre and South Bank Centre, which are on every visitor's list; Shakespeare's Globe, which should be; the "Gastrodrome"; and the Design Museum by Tower Bridge; Battersea Park and Clapham Common in which to escape other tourists; and entire neighborhoods to explore, such as Brixton.

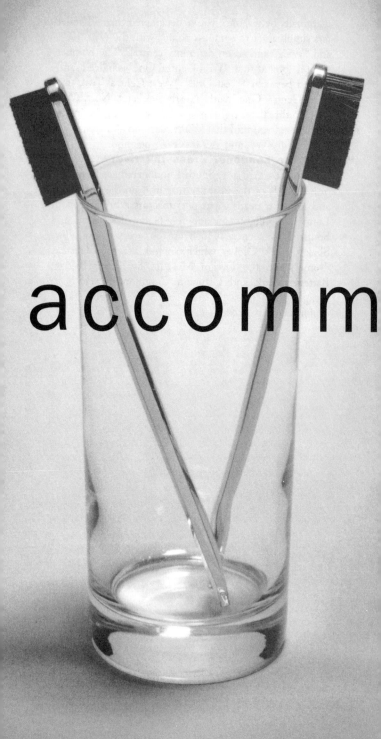

accomm

1

odations

Face it: This city
makes you pay
through the nose
for a place to lay
your head. You'll
have to capitulate
and consign half

your vacation funds to the hotel bed. Still, it pays to think ahead and spend those pounds wisely. London is blossoming with smaller, independent hotels, which often labor under the term "boutique hotel." We list several, and they're very good bets, offering so much deeper a London experience than those cookie-cutter chains or even some of the swankiest grand hotels. Of course, the best (and cheapest) way of all to get under London's skin is to stay with friends. If you don't have any, you can buy the next best thing—the hospitality of strangers in upscale B&Bs, still a relatively new concept in town.

Winning the Reservations Game

Try not to arrive roofless. Booking ahead not only gives you peace of mind, it also yields any special, weekend, or corporate rates that might be offered. Typically, though, it's the more expensive and bigger places that offer discounts, while the smaller hotels, guest houses, and B&Bs don't reduce their already lower rates. If you book a packaged holiday, you may be given a hotel's most boring, boxy, smallest room, but the rates are probably the lowest you could get for that property. Check into half-price programs—they're worth it if they include the hotel you like, which you can find out by calling ahead. Typically, you register, join, or buy a directory, which then accesses savings of up to 50% on the hotels in that program. Some to try are **Privilege Card International** (3391 Peachtree Rd. NE, Suite 110, Atlanta GA 30326, tel 800/236–9732), **Europe Hotel Directory** (Entertainment Publications, 40 Oakview St., Trumbull CT 06611, tel 800/445–4137), and **Great American Traveler** (Access, Box 27965, Salt Lake City UT 84127, tel 800/331–8867). You can also book hotels—more than one at a time, if you like—with a call to the London Tourist Board's Credit Card Hotline, which takes Access or Visa (tel 0171/824–8844). You will normally be asked for a deposit when you make a reservation, which will be deducted from the final bill. If you haven't made reservations in advance or are only booking a short stay, you may be asked to pay for the room on arrival. If so, check out the room before money changes hands.

Is There a Right Address?

To a certain sort of Londoner (they're usually called Sloane Rangers, after their Sloane Square stomping grounds, and Princess Di is the ultimate role model), **Knightsbridge** is the center not only of London, but of the world. For tourists, too, it's hard to beat, well served with tube, restaurants, and shopping—and Hyde Park on the doorstep. Just south of Knightsbridge, Belgravia is embassy territory, and some of the priciest real estate in town. As a tourist base it sure is peaceful, but there's not much more, except for pleasant strolls and Hyde Park.

Famously swinging in the sixties, **Chelsea**, a onetime artists' ghetto west of Belgravia, is expensive to live in and lovely to walk in. Its main drawback for visitors is inaccessibility, since there's a weird dearth of tube stops. There are buses galore, though, and attractions enough in the borough itself. Also west of the West End, green, peaceful, and expensive residential **Holland Park** is 10 minutes by tube from practically anywhere, yet has a distinctive out-of-the-maelstrom ambience, and one of London's loveliest small parks. **Kensington** is busier and more urban than neighboring Holland Park, while sharing some of its green and pleasant peaceful feel. South Kensington, with its tall-ceilinged houses, contains those giant Victorian cultural palaces—the museums. Streets are quieter and prices higher than farther north—except on the main roads (Brompton, Gloucester, Cromwell), where the opposite is the case. North of Holland Park, **Notting Hill** is the hippest district, centering on Portobello Road with its market. Antiques shops, a Caribbean-style carnival in August, and exciting young restaurants and galleries give Notting Hill a multicultural buzz. East of Notting Hill, **Bayswater**—an in-between-land—between Oxford Street and Queensway, between residential and midtown, between swanky and seedy—is full of cheapo hostelries in huge white wedding cake Victorians. Those we list are on the upper end of this spectrum, though still bargains, easy to get around from, and bang on Hyde Park.

Mayfair is London's true center, and you'll feel most urbane and sophisticated staying here. Bond Street shopping, Cork Street art galleries, tree-filled squares, restaurants—it's all here. Less expensive and less tony are Oxford Street and the streets to its north. Just across Piccadilly from Mayfair, **St. James's** has been known as "Gentleman's London" on account of its anachronistic clubs and its legions of shops selling hats, canes, shaving sets, ties, shirts, and handmade shoes. It retains an old-fashioned and courtly air, has two beautiful parks, its own palace, good restaurants, and top hotel rates. East of Regent Street, **Soho** on weekend nights is the nightclubbers' theme park, with hordes of youths, and a thriving gay scene.

Other times, the confusing grid of streets is restaurant paradise. Great fun; only one hotel.

On the east side of Charing Cross Road, **Covent Garden** is another center of London, not packed with hotel beds, but rife with shopping, strolling, eating places. It's as near as you can get to theaterland. North of Covent Garden lies **Bloomsbury**, made famous by Virginia Woolf and her circle. Convenient to the British Museum and lined with moderate small hotels, it's somewhat dusty and noisy but nevertheless a central place to stay. We list one hotel in the **Docklands**, a decidedly offbeat location way downstream on the Thames. This is London's new business district that never quite took off—part ghost town, part riverside theme park, it's a part of town that some people will love.

The Lowdown

Old faithfuls... The "Old Lady of Park Lane" is first in line. She is **Grosvenor House**, Forte's flagship, built on the grounds of the Earl of Grosvenor's late-18th-century estate. She's bulky, none too glamorous, and, like many an old friend, reassuringly homey and undemanding. The more glitzy **Savoy** never changes either, and we're glad of that, while the nearby **Fielding** is like the frumpy friend, dressed in sweats but seen in the right places. Some surprisingly wealthy people savor the continuity of the little Fielding. The **Hyde Park** has been efficient and pleasing for over a century, its quiet periods alternating with high-profile hosting (there's still a royal entrance). London's most egotistical chef now works here, which has trained the spotlight back on the place.

Grand duchesses... Masquerading as an old friend, but more of a snob than she cares to admit, is the **Connaught**, where you practically need a letter of introduction to get a room. It's considered very crass to ask for prices here. The **Dorchester** is the place to unpack your ballgown, or boogie in the nightclub if you lack an invitation to the ball. **Claridges** is the epitome of understated elegance—royalty feels at home on the sweeping marble stairs here, as do ancient dowagers lunching on smoked fish in its restaurant, the Causerie. For somewhere with the Palace of Versailles as role model, the **Ritz** is oddly egalitarian, especially since it was taken over by the Mandarin Oriental company, but it's still a good place to eat cake—as occasional guest Joan Collins would aver.

Favorite uncles... Slightly racy, a little unpredictable, these are relatively new guys in town. In brazen Soho, **Hazlitt's**, with its nooks and crannies, Victorian bathtubs, and many thousands of etchings, is popular with antique dealers and literary lions. Its younger but bigger brother the **Gore** shares its style. The **Stafford** has an interesting side—the carriage house rooms, which have the names of racehorses on their stable doors, are fun. The **Regent** is full of surprises—it's a fully-fledged grand dame with no dress code in an unstarchy part of town, with an outrageous atrium behind its unremarkable façade. More of a collection of pied à terres than a hotel, the slightly down-at-heel **Dolphin Square** is redolent of clandestine encounters, especially in the brasserie and in the bar overlooking the swimming pool with its fifties-era murals.

Where to misbehave... The **Savoy** has always had a louche air about it, perhaps because it has its own theater, or maybe it's the handmade beds or the breezes rolling in off the Thames. Many Londoners who had a rock 'n' roll phase mis-spent part of their youth in the bar of the **Columbia**, which never closes to the bands in residence; the bedrooms, meanwhile, host photo shoots for sleazy fashion articles in famous glossy magazines. At the **Portobello**, the round-bed suite with a fully functioning Edwardian brass bathing machine is practically perverted. If your age is still in the single figures, then **Pippa Pop-Ins**—a hotel that caters exclusively to children—is the place to be naughty.

Britishest... Every other hotel in London has a faux-Brit chintzy decor, a couple of four-poster beds, and afternoon tea, but no hotel is more genuinely English than the **Connaught**, where oils hang in oak-paneled hallways and you get the feeling that your nanny may be lurking around the corner to scold you for making too much noise. **Basil Street** is the cut-price version—it's like a dowager Knightsbridge aunt's house. The B&B agency **The Bulldog Club**, mind you, books you into actual dowager aunts' houses in Knightsbridge, Kensington, and all the best addresses; while taking an apartment at **Dolphin Square** will make you the temporary neighbor of many Members of Parliament, not to mention Princess Anne.

Worst simulated English... The clear winner of the Lionel Bart "London!" award is the **Lanesborough**. Great Britain was never as British as this—all with drawing rooms, frills and furbelows, and a genuine Jeeves on duty in every room (though the management is forever having to train new butlers, as American guests poach them). Honorable mention: **Brown's**, especially for the venerable afternoon tea service, heavy on scones with lashings of clotted cream. Tea is better elsewhere (see For Afternoon Tea, in Dining), but the tourists don't seem to know this.

Eurotrashiest... What with the Channel Tunnel and all, London now seems like Europe's latest capital. The question these days is more to ask what neighborhood is not Eurotrashy. The style kids with cash would only be seen dead in a few hotels, and, frankly, darling, they'd rather stay with friends, but if they have to buy a bed, they get it at **Sydney House**. The **Halcyon** and **Claridges** are OK, and while **Blakes** is a bit too music biz, the **Hempel** is probably a safe bet from the plebes—at least for a while.

Where the movie stars sleep... While it was closed for a two-year refurbishment, Hollywooders missed the **Dorchester** something rotten. A few got hooked on different hotels during its absence: Lauren Bacall and Charlton Heston went to the **Athenaeum**, which has always attracted the Californian actor. The **Halcyon** has many fans, too, William Hurt and Carrie Fisher among them.

Was that RuPaul in the elevator?... Again, the **Halcyon** wins hands down (everyone from RuPaul to Snoop Doggy Dogg stays here), with locals such as Sting or the members of Pink Floyd joining them there for dinner. The truly hip, however, slum it at the always so-out-it's-in **Columbia**. Madonna and Michael Jackson have been known to choose fittingly ungroovy hotels: Ms. Ciccone has queened it at the **Lanesborough**, while the Weird One went to the **Montcalm** (you'll notice we don't list it below, thanks to its frightening rates).

Suite deals… A person could move into the penthouse at **Dukes**—though not over-opulent, it's deeply carpeted, with plenty of space and a balcony, and you wake up looking at distant Westminster Abbey. **Hazlitt's** sole suite—a black oak Tudor fantasia with its own "Great Bed of Ware"—is fun for playing Lancelot and Guinevere, while Hazlitt's sister hotel the **Gore** has a suite with a bed Judy Garland once owned, and outrageous Grecian tiles in the bathroom. The **Stafford's** carriage rooms have fireplaces and Jacuzzis (downstairs), and entrances off their own cobbled mews. Two bargains in accidental suites (they don't claim to be, but they are virtual suites): the none-too-handsome basement (#77) at **Bryanston Court** and the **Commodore's** wonderfully quiet lemon-yellow duplex (#11).

Silent nights… Yes, the **Commodore** is quiet, as is the above-mentioned **Stafford** and its neighbor, the even quieter—since it's set in its own gaslit alley—**Dukes**. The huge **Kensington Close** is also secreted in its own streetlet. Another group of neighbors with peaceful postcodes are the **Beaufort**, the **Franklin**, and the **Claverley**, tucked on a residential South Kensington sidestreet just off the Brompton Road. Nearby in Chelsea, the **Sloane** and **Sydney House** won't keep you up late—neither will ambient noise at **Blakes** and the **Portobello**, though your fellow guests' partying might. High rooms at the **London Hilton** don't even need their sound insulation. The most peacefully positioned hostelry of all is **Holland House Youth Hostel**—too bad its dorm-style sleeping arrangements take away your privacy.

Best park view… **Holland House Youth Hostel**, being inside Holland Park, has to lead this category. If you like to look upon green, though, this is a fine city. All the Park Lane grands—**Grosvenor House**, the **London Hilton**, the **Dorchester**—and also the **Lanesborough** and the **Hyde Park** overlook (guess) Hyde Park—if you get a room on the park side, of course. From the **Hilton's** highest floors, you can also see a corner of the queen's private gardens at Buckingham Palace. A different side of Hyde Park is available for half the rates at the **Columbia** and the **London Elizabeth**. Peep into private squares from **Dorset Square**, **Egerton House**, the **Franklin**, and the **Porto-**

bello. Stay on the **Ritz's** west side or in rooms 201–205 at the **Athenaeum** to see into gorgeous Green Park.

Best river view... It's amazing how empty this category is considering the historic importance of London's great slow-flowing Thames. No secret are the river-view rooms and suites at the **Savoy**, which you should book ahead, and which will cost you dearly. The cheap version is available at the slightly strange **Scandic Crown** in Docklands: Get a room in Block #1, a converted warehouse with exposed brick and floor-to-ceiling windows onto the Thames (avoid Block #2, a pallid modern lump with no redeeming features).

May I get that for you, sir?... Service is a difficult commodity to pin down, since star individuals move on, but Donald and Alex, the pair of lovely concierges at the **Athenaeum**, have been there for a long time and show no sign of leaving. In general, this hotel apparently attracts kind people. The **Beaufort**, similarly, has an all-female staff that goes out of its way to make you happy, as does the neighboring crew at the **Claverley** (are they in deliberate competition?). The ferociously modern **Halkin** looks like the kind of place where you'd get snubbed for no reason, but the Armani-uniformed Euro types who work there are especially nice. The small **London Elizabeth** has a loyal team of Irishly smiling staff, while the tiny **Sloane** retains gorgeous and conscientious young Spaniards and Swedes until their wanderlust moves them onward.

Bargain beds... Top value prize goes to the high-end B&B agency the **Bulldog Club** for the ultimate in homey luxury. You get to live in the kind of house you'd want to own if you lived in London, and will probably be given the insights of the family that actually does live there. **London Homestead Service**s is the less tony version of the same thing, with truly inexpensive, very variable, but inspected and shipshape homes in all neighborhoods, including outlying boroughs and 'burbs. It goes without saying that the **Holland House Youth Hostel** is cheap; those allergic to communal living should note that there are a couple of rooms (as opposed to dormitories) here. Ditto the **Central Club**, only in reverse—there are hardly any dorms in this YWCA, aptly named for its central London location.

Single city... Lone travelers who are watching the pennies and don't need a bath of their own could do a whole lot worse than the **Claverley's** littlest, lowest-rate rooms (complete with one of London's biggest breakfasts). Alternatively, the **Portobello's** bargain cabins make a virtue of necessity by cramming TV, minibar, tea/coffee-makers, and phone, practically into the wood-paneled beds themselves, a set-up sort of like a Victorian cruise liner. Smaller still, and with no design feature to ease the pain, is room #14 at the **Edward Lear**, a family-run hotel with a homey atmosphere that might be very appealing to a single, youthful wanderer. At the other end of the size scale—other end of the price scale, too—the biggest single rooms in town are at **Claridges** and the **Regent**.

Budget West End... The **London Elizabeth** has nice new decor straight from *House & Garden*, and you don't pay a premium for a view over Hyde Park, nor even for a little balcony. **Bryanston Court** gives a great location—just north of Marble Arch—for the cash, though you shouldn't expect a vast room. The **YWCA**, **Central Club**, is even better located for even less cash, with the corollary that the decor is not fine and bathrooms are down the hall. The **Edward Lear** has lots of loyal repeat guests, mostly Australians and Europeans—the haphazard decor somehow seems to turn Americans off, though. Haphazard decor is something that the **Fielding** shares, though this is the best buy at the Covent Garden side of the West End. The **Hotel La Place** looks more the budget part, with all the modern conveniences of a Motel 6. Being a little off the beaten track, a half dozen blocks north of Oxford Street, it's pretty quiet, too.

The millionaire look, at Scrooge rates... All the hotels of David Naylor-Leyland and of Tim and Kit Kemps' Firmdale Hotels are beautiful to behold. **Egerton House** was Mr. N-L's first, and the one on which he lavished his best pieces and spared no expense. He takes the furniture home when it's too threadbare for his hotel—at least, he'll soon be gleaning one particularly stunning armchair from the Egerton's lounge. The penthouse suite at his **Dukes** hotel looks pricier than it is, and his **Franklin** hotel also gives a good deal of swank for the money. The Firmdale hotels we list are the **Pelham** and **Dorset Square**, the latter having slightly lower rates. Both are worthy of spreads in *Metropolitan Home* and have probably been in the British decor-porn magazine, *World of Interiors*. (We must have missed that issue.) The two tiny independents that run away with the honors in this category, however, are the **Sloane** and **Sydney House**. Each is the love child of its doting owner; each owner possesses such an eye! And at the Sloane, if you really love what Sue Rogers has done, you can take it home. Yes, every antique and gewgaw, along with the TV/VCRs and the beds, is for sale, and not at millionaire prices, either.

Family values... If your family wants to stay together in a family room, here are the best deals in town. The **Edward Lear** has three enormous rooms with very little in them but beds and thin carpets. Close by, but nearer Madame Tussauds and Regent's Park (the zoo!), **Hotel La Place's** five family rooms are a great value. Both properties are child-friendly, as is **Basil Street**. Some of the many family rooms at the **Columbia** are big enough to play hide-and-seek on a rainy afternoon; you can fit a family of five (one being a baby) in here for a hundred quid a night, English breakfast included. The **Commodore**, down the block, has better-looking multiple rooms, but they aren't the best rooms in the place—those are the two-level almost-duplexes, which you could easily fit a family into if you request a cot. For older kids who demand their own room, **Dolphin Square's** larger apartments are the business. Or, if younger kids are demanding their own room, give them their own hotel: Send them to **Pippa Pop-Ins**, a unique lodging where parents can drop off their youngsters for the night, almost as if at a babysitter's house. At the **Stafford**, there are some triples, or you could fit an extra bed in a carriage house room without feeling cramped. The way-out (of town) **Scandic Crown** also has large rooms for an offbeat family vacation.

For history buffs and anglophiles... It was founded by Lord Byron's butler, honeymooned in by FDR, and was the place where Alexander Graham Bell made his first experimental telephone call. No wonder **Brown's** is the number-one pick for amateur historians, especially when you consider the fame of its afternoon tea (you'd do better, actually, to take tea elsewhere). **Grosvenor House** has quite a history, or at least the land it stands on does.

See the oils in and around the fake library—they depict the former Earl of Grosvenor's estate on this site. And above the fireplace in the main lobby (the other end from Park Lane), see the painting of Victorian ice skaters on a rink that is now the Ballroom. Both the **Savoy** and the **Hyde Park** celebrated their centenaries during the past few years; both have had their share of rollicking parties, gatherings, and happenings. For a re-creation of the life-style of the late cousin-to-the-queen Lord Mountbatten, check in at, yes, the **Mountbatten**. (You'd have thought London's so rich in history, it wouldn't need to package it thus.) **Dorset Square**, conversely, has only little cricket bat motifs and some sporting memorabilia to remind guests that the first Lord's cricket ground was in the very square they're overlooking. The oldest house of all? The surviving Jacobean parts of the **Holland House Youth Hostel**.

For enemies of chintz and Regency... You're in trouble. Cabbage roses and Laura Ashley window treatments, brocade and Regency stripes are de rigueur, with the English-country-house look beating all others hands down. Obviously, relief is possible in places where low budgets forbid decor, like the youth hostels (**Central Club** and **Holland House**), and also at the **Edward Lear**, the **Columbia**, and certain floors of **Dolphin Square**. The **Portobello** has a faded Victorian look filtered through the owners' sixties heyday, all very reminiscent of sets from the Mick Jagger/James Fox cult movie *Performance*. But the two stand-outs for different decor are Anouska Hempel's also-slightly-sixties (and seventies) **Blakes**, and the stunning, Milano-modern **Halkin**.

Best health club... Among the swanky grands is a surprise winner, the **Kensington Close**, which has a bi-i-ig pool, two squash courts, and sauna/steam rooms, all for rock-bottom rates. **Dolphin Square** has an even bigger pool, lots of squash courts, tennis, and weight machines, but the public's allowed in, so it's busy. The **Grosvenor House** health club has another big pool, plus a good gym that also gets busy with non-residents. By contrast, the blindingly white, mirror-walled gym (adequate, but no free weights) in the **Hyde Park's** nether reaches never seems to have anyone in it. The **Regent** has a pool that's on the small side, but chlorine-free and pretty. Fitness on Five at the

London Hilton is the flashiest and newest facility. Although there's no pool, you do get personal trainers, plus such options as a session of acupuncture or hypnotherapy. Best for sybaritic spas, with the only sweat generated by the sauna, are the **Athenaeum's** little basement salon (there is a gym with cardio equipment, but it's minute) and the Elizabeth Arden-run pampering joint at the **Dorchester**. Finally, a great surprise: one of the best and biggest pools in central London is yours if you're a guest of the **Central Club**. Those who'd rather not stay at the YWCA can still use its pool by paying to join the club.

Taking care of business... The **Savoy** wins surprisingly many accolades from the corporate world; it's handily located, too, in a part of the West End that's as near to the City as the West End gets (10 minutes in a cab). The **Halkin** is a fantastic business base—rooms have two phone lines, with conference call capability, a fax (request it), and Reuters news service—and the very look seems so efficient, with none of the flounces and curlicues that are endemic to London hotels. The **London Hilton**, like most Hiltons, is OK for business stays, and there'll probably be a convention group around to prove it; ditto at **Grosvenor House**, where there's a huge business center. The **Athenaeum's** apartments are great for anyone who needs to entertain in a homey atmosphere, while the **Commodore**, which also has a business center, is a good pick for small businesses that don't splurge on expenses.

When the curtain comes down... For proximity to West End theater, you'll want to stay in or near Covent Garden and Charing Cross Road. Classics, on either end of the price scale, are the **Savoy** and the **Fielding**. The **Mountbatten** and its plainer sister the **Marlborough** are very near the theaters, too. So is the **Central Club**—and the cash you save on its rock-bottom rates could go towards several extra pairs of tickets. Many hotels offer theater packages, among them the little **London Elizabeth**, big **Brown's**, and the even bigger **Grosvenor House**.

Best redo... The **Athenaeum** had recent attention from basement to penthouse. Now there's a health club and an affordable, rather good restaurant (the old one was pink and empty), but nobody messed with the good bits—the leather-topped yew ship-style furniture and the whisky bar. The complete renovations at **Dukes** have transformed a dingy unwelcoming hostelry into a fine, quiet, patrician choice—lovely to look at, and with rates that don't cause palpitations. The **London Elizabeth** used to have hideous brown-and-beige rooms with vinyl chairs, until owner Peter Newman married an American with New England B&B sensibilities. Now it's pretty, and pretty inexpensive, too.

The outer limits... London's suburbs are as sprawling as those of Los Angeles, and there are hotels in outlying areas from Chiswick to Kentish Town—but we don't list them. **London Homestead Services**, however, probably has every one of the 32 boroughs represented on its books, and at extremely low rates, too. Through this B&B agency, you may be able to book a family home in, say, Barnes (gorgeous, big houses, trees, the river), or Islington (a trendy, liberal, partly Georgian neighborhood with good shopping and eating) for a truly authentic London experience. Don't go too far out, though. Cockfosters and Theydon Bois are fine for commuters, but stay there and you'll feel like you've drawn the short straw.

The twilight zone... There's eccentric on purpose and then there's plain weird. In the first category, the **Portobello** wins the "individual piece of furniture" award for the Edwardian bathing machine in its suite—a perverted though functional contraption of brass rods and faucets. The **Sloane** easily takes the conceptual prize for its bright idea of selling not only time in a room, but the furnishings of the room itself, should you be interested; **Pippa Pop-Ins** gets a special mention for providing rooms to people incapable of booking them or paying for them— namely children. Since the noncomformist is highly prized in England, it's not necessarily an insult to succeed in the "plain weird" category. **Basil Street** isn't weird at all, but it is deeply anachronistic, with its Parrot Club and its counterpanes and its slightly threadbare Persian rugs. **Dolphin Square** is a timewarp of a different stripe, with a mini-mall of shops that seems still stuck in the 1950s and an atmosphere to match. The **Fielding** has the charm of a warm-hearted person who dresses appallingly. If there were a London hotel that served smorgasbord in a dry-docked three-masted bark and offered insomniacs their money back, it would belong here. Oops, there is such a place. Hello again, **Scandic Crown**.

Try these when there's no room... You won't have a hope at the grands during those sold-out times, but the **Regent**, being newer and a little off-center, has been known to have a spare bed at the eleventh hour. So has the other newcomer, the very expensive **Lanesborough**. The **London Hilton** and the **Grosvenor House**, being huge, might have rooms, too. Paradoxically, some of the less-known tiniest places are worth calling at the last minute—specifically the **Sloane**, **Sydney House**, and **Hotel La Place**. Three Bayswater addresses that might yield a late-booking success are (in descending order of cost) **Whites**, the **London Elizabeth**, and the **Columbia**. Among more central properties, try the Edwardian-Radissons: the **Mountbatten** and the **Marlborough**.

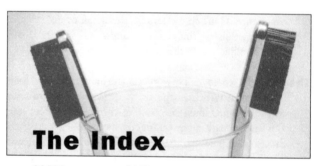

The Index

£££££	over $400	over £250
£££££	$300–$400	£190–£250
£££	$190–$300	£120–£190
££	$110–$190	£70–£120
£	under $110	under £70

Athenaeum. Independent owners gave this former Rank hotel a major rethink, in a Regency-meets-Art-Deco-at-Laura-Ashley style. Now it's the un-obvious Mayfair choice, scoring for low-attitude service, cute health club (steam, sauna, Jacuzzi, weights; no pool), and attention to detail (just look in the minibar); also good to remember for its apartments. Its restaurant, Bullochs, is Mediterranean-esque, semi-casual, and inexpensive.... *Tel 0171/499–3464 or 800/*

335–3300, fax 0171/493–1860. 116 Piccadilly W1V 0BJ, Green Park tube stop. 133 rms. £££–££££

Basil Street. Staying at this venerable hotel, you can breakfast at Harrods, yet it's peacefully set back from the Knightsbridge maelstrom. Many antiques are strewn, though it's not remotely designed. Guests—American academics and English country ladies (who get use of the private ladies' club)—come back and back and back, until they're "Basilites," and thus eligible for frequent-stayer miles.... *Tel 0171/581–3311, fax 0171/581–3693. Basil St. SW3 1AH, Knightsbridge tube stop. 92 rms. £££*

Beaufort. One of the first of the swelling genre of boutique hotels, where you have a latch key instead of a reception desk and a sitting room instead of a lounge, this one includes all drinks and room service. Run by a female team of fiendish efficiency, the Beaufort's even nearer to Harrods than Basil Street is. It gets top marks for friendliness, squashy-couch designer decor, and not charging premium phone rates.... *Tel 0171/584–5252, fax 0171/589–2834. 33 Beaufort Gardens SW3 1PP, Knightsbridge/South Kensington tube stops. 29 rms. ££££*

Blakes. Anouska Hempel, once synonymous with swinging Beatles London, became Lady Weinberg and opened this glamorous stage-set hotel. Her eclectic visual vocabulary (Biedermeier and black lacquer; moiré walls and halogen spotlights; oatmeal raw silk and wickerwork) has since been imitated to cliché, but despite some very tiny rooms, the Blakes style still stuns. So do the ridiculous prices in Blakes, the restaurant. Check out new sister the Hempel (tel 0171/298–9000) in Bayswater.... *Tel 0171/370–6701 or 800/926–3173, fax 0171/373–0442. 33 Roland Gardens SW7 3PF, South Kensington tube stop. 52 rms. ££££*

Browns. Ever-popular with Connecticut Yankees, Browns does the ersatz Victorian country house fairly well, though its soulless afternoon tea is overrated. Labyrinthine corridors and dark-stained wooden staircases connect the various townhouses that comprise this hotel begun in 1837 by Lord Byron's butler. It's about the only London Forte hotel with a boring restaurant, and there's no health club.... *Tel 0171/*

493–6020, fax 0171/493–9381. 34 Albermarle St. W1A 4SW, Green Park tube stop. 132 rms. £££££

Bryanston Court. Best Western affiliation brings Americans to this slightly-better-than-functional independent hotel. Most rooms are small with postage-stamp bathrooms, and some verge on shabby, but rates are great for this area behind Marble Arch. There's a rather elegant lounge with leather chesterfield sofa, oils, and a fireplace, plus a restaurant and a bar.... *Tel 0171/262–3141, fax 0171/262–7248. 56-60 Great Cumberland Place W1H 7FD, Marble Arch tube stop. 56 rms. ££–£££*

Bulldog Club. For a £25 annual membership, you can book a room in one of Amanda St. George's 20 friends' gorgeous houses in desirable neighborhoods. Accommodations will be similar to the best U.S. B&Bs, but most unusual in London. You'll get bargain deluxe treatment—full British breakfast (from a menu, in your private lounge), tea/coffee makers, mineral water, flowers, fruit, newspaper, and robe in your room, plus use of the family phone; sometimes the fax, too.... *Tel 0171/622–6935, or 905/737–2798 (Ontario, Canada), fax 0171/720–2748. 35 The Chase SW4 0NP (mailing address). 20 houses. ££*

Central Club. This YWCA is truly central—a street or two from the British Museum, and thus very near Covent Garden and theaterland. It's a listed (historic, preserved) building designed by Edwin Lutyens. On the premises is probably central London's most pleasant swimming pool. The vast majority of rooms are single or twin.... *Tel 0171/636–7512, fax 0171/383–4106. 16-22 Great Russell St. WC1B 3LR, Russell Square tube stop. 105 rms. AE, DC not accepted. £*

Claridges. Palatial, peaceful, and nearly perfect, this Savoy Group classic hosts royal, political, and business world personages in spacious rooms, some of which feel like 1930s ocean-liner staterooms, others like the setting for a fox-hunting or grouse-shooting weekend. Take tea in the foyer, dine in the pretty salmon-pink restaurant, or—best—do the smorgasbord in the cozy Causerie.... *Tel 0171/629–8860, 800/223–6800, fax 0171/499–2210. Brook St. W1A 2JQ, Bond Street tube stop. 200 rms. £££££*

Claverley. The Beaufort's neighbor, the quaint and friendly little Claverley has new decor of rampant color and occasional four-poster beds. An enormous English breakfast is included, plus tea, coffee, and hot chocolate anytime in the wood-paneled reading room or lounge. A very few single rooms without bath are inexpensive.... *Tel 0171/589–8541, fax 0171/584–3410. 13-14 Beaufort Gardens SW3 1PS Knightsbridge tube stop. 36 rms. £–£££*

Columbia. An anomaly—half rock 'n' roll hangout, half family tourist bargain—this vast Victorian opposite Hyde Park (which many rooms overlook) is clean and bright, if no great shakes in the decor department. Acres of first-floor lounges, a 24-hour bar, a breakfast room that serves dinner, too, and an echoing ice-blue lobby. Bedrooms are not all that big, but you do get a TV, safe, direct-dial phone, and beige bathroom.... *Tel 0171/402–0021, fax 0171/706–4691. 95-99 Lancaster Gate W2 3NS, Lancaster Gate tube stop. 100 rms. DC not accepted. £*

Commodore. Another bargain down the block from the Columbia (see above), this well run, quiet hotel has some special duplex rooms, freshly done in subdued colors. They come complete with sitting areas, tea/coffee-making facilities, hairdryers, TV, and direct-dial phones, plus the odd witticism such as a hat stand with models of hats instead of hooks. Rates include continental buffet breakfast in the separately owned Spanish restaurant in the basement.... *Tel 0171/402–5291, fax 0171/262–1088. 50 Lancaster Gate W2 3NA, Lancaster Gate tube stop. 90 rms. DC not accepted. ££*

Connaught. The honorary consul would feel at home here among the oak-paneled corridors, the invisible staff of old retainers, and the solid and sizeable rooms. Beneath the air of picturesque aristocratic decay, all is shipshape, spotless, and silent as Sunday. The eponymous Anglo-French restaurant and its Grill are among the best in town.... *Tel 0171/ 499–7070, 800/223–6800, fax 0171/495–3262. Carlos Place W1Y 6AL, Bond Street tube stop. 90 rms. £££££*

Dolphin Square. This thirties-era quadrangle a 5-minute cab ride from the Houses of Parliament (many MPs keep a pied à terre here) has functional rather than beautiful apartments

LONDON | ACCOMMODATIONS

and studios. What they lack in hotel services they make up for in the health club, with its famous pool mural, squash courts, and gym; its brasserie, with jazz brunches; and its unusual Thames-side perch. There are shops and a laundromat, too.... *Tel 0171/834–3800, fax 0171/798–8735. Dolphin Square SW1V 3LX, Pimlico tube stop. 151 rms. ££*

Dorchester. A legend among hotels, there is no faulting the opulent Dorchester, with its miles and miles of gold leaf, marble, and antiques. Renovation has brought the engines up to snuff, down to the climate control, dual voltage outlets, shiny marble bathrooms, cable TV, etc. There's not only a beauty spa and gym, but also a nightclub, lounges, bars, shops, ballrooms, and three restaurants.... *Tel 0171/629–8888, 800/223–6800, fax 0171/ 409–0114. Park Lane W1A 2HJ, Marble Arch tube stop. 253 rms. £££££*

Dorset Square. A designer/architect couple, Tim and Kit Kemp have a clutch of hotels around town (the **Covent Garden**, tel 0171/497–6600, is the newest), all distinctively English-countrified with loads of swagged drapes, lace antimacassars, antique cushions, and candlesticks and gewgaws, in the best possible taste. The Dorset Square is in a pair of Regency houses behind Oxford Street, overlooking the garden square where cricket was born.... *Tel 0171/ 723–7874, 800/553–6674, fax 0171/724–3328. 39-40 Dorset Square NW1 6QN, Baker Street tube stop. 37 rms. DC not accepted. ££–£££*

Dukes. In the heart of St. James's, this recent acquisition of small-hotel maven David Naylor-Leyland has its own gaslit driveway; oil portraits of assorted dukes in the foyer justify its name. Rooms have climate control, great detail (heated towel rack, real hairdryer, portable mirror, many outlets), and the staff is young, friendly, efficient. Green Park is steps away.... *Tel 0171/491–4840, 800/381–4702, fax 0171/ 493–1264. 35 St. James's Place SW1A 1NY, Green Park tube stop. 64 rms. £££*

Edward Lear. The former residence of Lear, a 19th-century artist and author of nonsense verse, lies behind Oxford Street at the Marble Arch end. There's nothing luxurious about the place, but it's survived for many years on friendliness and low rates, and continues to pull in a high percentage of repeat guests. Rooms have tea/coffee-making facilities and direct-dial phones; not all, but most, have TV and private bathroom, and some have refrigerators, too.... *Tel 0171/402–5401, fax 0171/706–3766. 30 Seymour St. W1H 5WD, Marble Arch tube stop. 21 rms. AE, DC not accepted. £*

Egerton House. The first Naylor-Leyland property (also see Dukes, above) is still strong, liked by bankers in particular, for some reason. Credit some good antiques, a lovely garden view in back (though there's no access), and a charming staff. Trademarks of these hotels are intimate size, no restaurant (but 24-hour room service), good value rates, and a greater tendency to vivid colors than your average English-country-style place.... *Tel 0171/589–2412, 800/473–9492, fax 0171/584–6540. Egerton Terrace SW3 2BX, Knightsbridge tube stop. 30 rms. £££*

Fielding. This eccentric guest house occupies an alleyway in the dead center of Covent Garden, where shopping and theater—and opera—collide. Expect rickety stairs instead of an elevator, showers instead of tubs in the tiny bathrooms, and no room service or restaurant, although there is a breakfast room.... *Tel 0171/836–8305, fax 0171/497–0064. 4 Broad Court, Bow St. WC2B 5QZ, Covent Garden tube stop. 26 rms. ££*

Franklin. Yet another Naylor–Leyland lodging, you can spit on this one from its sister Egerton House (see above), with which it shares most of its characteristics. There's a handsome double parlor for a lounge, with stairs leading down to a long private garden.... *Tel 0171/584–5533, 800/473–9487, fax 0171/584–5449. 28 Egerton Gardens SW3 2DB, Knightsbridge tube stop. 40 rms. £££*

The Gore. Very near the Albert Hall and Kensington Gardens is this big Victorian house hung with trillions of prints and strewn with antiques. Some rooms are funny follies—one with Judy Garland's former bed, another all leopard skins, another with a Tudor minstrels gallery and oaken four-poster. Bistrot 190 (see Dining) serves as restaurant.... *Tel 0171/584–6601, fax 0171/589–8127. 189 Queen's Gate SW7 5EX, Gloucester Rd. tube stop. 54 rms. £££*

Grosvenor House. Another Forte flagship, with another snob chef (Nico Ladenis), the "old lady of Park Lane" has been translated into the current London hotel idiom of English country—heavy color, marble floors and fireplaces, velvet couches, and floral arrangements. Best of all at this giant is one of the city's most impressive hotel health clubs, complete with pool. There's also a lounge for tea, and two more restaurants aside from Nico's domain.... *Tel 0171/499–6363, fax 0171/493–3341. Park Lane W1A 3AA, Marble Arch tube stop. 454 rms. ££££*

Halcyon. In lovely, leafy, residential Holland Park, the Halcyon quietly attracts celebrities. Light-filled, high-ceilinged rooms are dressed in swags of drapery, delicious colors (like mulberry and black, or lemon custard, apple-green, and white), and occasional themes, like the Egyptian Room (desert tent effect), the Blue Room (moon and stars in cobalt skies), and the Halcyon Suite with its heavenly conservatory. The Room at the Halcyon has an excellent kitchen.... *Tel 0171/727–7288, 800/457–4000, fax 0171/229–8516. 81 Holland Park W11 3RZ, Holland Park tube stop. 44 rms. ££££–£££££*

Halkin. The Halkin stands out a mile, with its exotic wood trim and paneling and many-hued marble, its non-fogging mirrors and keypad lighting controls. Totally Milanese, from the friendly Armani-wearing staff to the Italian restaurant (complète with garden; expensive), it's away from the traffic, behind the Lanesborough (see below) in tony Belgravia. In-room VCRs, faxes, and two-line phones please image-conscious Wall Street types.... *Tel 0171/333–1000, fax 0171/333–1100. Halkin Street SW1X 7DJ, Hyde Park Corner tube stop. 41 rms. ££££*

Hazlitt's. The only hotel in Soho has kept its fans, though its funky antiquey style has been appropriated by others. Visual trademarks include Victorian clawfoot tubs in the bathrooms and multitudes of prints on all walls; it has no elevator, no room service (except for breakfast), no lounge, and no restaurant (but that's the last thing you need on this street of restaurants).... *Tel 0171/434–1771, fax 0171/439–1524. 6 Frith Street W1V 5TZ, Leicester Square tube stop. 23 rms. £££*

The Hempel. See Blakes, above.

Holland House Youth Hostel. Possibly the world's best city youth hostel setting, though the accommodations themselves are as basic as dormitories get. It's housed partly in the remains of a Jacobean mansion and partly in a modern block, set in the middle of gorgeous little Holland Park.... *Tel 0171/937–0748, fax 0171/376–0667. Holland Walk W8 7QN, Holland Park tube stop. 187 beds. No credit cards.* £

Hotel La Place. Just-off-center, not far from Regent's Park—and the Regent (see below)—this small, sweet hotel has good facilities for the price. Refurbished rooms contain tea/coffee maker, direct dial phone, TV, hairdryer, pants press, and minibar, and breakfast is included.... *Tel 0171/486–2323, fax 0171/486–4335. 17 Nottingham Place W1M 3FB, Baker Street tube stop. 20 rms. AE, DC not accepted.* ££

Hyde Park Hotel. With the park behind and the shopping opportunities of Knightsbridge in front, this centenarian is glamorously positioned. It also harbors London's most glamorous chef in its restaurant, modestly entitled "Marco Pierre White, The Restaurant." Rooms contain all the stuff you'd expect from Forte's top property (and one with a separate royal entrance). The lobby's rich in eight kinds of marble; the health club's small but good.... *Tel 0171/235–2000, fax 0171/235–2000. 66 Knightsbridge SW1Y 7LA, Knightsbridge tube stop. 160 rms.* ££££–£££££

Kensington Close. The two best things about this large and utilitarian hotel are the location—set well back from the traffic, but steps away from Kensington High Street—and the fabulous health club, with squash courts, gym, and large pool. Boxy rooms are perfectly adequate; investing in an "executive" may be worthwhile, since they're twice the size. The two restaurants are worth avoiding.... *Tel 0171/937–8170, fax 0171/937–8289. Wrights Lane W8 5SP, Kensington High Street tube stop. 530 rms.* ££

Lanesborough. A Disney-esque version of Regency London, converted from the former St. George's Hospital. The bar is lined with random leather-bound books; check-in is achieved by signing the visitor's book; bedrooms contain fax machines, personalized stationery, an umbrella, big jars of bath unguents, a disturbing infrared security system—and (no joke) a butler of your own. The hotel's Conservatory restaurant is somewhat twee.... *Tel 0171/259–5599, fax 0171/259–5606. 1 Lanesborough Place SW1X 7TA, Hyde Park Corner tube stop. 95 rms. £££££*

London Elizabeth. Set near the depressing guest houses of Sussex Gardens, this likeable and friendly family-run hotel was redesigned by the owner's American wife. Rooms are fresh and English-chintzy in pale blues and yellows; some have tiny balconies, deluxe rooms have Hyde Park views, all have hairdryers, TVs, direct dial phones. There's an old-fashioned continental restaurant, Chez Joseph, and 24-hour room service.... *Tel 0171/402–6641, fax 0171/224–8900. Lancaster Terrace W2 3PF, Lancaster Gate tube stop. 55 rms. ££*

London Hilton on Park Lane. It's not the only grand hotel on the block, but it is the tallest, with great high-floor views for which you pay a premium. The boring room decor has Regency stripe brocade and repro Chippendale. The fabulous feature here is the Fitness on Five health club, with personal trainers, three studios, a gym, and spa. There's a brasserie/cafe, and a bar; on floor 28 is the restaurant Windows; in the basement, Trader Vic's hokey Polynesian.... *Tel 0171/493–8000, 800/445–8667, fax 0171/491–2751. 22 Park Lane W1Y 4BE, Hyde Park Corner tube stop. 448 rms. ££££–£££££*

London Homestead Services. A B&B agency, with fewer swanky uptown addresses than the Bulldog Club (see above), but far more in outer boroughs and residential neighborhoods. All homes have been inspected; the minimum stay is three nights; not all rooms have private bathrooms, in which cases rates are super-low. See London as she is lived.... *Tel 0181/949–4455, fax 0181/549–5492. Coombe Wood Rd. Kingston-Upon-Thames, Surrey KT2 7JY (mailing address). 500+ rms. Londonwide. £*

The Marlborough. From here you can spit on the British Museum, shop Covent Garden, and take in a few plays. It's an Edwardian Radisson—a reliable if unexciting chain—with decor that nods to that era. There's an unnecessary brasserie; rooms are fairly large and well insulated from traffic-heavy Gower Street.... *Tel 0171/636–5601, fax 0171/636–0532. Bloomsbury St. WC1B 3QD, Tottenham Court Road tube stop. 169 rms. £££–££££*

The Mountbatten. Sister to the Marlborough (see above), this hotel has a gimmicky theme—everything pays homage to Lord Mountbatten. It's in an absolutely central Covent Garden location, secreted in one of the winding lanes. There are so many restaurants nearby, you won't need the French brasserie, but the bar's handy.... *Tel 0171/836–4300, fax 0171/240–3540. Seven Dials WC2H 9HD, Covent Garden tube stop. 127 rms. ££££*

Pelham. Another, earlier number from Tim and Kit Kemp (see Dorset Square above), this one is slightly grander, being in a tall-ceilinged South Kensington townhouse, though the abundant antiques and drapery are familiar. In these rooms, you don't find chocolates and fruit, but you do get fresh flowers, a half bottle of claret, and a box of vitamin C tablets. Kemps restaurant is up to the neighborhood competition, and it offers round-the-clock room service.... *Tel 0171/589–8288, or 800/553–6674, fax 0171/584–8444. 15 Cromwell Place SW7 2LA, South Kensington tube stop. 37 rms. DC not accepted. £££*

Pippa Pop-Ins. Over 12? You can't stay here, then. It's a kids-only hotel where parents can drop off the children for the time of their little lives, and go out on the town knowing the kids are in safe and loving hands. Prices include meals, toys, and TLC.... *Tel 0171/385–2458, fax 0171/385–5706. 430 Fulham Rd. SW6 1DU, Parson's Green tube stop, 5 rms. DC not accepted. £*

The Portobello. Once the haunt of major rock stars and other celebs, the peaceful and still hip Portobello has seen better days. A beautiful lounge leads to huge private gardens (no access for hotel guests, but many rooms enjoy a view over it). Decor features such follies as freestanding canopied Victorian tubs, a four-poster bed with its own stairs, and wood-paneled cabin rooms which make a virtue out of being small. The place has style all right—plus breakfasts included in the rate and a 24-hour basement bar that serves food.... *Tel 0171/727–2777, fax 0171/792–9641. 22 Stanley Gardens W11 2NG, Notting Hill Gate tube stop. 25 rms. ££*

The Regent. The extraordinary feature of this relative newcomer—once the Great Central Hotel, then British Rail offices—is the soaring, palm-filled, skylit eight-story Winter Garden

LONDON | ACCOMMODATIONS

atrium, which about half the bedrooms overlook. Rooms are very spacious and there's a pretty pool in the basement health club. There's a good Italian restaurant, but many prefer the small menu served right in the Winter Garden itself.... *Tel 0171/631–8000, fax 0171/631–8080. 222 Marylebone Rd. NW1 6JQ, Baker St. tube stop, 309 rms. ££££–£££££*

The Ritz. Beautifully poised on the cusp of Green Park—its exquisite restaurant and secret Italian garden overlook the park—the Ritz, like cream, is rising back to the top under Mandarin Oriental management. The trademark Louis XVI style looks incongruously decadent under grey London skies, but it's easy on the eye and it's kept shapely by a young staff. Rooms are big, with bathrooms redone in manila marble. Tea at the Palm Court has been rescued from becoming forever a sad tourist trap by cutting the sittings to one.... *Tel 0171/493–8181, fax 0171/493–2687. 150 Piccadilly W1V 9DG, Green Park tube stop. 129 rms. ££££–£££££*

The Savoy. There's something especially glamorous about this over-a-century-old Thamesside Victorian/Art Deco palace, the only London hotel with its own theater. As with all the Savoy Group hotels, it has handmade beds, most staff are from its world-renowned training school, and the shower heads are the size of hubcaps. The Savoy Grill is one of London's power-lunch places; the Restaurant and more casual Upstairs (near the "Fitness Gallery") aren't at all bad, and the American Bar brought the martini to town.... *Tel 0171/836–4343, 800/223–6800, fax 0171/240–6040. Strand WC2R 0EU, Aldwych tube stop. 202 rms. £££££*

Scandic Crown. Fellow guests at this Docklands hotel are guaranteed to be conventioneers. Rooms in the old wing, a converted warehouse, are brick-walled and charming, and they boast the river views you came all this way out here for. Don't accept a room in the other wing. There's a health club, a courtesy bus (though it stops running too early), and two not-very-good restaurants; there are barbecues in summer, when the wide open grounds and Thames terraces come into their own. Beds are guaranteed comfortable—money back if you can't sleep.... *Tel 0171/231–1001, fax 0171/231–0599. 265 Rotherhithe St. SE16 1EJ, Rotherhithe tube stop. 386 rms. £££*

Sloane. Though you won't see price tags, everything here, from the 18th-century oaken tea pot or the Edwardian silver-backed hairbrushes to the canopied, carved four-poster bed, is for sale; you can even buy the TV. This gimmick is saved from being tacky by the incredibly good taste of owner and antique-auction-addict Sue Rogers. The decor is stunning, the young European staff disarming, the rooftop terrace charming, and the Chelsea location central. No restaurant, but there's 24-hour room service.... *Tel 0171/581–5757, 800/324–9960, fax 0171/584–1348. 29 Draycott Place SW3 2SH, Sloane Square tube stop. 12 rms. ££*

Stafford. Sandwiched between the Ritz and Dukes is this little place in an 18th-century townhouse. It's remarkable for its barrel-vaulted wine-cellar private dining salon, and for the dozen secluded Carriage House rooms in back, converted from stables and overlooking a cobbled mews. Decor here and in the main hotel tries too hard to be British, with displays of firearms and silverware and some overbearing color schemes, but everyone means well. The American Bar, its ceiling strung with toys, is a useful martini hideaway, and there's an English restaurant.... *Tel 0171/493–0111, 800/525–4800, fax 0171/493–7121. St. James's Place SW1A 1NJ, Green Park tube stop. 74 rms. ££££*

Sydney House. Super-chic but without pretensions, this Chelsea boutique hotel was designed and is run by young Jean-Luc Aeby, who has an eye for the witty antique—more of a flea market than a Sotheby's sensibility. There's 24-hour room service rather than a restaurant, and satellite TV in the rooms, some of which are pretty small.... *Tel 0171/376–7711, fax 0171/376–4233. 9-11 Sydney Street SW3 6PU, Sloane Square tube stop. 22 rms. £££*

Whites. One of the white palaces that line Bayswater road, this is the only one with any glitz. The hybrid Victorian-Louis XV decor leans heavily to the rococo, in lemon and rose and powder-blue colors. The best rooms have high ceilings and balconies overlooking Hyde Park. There's a little-known restaurant/bar with a pretty conservatory overlooking the park—great for breakfast, tea, or aperitifs.... *Tel 0171/262–2711, fax 0171/262–2147. Lancaster Gate W2 3NR, Lancaster Gate tube stop. 55 rms. £££–££££*

Central London Accommodations

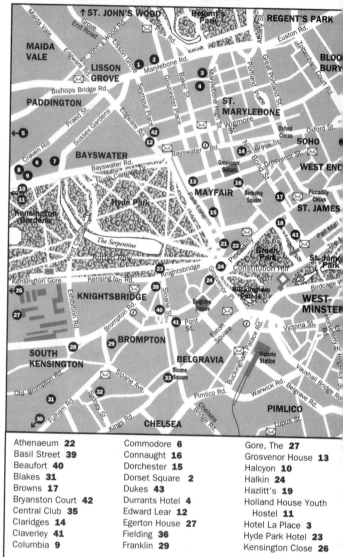

FINSBURY SHOREDITCH

CLERKENWELL
Clerkenwell Rd.

0 ____ 1 km
0 ____ 0.6 mi
N

ANCRAS
Gray's Inn Rd.
Curnan Fields
Guilford St.
Southampton Row
Theobald's Rd.
High Holborn
HOLBORN
Kingsway
Drury Lane
ENT
DEN
36
Aldwych
Strand
Law Courts
St. John's St.
Goswell Rd.
Farringdon Rd.
Beech St.
London Wall
Holborn Viaduct
Newgate St.
Fleet St.
City Rd.
Moorgate
Liverpool St. Station
BARBICAN
Bishopsgate
Cheapside
CITY
Queen Victoria St.
Cannon St.
Lower Thames St.

Victoria Embankment
Blackfriars Station
Blackfriars Bridge
Southwark Bridge
Cannon St. Station
London Bridge

STRAND
Charing Cross Station
37
Waterloo Bridge
Stamford St.
Southwark St.
SOUTHWARK
Union St.
Tooley St.
St. Thomas St.
London Bridge Station
38

Thames
York Rd.
Waterloo Station
The Cut
Blackfriars Rd.
Borough Rd.
Borough High St.
Long Lane
Great Dover St.
Tower Bridge Rd.

Westminster Bridge
River
Lambeth Palace Rd.
London Rd.
Lambeth Rd.
ELEPHANT & CASTLE
New Kent Rd.

Millbank
Lambeth Bridge
LAMBETH
Kennington Rd.
Kennington Park Rd.
Walworth Rd.
Old Kent Rd.

Albert Embankment
VAUXHALL
Kennington Lane
WALWORTH

Information ⓘ

Post Office ✉

ing 2

The true London cuisine is jellied eels, mashed potato, and an emerald green gravy known as liquor. If that doesn't whet your appetite, the better known great British dish is fish and chips—white, flaky fish battered and deep-fried, served with big, fat fries shaken with vinegar. Even more common is curry. A fixture on every high street in the British Isles, Indian tandoori houses serve marinated, spiced dishes cooked in the clay *tandoor* oven, as well as other bastardized dishes mostly of Bangladeshi origin. South Indian vegetarian food can be found in London, too, along with the latest craze—*balti*, a gloppy curry named after the Pakistani word for the iron wok-like *karahi* in which it is cooked.

Only in London

Higher up the culinary ladder, London food has evolved into a sophisticated hybrid cuisine, based (usually) on classical French, influenced heavily by the Mediterranean (olive oil, garlic, oregano) and northern Italy (polenta, risotto, and pasta, pasta, pasta), with its finger also dipped in the cooking pots of Thailand and the "Mediterranean Rim" (principally Morocco). You'll find restaurants serving any of these discrete cuisines, especially Thai.

As for beverages, the wines you'll find are French, first and foremost, but every restaurant that isn't making a point of its Gallic roots also has New World wines, as well as German, Italian, and other European (Spanish, Bulgarian, Portuguese) bottles on its list. English wine exists, but barely; beer is the British drink. Among the types of beer, bitter is less aerated, more hoppy, deeper, and, yes, more bitter than most American beers: Local brews include Fuller's, Young's, and beers called things like *Dogbolter* and *Rail Ale* from the Firkin division of Allied Breweries.

How to Dress

Unless we advise you otherwise in the listings below, dress however you like. Only the swankiest hotel dining rooms, and a few French throwbacks and food shrines, bother with a dress code, although lunch can be a business-dressy affair. The weather rules out shorts and tank tops nearly all the time, but if it ever gets hot enough to wear them to dinner, go ahead and do so—London's heatwaves are so rare, when they do occur the city loses its collective mind, taste, and sense of decorum.

When to Eat

Conservative mealtimes are the rule: Breakfast 7:30–9:30, lunch 12:30–2:30 (1pm is prime), dinner 7–9:30. Afternoon tea is from 3:30–5:30, though hardly anyone takes it. It is *not* "high tea": High tea is a nursery meal (what Mary Poppins would have served the Barks children at Cherry Tree Lane), a cross between tea and dinner that's eaten around 6pm, or else it's the northern English term for dinner (you may hear a Yorkshireman asking for his tea way after 5:30). Lunch is often called dinner, and dinner is frequently known as supper. The upstart meal of brunch is always called brunch, and where it exists (mostly in Covent Garden and South Kensington), it's served 1-ish to 4:30-ish on weekends.

Getting the Right Table

Unless a restaurant doesn't accept reservations (which we note below in The Index), it's always a good idea to call ahead to book a table. With the more exclusive restaurants, the trick to this is the same as anywhere: knowing which the right tables are, and being someone. The London *Evening Standard*'s weekly *ES* magazine carries a feature which deconstructs a restaurant, listing such mysteries as who dines there, where they sit, and where the Siberian regions are (though Brits don't have a term for "Siberia" in this context). Without those guidelines, you must rely on your insider friends to book the table for you.

Where the Chefs Are

London has grown to love its food, and chefs are revered more and more. One who reveres himself so much that there is little space left for anyone else's superlatives is **Marco Pierre White** who has found a suitably grand home in the Hyde Park Hotel, *The* Restaurant (our italics). He was the protegé of superfamous (from TV) **Michel Roux**, whose son of the same name now handles the two-Michelin-star cuisine at Le Gavroche (see below). Other hotels with superchefs include Grosvenor House, where the self-taught **Nico Ladenis** holds court at Chez Nico at Ninety Park Lane, and The Four Seasons, where young dreamboat **Jean-Christophe Novelli**, former private chef to the Paris Rothschilds, does amazing things with game. **Bruno Loubet** used to hold the reins in that silver-cloche establishment, but left to open Bistrot Bruno. One of the very rare three-Michelin-starred establishments in town is Chelsea's La Tante Claire, where gifted Gascon **Pierre Koffman** has been making foodies faint for years now. Unlike many grand chefs, he still gets his hands on the pans. The vastly praised **Simon Hopkinson**, late of Bibendum, used to do that, too, but now he handles the pen as a food writer.

LONDON | DINING

Chefs of less exalted price are no less revered by the cognoscenti. Currently riding a wave of attention are **Fergus Henderson**, who comes to food via architecture, as his very own restaurant refit at St. John shows, and former soccer player (and Marco Pierre White sous-chef) **Gordon Ramsay** at Aubergine. Also notable, though not this year's models, are the still innovative and exciting **Alastair Little** with his eponymous restaurant, The Square's **Philip Howard**, and the duo at The River Cafe who put modern Italian food on the map, **Ruth Rogers** and **Rose Gray**. **Sally Clarke** of Clarke's is another woman chef of London doing great things. Her near neighbor at Kensington Place, **Rowley Leigh**, is patchy but still worth watching.

The Lowdown

Book before you fly... London isn't quite New York in this respect. Even the most elevated gastronomic temples and hottest hangouts du jour shouldn't make you wait longer than a week for a reservation, and you can usually get a table at short notice. One exception used to be **Bibendum**, but now that the great Simon Hopkinson has laid aside his toque, the current state of things remains to be seen. Other joints that demand several days' warning before they feed you include **Aubergine** and the **River Cafe**. Gorgeous sister restaurants **Le Caprice** and **The Ivy** are perennial sellouts, too, as is the lunching-lady-style **Daphne's**. In the neighborhoods, **The Brackenbury** in Hammersmith is deservedly popular, as is **Wódka** in Kensington, and **St. John** in the City needs booking, even though it's so big. Weekends find **Belgo** and **Casale Franco** mobbed by north London locals, while weekday lunches are impossible at the **Savoy Grill** and **Orso**—same reason, different clientele.

Celebrate here... The hokey choice is **Quaglino's**—the watchword for a big night on the town in the twenties, it was resurrected by Sir Terence Conran in the early 1990s, when all London talked about it again. But there's a risk there of feeling like one of the herd, and who wants that on their special day? Better to go for the terrace overlooking Tower Bridge at another Conran special, the **Pont de la Tour**. If you're pulling out all the stops, the

Ritz is so pretty, and the waiters are properly pampering. For something completely different, the original **Belgo** has stark concrete (carved with quotes from Rabelais) and is cheap and suitably raucous. For the daytime, **Belvedere** in Holland Park is heavenly; or you could eat there early on a summer's evening before a performance at the open-air theater nearby in the park. Champagne and oysters at **Green's** is especially and seriously British, followed by tea and cake at **The Fountain**. For a precious lunch, perch on a love seat at **The Causerie** and have the waiters refresh your smorgasbord plate frequently. And from the sublime to the ridiculous, the Chinese restaurant **Gracelands Palace** is forever full of hen nights and birthdays, come to worship at the court of the King, a.k.a. owner and Elvis impersonator Paul Chan.

Suddenly starving in Covent Garden... There *seem* to be so many places to eat in this neighborhood, yet few are worthy. **Joe Allen** is good for any time, but impossible to locate: Walk down Exeter Street and when you think you're close, look for a small brass plaque and follow the staircase down. In another back alley, but obvious when you're upon it, is **Fatboy's Diner**, good for a simple and cheap refuel. Right by the tube station is **Maxwell's**, also simple and cheap, but stick to the burgers and fries. Bigger, French food is fine at the brasserie **Le Palais du Jardin**, where the crowd is a good sign (not always the case around here); small or big food is excellent, and very healthy, at the casual vegetarians, **Neal's Yard Dining Room** and **Food For Thought**.

Caught in Portobello with low blood sugar... The **Brasserie du Marché aux Puces** was made for this purpose. It's way up in the Goldborne Road regions, past the Westway flea market, and a long, long way from the antique market you came for, but it's a worthy destination, serving food with a French accent. Closer to the antique stalls, the shabby-chic **All Saints** is still a popular neighborhood hangout after a few years of constantly changing chefs and food styles. It seems now to have settled with slightly elevated home-cooking. If you want a cocktail for unwinding, crowded **Beach Blanket Babylon** is the place; its restaurant—fantastical-looking, in its Antoni Gaudi-meets-the-Addams-Family style—serves good grilled meat and fish, salads, and pasta. The absolute, all-purpose, favorite dive of the area, however, is **192**. Whatever the time of day (as long as it isn't Sunday), there'll be hangers-out at this wine bar to the stars (or people who think they are).

Most comforting... At the **Gay Hussar**, a long-lived Hungarian restaurant in Soho, bouncy banquettes envelop people wearing tweed jackets with leather elbow patches, who consume vast portions of cold cherry soup, goulash, and *paprikás töltött palacsinta* (chicken-veal-paprika pancakes). Knightsbridge's **St. Quentin** is pure Paris, elegant yet unstuffy, handsome yet undesigned, serving wonderful unfashionable food without attitude. In Hampstead, the charmingly dingy **The Coffee Cup** is especially comforting to Brits, harking back to the England of their childhood or even earlier. The menu? Things on toast with overbrewed tea. Lovely, friendly **Costa's Grill**, on the other side of town in Notting Hill, is the Greek taverna version, with a matching garden. Shabby **Daquise** serves South Kensington nostalgia and Polish nursery food. A high class of nursery tea can be relived (or discovered) at **The Fountain** in Fortnum & Mason, where auntly waitresses serve "Elegant Rarebit" (cheese on toast with bacon and tomato), ice cream with tiny jugs of hot butterscotch sauce, and pots of Earl Grey tea.

For grown-ups... When your parents dressed up and left you with the babysitter, such are the places you imagined they went. A sophisticated place, sober of mien, where anything less than jacket and tie (and 40-something years) feels underdresssed, is **Shaw's**, which serves the serious English food of chef Frances Atkins. At **The Square**, diners dress expensively to partake of Philip Howard's inspired prix-fixe menus. You'd better be mature enough at **Clarke's** not to mind eating what you're given, because Sally C. sets the menus herself, based on what's best available fresh today. Her wellheeled patrons are rarely disappointed. At **Alastair Little**, the minimal decor leaves you free to concentrate totally on your plate, where the excellent hybrid Modern Brit/Med/Pacific Rim cuisine features a lot of fish. The high-priced blue-and-yellow Chelsea salon that is **La Tante Claire** attracts grown-up and wealthy palates to the inventive cooking of chef Pierre Koffman. Pizza is tailored to restrained and genteel tastes at Mayfair's **Condotti**, with its walls full of Paolozzi paintings; likewise the burgers at Covent Garden's **Christopher's**. The **Savoy Grill** exists for captains of industry, newspaper editors, and parliamentarians who eat only the most British foods—beef Wellington, liver and bacon, fish pie.

For kids... Actual kids are happy with the burgers at **Tootsies**, **Maxwell's**, and the two diners **Ed's Easy** and—especially—**Fatboy's**, whose steel trailer and astroturf yard are a thrill. If it's pizza they're longing for, the noisy American-style **Chicago Pizza Pie Factory** is ideal. **Marine Ices**, an ice-cream parlor near Camden Lock, and **Lauderdale House**, a park cafe next to Highgate Cemetery, seem to have been simply made for kids. Somewhat higher on the culinary scale, Antony Worrall Thompson's casual **Bistrot 190** and its sister **Zoe** are pretty kid-friendly, and the exalted **River Cafe** extends a surprisingly warm welcome to small people, though they'd better be budding gourmets. **The Fountain** at Fortnum & Mason is a useful good-behavior bribe—a dress-up and sit-tall place for ice-cream sundae special occasions.

Party hearties... The *patron* of **Wódka** brews his own stickily wicked cherry vodka, which—along with *ziborowa* and *krupnik*, and wines from everywhere but Poland—fuels many a private-room party. See the bachelors stagger upstairs around midnight. An insidery but jolly atmosphere goes down in the restaurant itself, too. **Belgo** is the opposite of a serious salon, what with waiters dressed as medieval monks, and vast quantities of *moules-frites* and Belgian *kriek* beer around. Noise level is high, as it is at **St. John**, which looks like a supercool school refectory with a buzz that invites good times.

Pre- and post-theater... For West End theaterland, Japanese-y **Wagamama** is perfect for fast-fueling before curtain up, though it closes too early for after. The **Savoy Grill** shifts gears and ceases to be the power players' canteen in the evenings, when it offers a two-part before-and-after theater supper. *The* place for late-night after-the-curtain-calls dining is where the actors themselves go (in London as in New York), **Joe Allen**. A bargain, speed-

delivered pre-theater deal is offered 6–7pm at that toniest of American transplants, **Christopher's**. On the other
side of Charing Cross Road, in Soho, are several options
that will feed you late at night. At **Soho Soho**, the first-
(ground-) floor rotisserie is perennially loud and full, and
there's similarly French-ish bistro food at **Café Bohème**,
if you can squeeze in past the crowds of drinkers. **Melati**
serves good Malaysian food, but lacks the bar scene of
the other two. The place to drink, eat, people-watch, and
extend your evening almost as long as you like is **The
Atlantic Bar and Grill**, with its eclectic menu and late-
night weekend crowds. Less frenetic than that, the beautiful and trendy **Criterion** across the street serves only
until 11:30, but it's easy to reach fast from any of the
West End houses. Up in Islington, the "Off-West End"
Almeida Theatre has the divine, upscale pizzas of **Casale
Franco** in a hidden courtyard nearby, though be warned
that you're not allowed to order only the pizza, and
there's no reservations, so come very early to make the
play on time.

Stargazing... It helps to watch a little British TV before
attempting to celebrity-spot in this town—this ain't no
L.A. Movie folk and especially rock people do visit,
though, and seem to feel at home among the leafier parts
of town, generally toward the west. **Room at the
Halcyon** in Holland Park harbors many a local celeb,
some of whom have fame that spread farther than Dover:
John Cleese, for instance, and Sting, and Elton John.
Nearby in groovy Notting Hill, the wine bar **192** hosts
fashion designers, writers, and anyone with the last name
Freud (author Esther and sister designer Bella) or
Conran (Jasper the designer, Shirley the sometime
superwoman, not Terence the patriarch), although many
will have defected to Tom Conran's **The Cow** around the
corner (unreviewed here, since it opened too late).
Daphne's hosts glitzy ladies of the Ivana Trump ilk, and
Le Caprice and **The Ivy** attract movers and shakers in
the worlds of architecture, business, art dealing, publish-
ing—you name it. The latter is also a thespian haunt,
being in theaterland, a tonier choice than the perennial
actor's hangout **Joe Allen**, another West End option. If
you know their faces, you can spot homegrown politicians and bigtime reporters and columnists at power

lunches at **The Savoy Grill**, while Labour left-wingers favor the **Gay Hussar** in Soho; architects and anyone writing for the *Guardian* go to **St. John**, in the City. **Wódka** is the secret Kensington hangout of people from all strata—Jerry Hall and Charles Saatchi to name two utterly unrelated sometime regulars. Magazine mavens like Joe Allen's sister restaurant **Orso** for lunch—go there to spot future New York editors.

Beautiful people... London doesn't really go for this idea, and thankfully is not currently a models' center. What you have instead are incredibly cool and interestingly dressed people posing for all they're worth. Apologies for the unavoidable past-the-"sell-by"-date on this list of their hangouts: **The Atlantic** is the central London Piccadilly posing palace, thanks to its late drinking license. Hipper than that, and open all night, though fuelled by caffeine instead of alcohol, is **Bar Italia**. All around it, Soho attracts youth and the best looking gay men in town. Proper restaurants with tables full of pulchritude include **Aubergine** and **The Canteen**; **Daphne's** has the mon-eyed crowd whose clothes, at least, are good-looking. Both **Kensington Place** and **Wódka** attract professional-ly groomed fashion biz characters.

Most romantique... Any place whose name translates into "the love apple" is probably conducive to amorous encounters, and so it is at **La Pomme d'Amour**, with its conservatory garden and classic but light French cui-sine—even its Holland Park location, reminiscent of a Paris boulevard, is kinda cute. Near neighbor **The Belvedere** outdoes it for setting, however, since it has one of the most gorgeous London locations, in Holland Park itself. Yet another Holland Park French restaurant, the venerable **Chez Moi** is quaintly cozy and old-fashioned, all in pink, with waiters who delight in heightening your romantic drama—a "flower-for-the-lady" place. In town, **Le Caprice** feels delicious and decadent with its modern black-and-silver color scheme and its well-spaced, white-dressed tables. The service here tends to pamper diners, too. There's something illicit about Soho's **French House**, hidden above the ever-crammed pub of the same name, with its photos of French boxers, lined with mirrors and upholstered in vermillion. It's the earlier success of Fergus

Henderson and Margot Clayton, the pair responsible for St. John, so the food's great, too, in a hearty, naked way. Way north, **Lemonia** is a breath of the Aegean, lighter and leafier of decor than most London Greek places, and so authentic you'll imagine you're getting a suntan.

Britburgers... Oh yes there is such a thing, and there are a few good examples of the art of short order cooking around town, most of them in Covent Garden, burger capital of London. Conveniently close to that tube stop is **Maxwell's**, the (relocated) place that brought the trendyburger to London in the seventies. Between here and the Strand is tony **Christopher's**—decidedly not a burger joint, but the downstairs cafe serves good burgers for less money with less swank and swagger. Just around the corner, **Joe Allen**, as you'd expect from the twin brother of Joe's New York original, turns out a near-perfect patty, too. Those who know, however, often claim that the best burger in town is the "Fatburger" at **Fatboy's Diner**. The West London chain **Tootsies** is well worth remembering, too, and it has crinkle-cut fries to die for.

Really old but still alive... This is usually a recommendation in the world of restaurants–they have to be doing *something* right to stay in business so long. London has fewer very venerable eating houses than you might expect in such an historic city, but the oldest of all, **Rules**, is *very* old. Founded in 1798, it's probably serving the same game-laden menu, give or take the odd fruit sauce and sprig of lemongrass. Younger by far, but showing tenacity, are the beautifully preserved Victorian **F Cooke & Sons** and the **Manze's** by Tower Bridge, for traditional dishes such as jellied eels and pie and mash. (See "Cockneys and East Enders" for more about London eels.) Some of London's loveliest places are those that persisted through decades of low profile, only to attain a sort of hipness again by accident. **The Gay Hussar**, in Soho, is one such—never in fashion and never out of it. **Bahn Thai**, nearby, was one of the pioneers of a cuisine that now challenges Indian as London's native nosh. **St. Quentin's** exact simulation of a Paris brasserie only improves with the patina of age.

Overrated... Not so much overrated as overused (there's so little competition in the environs of the South Bank

Centre, where it's sorely needed), the **Archduke** continues to attract custom it barely deserves for its international sausage collection and underwhelming self-served soups, salads, and quiches. **Quaglino's** is glamorous and fun and very big, but it's not the culinary heaven the out-of-towners that pack it every night seem to think it is, and the service can be decidedly offhand. Opinion is divided over **St. John**, the big splash of early 1995. Some hate Fergus Henderson's style—scorn was heaped on his early appetizer of a bunch of carrots and a boiled egg on a plate— but many dishes are stunningly original without gimmick, like his signature salad of bone marrow and parsley. The food at clamorous table-hopping **Kensington Place** isn't what it used to be either. Sometimes boring foodwise, you might say. As for **Marco Pierre White: The Restaurant**, does it really deserve its three Michelin stars? The reverence accorded to chef Marco by his elderly lady groupies (there's always a table of them in) would attest to its success, but only they and professional restaurant critics can judge the place with any consistency—the prices, among the highest in the land, prohibit frequent visits by anyone else, so who can know?

Auld London towne... Rules (see above) is the auldest of all, serving deer and grouse to the gentry and the hoi polloi for two centuries. A handful of other places, often in the grand old hotels, serve once-reviled English food and serve it right. **The Savoy Grill** has two sides to its menu—literally: There's a French side and a British one, both good, but you're safe with the steak-and-kidney here. The **Ritz** does classic roast beef at not inconsiderable expense (more affordably at lunchtime). **Simpson's-in-the-Strand** is the master carver, where great trolleys bearing joints of roasted meat are wheeled to your table and served with spuds (potatoes), gravy, and the correct accompaniments (Yorkshire pud and horseradish for beef, mint sauce for lamb, applesauce for pork). This 1828 wood-paneled Edwardian also offers "pig's nose with parsley and onion sauce" for breakfast. The seafood soul of Britain is expressed beautifully at **Green's Restaurant and Oyster Bar**, another wood-paneled establishment, where native oysters (small and strong) or "big" ones precede Devon crab salad or something with meat if you insist. Finally, if your credit cards can take some pounding, don't forego the **Connaught**. There's the (again) wood-paneled

Restaurant and the smaller green-and-gold Grill, both serving perfect English food from a kitchen presided over by Frenchman Michel Bourdin for over 20 years. Everything tastes as it might at the very grandest of country weekend houseparties (think *Brideshead* and all those other *Masterpiece Theater* pieces).

Cockneys and East Enders... It's easily argued that this stuff is the real London cuisine: fish and chips, pie and mash, breakfast fry-ups, and mixed grills. When it's good, it's very, very good, and mostly very, very bad for you. Fish and chips—cod, plaice, or haddock deep-fried in batter and served with thick, slightly flabby french fries, golden tan outside, fluffy white inside—has been appropriated by trendy restaurateurs not just in England, but on the other side of the pond, too. London's best are found at **Geales** and the **Sea-Shell**, and—if you like the dish—are worth a special trip. In Covent Garden, you could do worse than the **Rock & Sole Plaice**. Even if you're squeamish about grease, you'll probably like the sound of fish 'n' chips better than the other London dish: eels, stewed or jellied, and served with emerald green "liquor"—a kind of parsley broth. Pie and mash is more easily envisaged: ground beef with a pastry lid, and mashed potato—not creamed, not whipped, but mashed, and sliced like cake. Two London families share the eel monopoly, the Cookes and the Manzes (see **F Cooke & Sons** and **Manze's** in the Index below). Their shops, in or around street markets whose traders live on this stuff, are worth visiting for the beauty of the functional decor alone—the wooden high-backed benches, ornate green-brown-and-white ceramic tiles, sawdust-covered floor, and marble-topped wrought-iron tables haven't changed a bit since the Victorian era. Also little changed is the way business is conducted at Smithfield, the main meat market; after 8am, when the selling's over, the porters repair to the **Fox and Anchor** for the biggest British breakfast in town, black pudding (sausage made from boiled blood) and pints of bitter (there's a unique licensing situation here).

Bagels, who knew?... Near Petticoat Lane, the East End antiques and junk market, Jewish East Enders (many of whom ended up in New York and Hollywood, but that's another story) get their bagels—yes, bagels—from the **Brick Lane Beigel Bake**. Available hot from the oven 24 hours a day, these bagels are filled with lox and cream cheese (and a margarine schmear, unfortunately), or bright pink salami, or cheddar cheese. They're smaller than the New York kind, but just as good.

Vegging out... No city restaurant completely ignores the increasing ranks of people who don't eat things with faces, but some cater more than others. Among totally vegetarian restaurants, not too many enjoy gourmet ambience, however good the food. One unlikely exception is **The Place Below**—below, that is, a Wren church, in the crypt. Two nights a week, this wonderful cafe becomes a candlelit real restaurant, serving a divine set dinner. For lunch or tea, the spring blossom-canopied church courtyard of **The Wren at St. James's** is also a veggie haven. For a most haute meal, try the **Room at the Halcyon**, where up-and-coming chef Martin Hadden thoughtfully provides an entirely separate menu for veggies. In Covent Garden are two places which, though the food is fresh and delicious, close early, presumably following the weird *idée fixe* that vegetarians don't eat out at night. **Food For Thought** has horrible chunky yellow pine decor and 1,000-watt lighting, whereas at least, **Neal's Yard Dining Room** makes an attempt at ambience, with an on-view kitchen and natural light. Another misconception about vegetarianism is that veggies are fanatics who ascribe to religious cults. **Govinda's**, one of Soho's best bargains, has fresh, international, mostly Indian-style veg dishes, but is run by the Hare Krishnas—yes, they still exist. At least they don't bother you while you eat. In the City, **East West** has no religious affiliations, unless you count New Agery, but it does serve pure macrobiotic meals. Amazingly, it continues to serve till 10pm and has a liquor license. A great way for vegetarians to feed is on the cuisine of South India, at **Diwana Bhel Poori** and other places along Drummond Street, not far from the British Museum.

Something fishy... **Alastair Little** has a special affinity with fish, always doing something interesting and pan-Pacific with it. The best feature of **Quaglino's**—better than the glamorous staircase—is the "Crustacea Altar," which serves plateaux de fruits de mer that approximate the ur-plateaux of La Coupole and its ilk. So does that other Sir Terence palace, **Le Pont de la Tour**. Oysters are best at **Green's**; at yet another Conran shop, the **Bibendum Oyster Bar**; and at **Daphne's**, where shellfish are still on the diets of the ladies who lunch. **Belgo**, living up to its Belgian provenance, has the most fun with mussels. Near Piccadilly Circus is a useful, relatively budget piscine emporium, **Cafe Fish**. It's no great gourmet shakes, but the fish is fresh, the execution reliable. Broiled fish is wonderful at a good Greek, like **Lemonia** and both **Micro** (small) and **Mega** (big) **Kalamares** in Queensway. **Costa's Grill** on a fine summer's night in the small garden is evocative of Greek island vacations, if you drink enough retsina with your *psari*. The *pulpo* (octopus) tapa and the *zarzuela* (seafood and fish stew) at **Rebato's** are memorable, as was the carp in aspic at **Wódka**, which may or may not be back on the menu. Sushi is just not worth bothering with in London, but if you can't live without raw fish, **Moshi Moshi Sushi** is silly silly funny, with its countertop train delivery and its system of counting up the plates to tally the check. There's also an attractive view of Platform One of Liverpool Street Station.

For oenophiles... Wine lists in London used to be all French, and mostly Bordeaux and Burgundy at that, but this is far from true now. New World wines—from Australia, Chile, and, yes, even California—are ubiquitous, and you'll see Italian, German, and some Spanish wines, plus various eastern European bottles on many a list. All the grand dining salons fulfill the Important Wines requirement, of course, with only French on the list at **Le Gavroche** and **Chez Nico**; mostly French, with a little German and Italian, at the **Connaught**. The requisite Places with Interesting Lists include **192**, which picks out seasonal selections on your behalf.

But is it pizza?... There is, contrary to the opinion of any yankee expat you may encounter, good pizza in London. It's not necessarily the New York style—thin crisp-crusted, oregano-laden pie—nor Chicago's thick, chewy, doughy variety, though both are available. Instead, what you get here is a hybrid that owes its provenance directly to Sicily. **Casale Franco**, in far-off Islington, serves amazing, irregularly-shaped pies with bubbles and charred bits on the crust; piled on top are whole basil leaves and roasted tomatoes and slices of prosciutto and artichoke hearts and other good stuff. The trouble is the restaurant's absurd and greedy policy of not allowing these to be your entrée at peak hours. They don't take reservations, either. So forget that, and head to the reliable **Pizza Express** chain. Ordering anything but pizza here is a grave error, but the thin, crisp, Italian pies are fine. Get the Veneziana (onions, raisins) and have 10p donated to the "Venice in Peril" fund. **Condotti**, in the heart of Mayfair, is the Rolls Royce of pizza joints, serving the usual suspects, plus a potato-crusted four-cheese pie, between art-encrusted walls. There are other pizzerias of note, but they're too outlying to appear in a city guide.

Neighborhood places where Londoners go... The **Brackenbury** is hidden in a back street in Hammersmith (the up-and-coming restaurant row), yet is packed every night. Not only is its "new British" food always interesting and sometimes stellar, the atmosphere is warm and homey, the service sweet. Likewise at the miniscule **Al San Vincenzo**, just north of Marble Arch, where Vincenzo Borgonzola is inventive with Umbrian recipes and his English wife takes the orders. In Soho, **Bistrot Bruno** serves robust-is-an-understatement dishes that Bruno Loubet has extrapolated from *cuisine de terroir* (French regional cooking) classics. This neighborhood also offers the only Chinatown restaurant that foodies don't snub, **Fung Shing**, and **The French House**, the previous incarnation of St. John, with Margot Clayton (Fergus Henderson's partner) in charge.

Is this a bar or a restaurant?... In this land of strange alcohol licensing laws—land of the 11pm closing time—a few places that claim to be restaurants are overwhelmed by their bar scenes. (See also Nightlife for good drinking spots.) First up is the vast **Atlantic Bar and Grill**, the Piccadilly Circus of late-night bars, located just off Piccadilly Circus itself. The food ranges from acceptable to good (get the appetizer plates to share), but the reason to eat here is to secure a good table during rush hour. **192** is Notting Hill's social club, mobbed with bar flies most nights—although the food is good, the wine

LONDON | DINING

list (it's officially a wine bar) is even better. **Bar Italia** in SoHo is a coffee bar, period—no alcohol, little food, much posing. Nearby is **Café Bohème**, which *is* a bar, except it does pretty OK food—just don't try eating it at 11:30pm on a Friday. In Camden, the **Crown & Goose** is a pub, but a pub serving big food and coffee, and always packed to the gills. It's the sister of **Bar Gansa**, another bar-restaurant, this one with tapas. **Joe Allen** has a New York-style proper bar with bar stools, as this true Manhattan transfer should. Nearby, **Maxwell's** does those sugary, blender cocktails for office workers, and the **Palais du Jardin** has a civilized U-shaped bar for sipping wine while awaiting a table.

Tapas: The craze that stayed... Somewhere around the end of the eighties, somebody wheeled those Spanish tidbits called *tapas* into London, and soon it seemed every restaurant had a little dish of *boquerones* (marinated fresh anchovies) and a slice of *tortilla* (potato omelet) on the table. (The word *tapas* means "lids", because the first tapa was a slice of bread to keep the flies out of the sherry.) Suddenly Iberian was in. **Rebato's**, just south of the river, and **Galicia**, in the nether regions of Portobello, are both long-, long-standing Spanish restaurants that do tapas (as opposed to tapas bars), both *muy autentico* and—especially Rebato's—hopping on weekends. The food at Rebato's is much better than at Galicia, but Galicia has a sweet, homey ambience. Among the onslaught of inauthentic tapas bars, the most consistently popular is Camden Town's **Bar Gansa** (the only tapas bar to sponsor a softball team that includes a member of the band Madness), serving a bigger range of little food than most, with particularly inauthentic but essential giant fries.

Cheap 'n' cheerful... Fish and chips, pie and mash, these are always bargains, but there are other things to eat when belts are tight. Indian food, as we've noted, is the unofficial British cuisine, and virtually any high street tandoori house will be good. For English diner-equivalent food, the **Chelsea Kitchen** has been there since Chelsea was the swinging center of the world, and it's still likeable. There's good French diner food, and a lovely, casual ambience at the wine bar in picturesque Shepherd's Market, **L'Artiste Musclé**, while Thai bargains are offered at **Ben's Thai**, above a big pub in untouristy Maida Vale. There's always a line in Bloomsbury for the noodles and "health dishes" and communal fun food of the frighteningly popular **Wagamama**, which is near Belgo Central (yet to open at press time). The original **Belgo** is a bargain if you stick to mussels and fries (which is what they do best), and both **The Criterion** and **Joe Allen** do two-dishes-for-a-tenner deals, the latter at weekend brunchtime only. **Daquise**, the ancient Polish cafe by South Ken tube, is a bargain place in which to kill hunger for hours. In Piccadilly, as central as can be, the spring blossom-canopied church courtyard of **The Wren at St. James's** is perfect for lunch or tea. All around town you'll see Paris-style brasseries, which seem to offer a great value, though they are almost interchangeable, with their baguette sandwiches and goat's cheese salads and Toulouse sausages. Out of the **Dôme**, **Café Rouge**, and **Café Flo** chains, the last is marginally the best, useful for its "Idée Flo" two-course simple meal—useful, but dull. They all are. **Tuttons**, a very handily-located brasserie off the Covent Garden Piazza, used to be bad, but got revamped soup to nuts in 1995, and does a two-course prix-fixe deal, and a bargain "Express Menu."

Indian institutions... There are so many good neighborhood curry houses that they alone could fill this book, but we single out this pair as examples of their genre: On a Notting Hill strip of several Indians, find the frenetic institution **Khan's**. It retains its popularity because of its soaring sky-like ceilings, palms, and low prices, but mostly because of its popularity. (Nothing succeeds like success.) Over in the East End Bangladeshi community around Brick Lane, the same role is fulfilled by the **Nazrul**, whose waiters' jackets say on the pocket "Naz Rules," and which is almost embarrassingly inexpensive. Near Euston Station, **Diwana Bhel Poori** isn't much on ambience, but does great South Indian meals. Nearby, rock-bottom cost and complete immersion in another culture is available at the **Indian YMCA**.

Best Asian... London has ambassadors from most Asian kitchens, and has had for decades. First to arrive were the Cantonese; now, in preparation for (or avoidance of) the return of Hong Kong to Chinese rule in 1997, chefs from that city are flocking in, and the Chinese food scene is changing again. Dim sum here have a reputation that rivals Hong Kong's, and the biggest, most ornate, and best known place to partake of those unrecognizable steamed things on trolleys is **New World**. Among Chinatown Cantonese, **Fung Shing** is not only reliable, but prettier than most, in restful pale green. Malaysian food is not available everywhere, but its satays and noodle dishes are easy to eat, as Londoners have been doing for years at **Melati**. The *Tom yam koong* (very spicy shrimp soup), *pad Thai* (noodles with everything), green and red curries, and so on of Thailand have been thoroughly adopted in this town. Try Thai in Soho at **Sri Siam** and **Bahn Thai**, or make an outing to far-flung Maida Vale and the non-gourmet but pleasing **Ben's Thai**.

The French connection... Time was, going to a London restaurant was a big night out, and the restaurant was Escoffier-French, with great batteries of flatware and waiters who said "*et pour madame?*" and served the veg-etables from the left. Now, of course, we understand that French is not the only cuisine, even if France is still the most food-obsessed nation of Europe, and we under-stand this partly because there aren't so very many French restaurants left. One holdover is **Chez Moi**. Its attempts at staying à la mode are sadly misguided—it serves what must be the most overdressed and crouton-ed Caesar in the western world—but the more classical French dishes are satisfying. **L'Artiste Musclé** may be the least preten-tious, most basic (in a good way) French place in town, apart from **Surinder's**, a little *mère-et-père* place near Portobello that does a great-value rich and Gallic prix fixe. The check is also reasonable at Covent Garden's **Le Palais du Jardin**, a creditable simulated French brasserie. Going up the scale, the *comme il faut* award for all-round French authenticity, loveability, and understated charm has to go to the Knightsbridge **St. Quentin**. **Bistrot Bruno** has the most inventive *cuisine de terroir* you'll find outside the French regions themselves, while **La Pomme d'Amour** is best for its beauteous, summery setting, and its unadventurous menus come out well on the plate. The even more gorgeous **Ritz**'s French side is classical, laden with foie gras, lobster, caviar, and so on, and priced accordingly. If you're going to lavish many pounds on the French meal-fairly-near-France of your life, though, do it at **La Tante Claire**. It never misses. Those who crave extra waiterly flourishes, a surfeit of very rich people, and even richer ingredients favor **Le Gavroche**, where Michel Roux, Jr.'s cuisine is as Classical as you'll find. Then there are those who worship **Chez Nico**, a serious Park Lane salon that impresses without being much fun.

Old Italian... Soho was originally the home of London's Italian community, and a few red-sauce survivors of the rent wars remain in this groovy schmoozy neighborhood. Some we don't recommend, but you've gotta love **Pollo** for its grungy plastic-ivy, pine-paneled decor, and hordes of art student club kids feeding on chicken cacciatore, ravioli in brodo, and cassata. London's biggest bargain in old-fashioned pasta is still served at **Centrale**, which is lesser-known, better, and hipper than Pollo. The late lamented film director Derek Jarman was a fixture there when in London. While in Soho, don't forget to drop in at **Bar Italia**, which functioned for years as the Soho Italian community's center before being adopted forever by clubbers. It got an architect's redesign recently, but much to the relief of old and new fans alike, it looks exactly the same afterwards. One venerable Italian place that has kept up with the times is **Bertorelli's**, where some of the kind waitresses have remained loyal through redecorations and chef changes and everything. They still offer the fabulous olive bread with big smiles.

Noov Italian... Actually, **Bertorelli's** has kept up so well, it belongs in this category, too, for the inventive but not over-challenging food of Maddalena Bonino. Conran has one Italian in his trendy stable, the **Cantina del Ponte** (next to its French translation, Le Pont de la Tour); it's well-supplied with terrace tables, which are more of a reason to come than the predictable, not always great, sun-dried-balsamic cooking. Queen of the sturdy southern style that replaced the creamy-ragù-giant-peppermill Italians is the **River Cafe**. Anyone who went there before 1994 will be surprised at the new lighter, bigger room, with its long, mirrored bar; anyone who's never been there before will be surprised at the lack of any river view. Its prices, which used to seem outrageous, haven't risen much

LONDON | DINING

and now appear more reasonable in the big picture, especially for food of this quality. More central, and close to Bertorelli's, is Joe Allen's Italian cousin **Orso**, also a carbon copy of the New York version. Astonishingly, it manages to attract a similar crowd to its NYC model, though London's has fewer thespians and more magazine editors. In Portobello land, find its little sister **Orsino**.

Somewhere in between France and Italy... Mediterranean madness was caused partly by Antony Worral Thompson, who has London on a leash (see sidebar). The menus at all his places (**Bistrot 190, Zoe, dell'Ugo**) begin with "country bread, tapenade, anchoïade, and olives"—and so, it seems, do half the newer restaurants in town. **Brasserie du Marché aux Puces**, for instance, which has a French name, but is pan-European, as is its new Notting Hill sibling, **Avenue West Eleven. Soho Soho's Rotisserie**, the adjacent **Café Bohème, Daphne's**, the **Belvedere**—these are all Mediterraneanesque.

Best prix-fixe lunch... The places presenting the most shocking checks are the hotel dining rooms, the big star chefs, the haute French places, and permutations of same. But at any of these, big savings can be harvested over lunch—a lunch that could run for hours. **Chez Nico, The Connaught, Marco Pierre White: The Restaurant, Bibendum**, and **La Tante Claire** all offer a three-course lunch for £25, while the **Ritz** has the same for £26. Some of those include coffee, but none the half bottle of wine that **Le Gavroche** throws in for £36. At **The Four Seasons**, £25 buys you four courses. Both **The Ivy**, and **Alastair Little** do three-course lunches for half that, the former only on weekends, and **Quaglino's** does one for only a little more.

The great British breakfast... If your hotel only does continental, repair for morning sustenance to any greasy-spoon caff you happen upon. Good luck—they're a dying breed. For under a fiver, you can order: bacon, egg (fried), sausage, black pudding, a slice (fried bread), beans (baked), mushrooms (fried or poached), tomatoes (griddled), and toast. If that's not enough, add kippers, liver, kidneys, porridge (oatmeal). If you can't find a caff, head to **Simpson's-in-the-Strand**, which offers the works in

Edwardian splendor at well under a tenner. It comes with coffee, oj, newspaper, and pastries. In St. James's are two genteel purveyors of the traditional breakfast: the **Fountain** and the **Ritz** (at its most affordable time of day). Early risers (or night people) can try the **Fox and Anchor** pub, at its best very early when the meat porters from nearby Smithfield market are still there.

Tea for two... Let's say it again: The meal the British take around 4pm is not "high tea." Actually, you'd have trouble locating a single Londoner who takes tea at all, except for the hot beverage, which is still widely drunk pot after pot after pot. "A proper tea" consists of tiny, delicate, crustless sandwiches—usually filled with cucumber, egg, or salmon—then scones with strawberry jam and clotted cream (as thick as cream can be before it's butter), then cake; and tea, of course, made with loose leaves, of course. The **Ritz**'s tea in the pretty Palm Court had become a tourist trap until new owners took over the hotel. Now the two-sitting crush has been abolished, and you can sit there sipping champagne along with the scones, if you want, from 3:30 to 6:30. The **Savoy** does a lovely tea, with attentive uniformed service and endless refills, not just of tea but of all the tiers of the cakestand, too. The timeless and elegant **Fountain**, which is behind Fortnum & Mason and belongs to it, serves its own blends of tea; it's quite suitable for dowagers and Little Lord Fauntleroys. For a more continental tea, with palmiers and éclairs and milles feuilles, try **Patisserie Valerie**'s original Soho branch and its outposts, or **Maison Bertaux** around the corner—these two stalwarts have gone head-to-head in the cake wars for decades, and still nobody wins, nobody loses. If in Hampstead, try the local tea-time institution, the Hungarian **Louis Patisserie**.

LONDON | DINING

The Index

£££££	over $65	over £40
£££€	$40–$65	£25–£40
£££	$28–$40	£18–£25
££	$16–$28	£10–£18
£	under $16	under £10

(Per person for three courses and coffee, no wine)

Al San Vincenzo. Hidden in nowheresville, behind Marble Arch, this piccolo salon (only eight tables) serves Umbrian dishes, some of them unusual: *risotto al vino Rubesco* (made with the red wine of Umbria, Rubesco Torgiano); octopus, snails, squab, or tongue, in salty cannellini bean puree, or with piquant salsa verde; and a dessert—*melanzane alla cioccolata*—of sweet sautéed eggplant enrobed in dark chocolate sauce.... *Tel 0171/262–9623. 30 Connaught St. W2, Marble Arch tube stop. AE, DC not accepted. £££–££££*

Alastair Little. Chef/owner Little has been prominent on the culinary scene for some years, serving his own hybrid modern Brit/Med/Pacific Rim cuisine to groovy foodies in this minimalist, none-too-comfortable, two-level Soho salon. Fish is prominent; menus change twice a day.... *Tel 0171/734–5183. 49 Frith St. W1, Leicester Sq. tube stop. DC not accepted. ££££*

All Saints. A good night at this bare-plaster-walled, wooden-chaired, neighborhood place is like dinner at somebody's house, with an eclectic selection of media types, band members, and bankers on hand. Food matches the informal mood—gazpacho; Tuscan chicken on herbed polenta; crispy duck pancake; a tall, creamy lemon tart.... *Tel 0171/243–2808. 12 All Saints Rd. W11, Westbourne Park tube stop. Reservations for dinner. AE, DC not accepted. ££*

LONDON | DINING

Archduke. A wine bar in a converted brick-walled warehouse, whose main attraction is its proximity to the South Bank Center, where food options are sad. Stand in line downstairs for quiches, pâtés, salads, soups, or go up to the restaurant for a large variety of sausages. The food's OK, the atmosphere—especially when there's live jazz—can be great.... *Tel 0171/928–9370. Concert Hall Approach, South Bank SE1, Waterloo tube stop. Reservations for dinner in restaurant. ££*

L'Artiste Musclé. A sweet little *tranche* of provincial France in a picturesque Mayfair tangle of car-free streets, this simple wood-floored, bentwood-chaired wine bar is best experienced from a sidewalk table in summer, and least successful in the cramped basement. Beef bourguignon, *saucisse* (smoked sausage) and flageolet beans, French bread and pâté are always on the blackboard menu.... *Tel 0171/493–6150. 1 Shepherd Market W1, Green Park tube stop. Reservations for 5 or more. DC not accepted. ££*

Atlantic Bar & Grill. Benefiting from an anomaly in the licensing laws, this late-night spot looks like a jazzed-up, parquet-floored ocean liner. Despite being the size of a small village, it gets packed most nights, and weekends are a zoo. Some food's good—Mediterranean or Asian appetizer platters; linguini with cashew-cilantro pesto.... *Tel 0171/734–4888. 20 Glasshouse St. W1, Piccadilly Circus tube stop. Reservations weekends. DC not accepted. £££*

Aubergine. A raving success in its opening year (1994), this small, Provençal-looking foodie haunt in Chelsea has an inventive Franglais menu (literally—viz: "sea bass with jus vanille"; "pan-fried red mullet, sauce épices, pommes frites"), the work of young Scottish star Gordon Ramsay.... *Tel 0171/352–3449. 11 Park Walk SW10, Sloane Sq. tube stop. ££££*

Avenue West Eleven. This light-filled, stone-floored, hessian-and-adobe-decorated room is brought to you by the Brasserie du Marché aux Puces people, and therefore, it's in fashion. Many things can be ordered in two sizes (a growing trend)—things like cäpes on brioche toast; parrot fish with dill and lemon gin.... *Tel 0171/221–8144. 157 Notting Hill Gate W11, Notting Hill Gate tube stop. ££–£££*

Bahn Thai. A longstanding Soho Thai, this is often accused of being the best in town, with a menu several pages long, studded with chili symbols to denote what's spicy hot. Soft shell crab, duck with honey dipping sauce—and hundreds more additions to the usual noodles and soups are enticing. It got a recent redesign, and now looks far better, with a decor of bamboo chairs and halogen spotlights.... *Tel 0171/437–8504. 21A Frith St. W1, Leicester Sq. tube stop. Reservations for dinner. £££*

Bar Gansa. Plainly decked out in lemony hues and some Iberian gewgaws, this very successful tapas bar in Camden Town is not for quiet conversation on weekends. *Albondigas* (meatballs), *boquerones* (fresh anchovies), tortilla, and chorizo are among many little dishes.... *Tel 0171/267–8909. 2 Inverness St. NW1, Camden Town tube stop. No reservations. £*

Bar Italia. This Soho institution is the ur-espresso bar, always open, nearly always full of life, and lined with Rocky Marciano-abilia. Sandwiches, panetone, and unmemorable gelati are the meager food choices, but the espresso and cappuccino are the business.... *Tel 0171/437–4520. 22 Frith St. W1, Leicester Sq. tube stop. No reservations. No credit cards. £*

Beach Blanket Babylon. This outrageous-looking dungeon-like fantasy is the nearest thing to a singles bar you'll find in hip Notting Hill. Cross the drawbridge to the restaurant to pick up a good meal here, too—glass noodle and crab salad with sweet chilli dressing; duck with gnocchi and cèpes.... *Tel 0171/229–2907. 45 Ledbury Rd. W11, Notting Hill Gate tube stop. Reservations for dinner. AE, DC not accepted. ££–£££*

Belgo. This Belgian-style faux-refectory in Camden has now spawned a branch in Covent Garden, which had just opened at press time. Order mussels and fries, waterzooi (fish stew), or cherry beer from waiters dressed as monks, in a steel, concrete, and pine chamber, entered via another drawbridge.... *Tel 0171/267–9718. 72 Chalk Farm Rd. NW1, Chalk Farm tube stop. DC not accepted. ££*

Belvedere. A beautiful midpark setting for this serene room of huge windows and white linens far outstrips the Med-Brit menu (blackened tuna; confit of duck, garlic mash; welsh rarebit; chocolate marquise).... *Tel 0171/602–1238. Holland Park, Abbotsbury Rd. W8, Holland Park tube stop. ££££*

Ben's Thai. A big off-the-beaten-track Art Nouveau pub harbors this wood-paneled dining room upstairs. There's better Thai food in town than Ben's *tom yam koong* (shrimp soup), *kwaitiew pad si-ewe* (egg-veg-beef noodles), etc., but value and casual ambience this has got.... *Tel 0171/266–3134. The Warrington Hotel, 93 Warrington Crescent W9; Warwick Ave. tube stop. Reservations for dinner. AE, DC not accepted. ££*

Bertorelli's. Been around for ever, but you'd never know from the white walls and cobalt-blue lamps, the great service, the friendly buzz, and the modish (but not *too*) menu—garganelli with green beans and cobb nuts; monkfish ragout; panna cotta.... *Tel 0171/836–3969. 44A Floral St. WC2, Covent Garden tube stop. £££*

Bibendum. The moment of transition after the departure of Simon Hopkinson—the chef and partner (with Sir Terence Conran) who put this on the map—occurred as we went to press. Still, this cherished French (with British accent) treat, beneath the stained-glass windows of the Michelin tire man (this was that company's HQ), is bound to come out right.... *Tel 0171/581–5817. Michelin House, 81 Fulham Rd. SW3, South Kensington tube stop. DC not accepted. £££££*

Bibendum Oyster Bar. In the same exquisite, exuberantly tiled Art Nouveau building as the Bibendum restaurant (and the Conran Shop), eat *plateaux de fruits de mer*, crab or Caesar salads, as well as oysters, in great style.... *Tel 0171/589–1480. Michelin House, 81 Fulham Rd. SW3, South Kensington tube stop. No reservations. DC not accepted. £££*

Bistrot 190. This is the original of ubiquitous Antony Worrall Thompson's several Med-style cool and casual places. Near the big South Ken museums, it's got a permanent well-heeled crowd feasting on big food. The menu describes dishes by listing every ingredient: e.g. pork chop with rhubarb compote and cheese-and-mustard mash. The lemon tart here is the sine qua non.... *Tel 0171/581–5666. 190 Queensgate SW7, South Kensington tube stop. No reservations. £££*

LONDON | DINING

Bistrot Bruno. How glad we are that Bruno Loubet embraces unusual meats and peasant cooking techniques (in, say, neck of lamb and tripe-stuffed potato); his onion tarte tatin is swoon-inducing, and ah, those chocolate-enrobed sorbets with coffee! Look for his new place, l'Odeon, too. The adjacent Cafe charges less money for less Loubet.... *Tel 0171/ 734–4545. 63 Frith St. W1, Leicester Sq. tube stop. £££*

Brackenbury. Take a cab to reach this peach-colored peach in a secret Hammersmith pocket, featuring the vivid, fun food of young Adam and Katie Robinson. An assiette of all the fishy appetizers is always offered; otherwise, market availability dictates—saffron turbot and mussel stew, onion-thyme tart, sautéed brains, a burger, blood-orange sorbet. It's loud and friendly.... *Tel 0181/748–0107. 129 Brackenbury Rd. W6, Hammersmith tube stop. ££*

Brasserie du Marché aux Puces. Punctuating the end of Portobello Road, this big-windowed, wood-floored, all-purpose eatery does laid-back French-ish food, like vichyssoise; ox tongue with capers; steak; bread-and-butter pudding; or endive, pear, and walnut salad.... *Tel 0181/968– 5828. 349 Portobello Rd. W10, Ladbroke Grove tube stop. No credit cards. ££*

Brick Lane Beigel Bake. An East End institution, this 24-hour boil-then-bake-ery offers standing room only for noshing on filled bagels and terrible coffee at giveaway rates.... *Tel 0171/729–0616. 159 Brick Lane, E1, Whitechapel tube stop. No credit cards. £*

Café Bohème. Most useful as a Soho rendezvous and after-hours drinking den (as your bruised elbows will notice), this continental brasserie nevertheless has perfectly fine food, along the ciabatta-roast-veg-goat's cheese sandwich axis.... *Tel 0171/734–0623. 13 Old Compton St. W1, Leicester Sq. tube stop. Reservations for dinner. DC not accepted. ££*

Cafe Fish. A most handy stop in the middle of town, with a menu divided into cooking methods (steamed, *meuniàre*, fried, grilled), this spot plays the greatest fish hits—bouillaibaisse, *moules mariniàre, plateaux de fruits de mer* (available for one person). It's bustling and plain-looking with a fast, cheap, busy-busy basement wine bar.... *Tel 0171/930–3999. 39 Panton St. SW1, Piccadilly Circus tube stop. ££ (wine bar), £££ (restaurant)*

Café Flo. The best of the nearly identical Parisian wannabes, this cafe—and its branches—does a good, fast, cheap soup-or-salad, steak-or-fish-with-fries deal. Many other dishes from cassoulet to goat's cheese salad are augmented by the occasional regional wine and food promotion.... *Tel 0171/836–8289. 51 St Martin's Lane WC2, Charing Cross tube stop. DC not accepted. £–££*

Cantina del Ponte. Gorgeously perched on the right bank by Tower Bridge—part of Sir Terry's "Gastrodrome"—this supplies not the best, but a creditable (and large) modish southern Italian menu. Eat in a big Tuscan-rustic terracotta-tiled room, or on the terrace. Wild mushroom soup; stuffed zucchini flowers; grilled squid on rocket (arugula).... *Tel 0171/403–5403. Butlers Wharf, 36c Shad Thames SE1, Tower Hill tube stop. ££££*

Le Caprice. It has been a wonderful experience to spend time here since the old London fave was reopened by the classy Corbin-King duo (see also the Ivy, below). Shiny 1980s black furnishings, sparkly lighting, Japanese-y flowers, starched white cloths set the scene for a round-the-world menu (bisque of Dublin Bay prawns; champagne risotto with Perigord truffles; deep-fried cod and chips). Service is perfect.... *Tel 0171/629–2239. Arlington House, Arlington St. SW1, Green Park tube stop. ££££*

Casale Franco. Ask, or you'll never find the cobbled courtyard entrance (with hotly-contested summer tables) to this Islington staple. Famous for great pizza, it has an arrogant no-pizza-only policy, no reservations, and a sometimes surly staff, but the brick-walled warehouse chic and the compulsory other food (calves liver, cuttlefish in its ink, polenta, salads) is fine.... *Tel 0171/226–8994. Behind 134 Upper St. N1, Highbury and Islington tube stop. No reservations. AE, DC not accepted. ££–£££*

The Causerie. How sweet it is to perch on delicate couches at low oval tables and be cosseted by charming French waiters, as you load up at this 30-dish smorgasbord (smoked fish, marinated herring, salads, chicken mousse). An unexpected bargain.... *Tel 0171/629–8860. Claridge's Hotel, Brook St. W1, Bond St. tube stop. Jacket and tie required for men. ££*

Centrale. Basic as it gets—there's not even a bathroom—this Italian Soho diner nevertheless serves great pasta (the usual sorts) and minestrone; the risotti you can live without, though.... *Tel 0171/437–5513. 16 Moor St. W1, Leicester Sq. tube stop. No reservations. No credit cards. £*

Chelsea Kitchen. They do not lie: since Chelsea swung in the sixties, this has been its kitchen, filling folks up with wholesome fodder—from egg and chips to beef stew with veg, moussaka, chicken curry, and apple crumble and custard.... *Tel 0171/589–1330. 98 King's Rd. SW3, Sloane Sq. tube stop. No reservations. No credit cards. £*

Chez Moi. This gentle, pink-walled anachronism comes from the days when French meant fancy. Ordering wisely still gets you a fine meal—*pot-au-feu de poussin* (poached vegetables and boned young chicken); tournedos with béarnaise; salmon quenelles. Skip dessert. The waiters are lovely.... *Tel 0171/603–8267. 1 Addison Ave. W11, Holland Park tube stop. ££££*

Chez Nico at Ninety Park Lane. Nico Ladenis, self-taught superstar of London cuisine, keeps a lower profile than he used to, maybe because he's finally settled down in the patrician salon he deserves. Here you'll find well-padded seats and patrons, obsequious service, and complicated perfection on the plate, replete with foie gras. Dress smart.... *Tel 0171/409–1290. Grosvenor House, 90 Park Lane W1, Marble Arch tube stop. £££££*

Chicago Pizza Pie Factory. Where deep-dish lives in London. Chicago pop radio blares and it's pretty authentically American, down to the eager service. Expat Bob Payton, who opened this place and brought this style to town, died suddenly and prematurely in 1994; his energy is missed.... *Tel 0171/629–2669. 17 Hanover Sq. W1, Oxford Circus tube stop. Reservations for kids' Sunday lunch. DC not accepted. ££*

Christopher's. The diametric opposite of the above, this is upscale East Coast dining transplanted, uncut, to Covent Garden. Up the stone stair is a soaring mirrored space, where opera music fills the air and you can dine on plain broiled steak, chicken, and fish; fries, creamed spinach, or nutmeggy mashed potatoes; and salsas and salads. Below is a cafe that halves the check. Brunch is the best meal here.... *Tel 0171/240–4222. 18 Wellington St. WC2, Covent Garden tube stop. ££ (cafe), ££££ (restaurant)*

Clarke's. Chef/owner Sally C. trained in Paris and California, and duly displays both influences in food that's classically treated and tastes fresh. Ingredients are respected so much that each night's menu is dictated by the best available—one set menu, whatever Sally has chosen, period.... *Tel 0171/221–9225. 124 Kensington Church St. W8, Notting Hill Gate tube stop. No AE, DC. ££££*

The Coffee Cup. Dingy and wood-lined with ancient vinyl banquettes, this adored "caff" (Brit slang for cafe) is so unfashionable that it's going to start a trend any second. You can order beans and eggs on toast, gateaux with aerosol frosting, hot buttered crumpets (like griddle cakes), mixed grills, and fry-ups; there's no espresso.... *Tel 0171/435–7565. 74 Hampstead High St. NW3, Hampstead tube stop. No reservations. No credit cards. £.*

Condotti. This is Mayfair pizza, meaning art on the walls, an extra quid on the check, and a most unusual potato-crusted four-cheese pie on the list of usuals; salads are mercifully better than at Pizza Express.... *Tel 0171/499–1308. 4 Mill St. W1, Oxford Circus tube stop. Reservations for lunch. ££*

The Connaught. This correct dining room is the ultimate purveyor of one sort of English experience—the aristocratic one (not even a fantasy for many regulars here). The Restaurant is bigger and clubbier, the Grill lighter, more intimate, but both serve the French master chef's British dishes—pickled tongue and boiled silverside (brisket), game, roasts—plus some classic French (tournedos Rossini, for example). All comes *complet* (with side dishes and appetizer), so the prices aren't quite as fierce as they seem.... *Tel 0171/499–7070. Carlos Place W1, Green Park tube stop. Jacket and tie required for men. ££££*

LONDON | DINING

Costas Grill. This welcoming Greek taverna-diner, some blocks from the trendy parts of Notting Hill, serves good Hellenic staples (homemade hummus with hot pita, moussaka, Greek salad with feta). Garden's a polite word for the yard in back, but it's most useful on a warm night.... *Tel 0171/229–3794. 14 Hillgate St. W8, Notting Hill Gate tube stop. Reservations for dinner. No credit cards. £*

The Criterion. Byzantine splendor in Piccadilly Circus, it is another domain of Marco Pierre White. A grown-up atmosphere, a certain percentage of beautiful people, and a wide selection of fairly classical French dishes with interesting bits, like Gravadlax and Beignetes of Oyster with Citrus Butter, or Roast Leg of Rabbit Farci with Calamari, Pearl Barley Risotto. The hangar-sized place really is a beauty, with its golden mosaic ceiling and cerulean drapes.... *Tel 0171/925–0909. 224 Piccadilly W1, Piccadilly Circus tube stop. ££££*

Crown & Goose. It is, as its name implies, a pub, but one with a roaring fire, art, squashy sofas for winter, and sidewalk tables for summer. Food includes risotto, steak sandwich with dijon mayo, and stuffed mushrooms. The place is usually packed.... *Tel 0171/485–2342. 100 Arlington Rd. NW1, Camden Town tube stop. No reservations. No credit cards. £*

Daphne's. Where the lady lunches: big hair and gilt buttons are de rigueur after dark, when your baubles should be real. Food is from the Mediterranean hit parade (fritto misto, sea bass baked with fennel, an unctuous Caesar salad, shellfish, and risotti); what really matters is which flagstone-floored conservatory you're seated in.... *Tel 0171/589–4257. 112 Draycott Ave. SW3, South Kensington tube stop. ££££*

Daquise. Ancient and fusty Polish Daquise squats contentedly by the South Ken tube, oblivious of her upscale neighborhood. The mushy *koulebiak* (salmon pastry) and *bigos* (sauerkraut and leftovers) seem like they've been simmering for years. Borscht is OK; tea, pastries, and vodka better.... *Tel 0171/589–6117. 20 Thurloe St. SW7, South Kensington tube stop. No reservations. No credit cards. £*

dell'Ugo. Another Anthony Worrall Thompson success, this one in Soho central caters to diners upstairs, drinkers and grazers down on the first floor. There's the expected menu:

country bread, tapenade, anchoäde, and olives; crostini; lamb shank with rosemary, garlic, and flageolet beans.... *Tel 0171/734–8300. 56 Frith St. W1, Leicester Sq. tube stop. No reservations downstairs. DC not accepted. ££–£££*

Diwana Bhel Poori. Staples of the South Indian menu include the *masala dosa* (a paper-thin rice/lentil flour pancake encircling spiced potato and green coconut chutney) and *bhel poori* mixtures (tortilla chip-like bits mixed with tamarind and coconut chutneys and spiced yogurt). It's delicious, enlivening food, served in a basic pine table cafe.... *Tel 0171/387–5556. 121 Drummond St. NW1, Euston Sq. tube stop. No reservations. £*

East West. In a holistic health center on the City's edge, this slightly smug and holy macrobiotic restaurant serves semi-delicious, semi-taste-free set meals. The food groups couldn't be more balanced if they were Baryshnikov, though you're welcome to mess with your chakras and order the organic wine.... *Tel 0171/608–0300. 188 Old St. EC1, Old St. tube stop. £*

Ed's Easy Diner. Some say this is a great burger, others accuse Ed of grease-mongering, but you also get a fifties decor with jukebox, cheese fries, kosher dogs, and peanut butter shakes.... *Tel 0171/439–1955. 12 Moor St. W1, Leicester Sq. tube stop. AE, DC not accepted. £*

Fatboy's Diner. This one is unmistakeably a diner—a chrome trailer shipped from Pennsylvania and planted with an astroturf yard. Progress from your basic Fatburger to the kitchen sinkburger known as the Hillbilly, and wash it down with an ice-cream float.... *Tel 0171/240–1902. 21 Maiden Lane WC2, Covent Garden tube stop. No reservations. No credit cards. £*

F Cooke & Sons. London's only true indigenous food is stewed or jellied eels (see the precooked ones writhing at the counter), pie (of ground beef), mash (mashed potatoes), and liquor (parsley sauce), and here is its most perfectly preserved purveyor (call for other locations). It's not just a meal, but a culture—a workingmen's caff, sawdust-floored, Victorian tiled.... *Tel 0171/254–2878. 41 Kingsland High St. E8, British Rail station, Dalston Kingsland. No reservations. No credit cards. £*

Food For Thought. Near to Fatboy's (see above) and a million miles away, here is meatless, microwaveless, nearly guiltless vegetarian happy food—happy because it's good, cheap, generous, and fresh. Thick slices of wholemeal bread, stir fries, and maybe spinach-ricotta filo, followed by cakes and cookies.... *Tel 0171/836–0239. 31 Neal St. WC2, Covent Garden tube stop. No reservations. No credit cards. £*

The Fountain. It's even more English than Mary Poppins, who would feel at home on the comfy chairs here. Order quaint food (things on toast, pies, genteel salads, and poached dover sole) and/or Vesuvian sundaes oozing with sauces and cream and fruit, with teas from mothership Fortnum & Mason to assuage the sugar rush.... *Tel 0171/734–8040. Back of Fortnum & Mason, 181 Piccadilly W1 (entrance on Duke/Jermyn St.), Green Park tube stop. £–££*

The Four Seasons. A grand hotel dining room, with a park view that helps the lunch be an even better value. Young Jean Christophe Novelli has made a name in game (lettuce-wrapped saddle of rabbit with white bean jus and truffle oil is a recent invention), and is thought bold.... *Tel 0171/499–0888. Hamilton Place, Park Lane W1, Hyde Park Corner tube stop. Jacket and tie required for men at dinner. £££££*

Fox & Anchor. This pub by Smithfield, the meat market, serves big plates of meat. It opens at 7am, and has a unique license to serve alcohol with breakfast.... *Tel 0171/253–4838. 115 Charterhouse St. EC1M; Farringdon tube stop. No reservations. DC not accepted. £*

French House Dining Room. Above the Soho pub of the same name is a tiny, cozy dining salon, all red banquettes and mirror, where Fergus Henderson and Margot Clayton of St. John honed their craft. It still serves their kind of Scottish-French nursery food—crab and mayonnaise, garlicky salads, giant lamb shanks, homemade cake, and ice cream.... *Tel 0171/437–2477. 49 Dean St. W1, Leicester Sq. tube stop. ££–£££*

Fung Shing. London's Chinatown, though improving, is not a patch on New York's or San Francisco's, but this cool green place has authentic dishes like salt-baked chicken, fried intestines, and stewed duck with yam, available even to those who can't decipher pictograms.... *Tel 0171/437–1539. 15 Lisle St. WC2, Leicester Sq. tube stop. Reservations for dinner. £££*

Galicia. In the Notting Hill netherlands is this easygoing family-run Spanish restaurant, with a tapas bar in front. The food is hit-or-miss—the more Iberian the dish, the better it is. Tapas outshine entrées, which is OK, because it's a good place to shoot the breeze for hours.... *Tel 0181/969–3539. 323 Portobello Rd. W10, Ladbroke Grove tube stop. AE not accepted. £–££*

Le Gavroche. A very well-known center of gastroporn, run by the Roux brothers (the Julia Childs—Children?—of the U.K.). Son of Albert, Michel Roux, Jr., now wears the toque in this dark-green subterranean *boîte*, keeping the family recipes warm. These are welded to the highest Classical tradition, littered with foie gras, truffles, and lobster, but certified best of breed.... *Tel 0171/408–0881. 43 Upper Brook St. W1, Marble Arch tube stop. Jacket and tie required. £££££*

Gay Hussar. Rub elbows with Labour politicians and other lefty intelligentsia at this beloved old Soho Hungarian—probably rub elbows literally, since the enveloping banquettes are shared. Eat big: "heroic goose" is one item on the menu, appropriately. Expect dishes to have cream in them whenever possible.... *Tel 0171/437–0973. 2 Greek St. W1, Leicester Sq. tube stop. £££*

Geales. One of the best places to get ye famous British fish n' chips, it even has a restaurant attached—they're usually takeout only. Ordering anything else would defeat the object, but you could try a side of mushy peas (it's just what it sounds like).... *Tel 0171/727–7969. 2 Farmer St. W8, Notting Hill Gate tube stop. AE, DC not accepted. £*

Gracelands Palace. Paul Chan is the only Chinese restaurateur to perform Elvis impersonations. His place is not famous for food, so make sure you're booking your table for a show night.... *Tel 0171/639–3961. 881 Old Kent Rd. SE15, Elephant and Castle tube stop, then bus #53, 172, or 173. AE not accepted. £–££*

Green's. A manly set of darkly wood-panelled rooms provides a surprisingly sybaritic time among nobs and establishmentarians. You can quaff champagne from London's best list of them (other wines aren't bad either) and feast on oysters (there's a separate bivalve bar) as well as shellfish, grilled halibut, or calves liver. Try the amazing claret ice cream.... *Tel 0171/930–4566. 36 Duke St. SW1, Green Park tube stop. Jacket and tie for men. ££££*

Indian YMCA. Imagine the dining hall at Delhi University—that's what you have here, only it's less humid. Get thoroughly, spicily fed for very little; stand in line for a meal ticket first.... *Tel 0171/387–0411. 41 Fitzroy Sq. W1, Great Portland St. tube stop. No reservations. No credit cards. £*

The Ivy. There is nothing wrong with The Ivy: No nastiness toward nobodies, lots of eclectic dishes you want to eat (blinis and caviar to shepherd's pie, and irresistible Desserts R Us); and nearly every night, a glamorous feeling that you're in the place where things happen.... *Tel 0171/836–4751. 1 West St. WC2, Leicester Sq. tube stop. ££££*

Joe Allen. You could be at the original on Manhattan's 46th Street restaurant row, from the brick walls to the corn muffin with broiled chicken breast and salsa; from the cobb salad and warm banana bread with caramel sauce to the theatrical flock after curtain.... *Tel 0171/836–0651. 13 Exeter St. WC2, Covent Garden tube stop. No credit cards. £££*

Kensington Place. Chef Rowley Leigh has had his turn as flavor of the month, but now he's settled into being just hugely liked by the legion of table-hopping regulars, who call this glass-walled echo chamber "KP." Grilled foie gras on sweetcorn blini is his signature appetizer; baked tamarillo with vanilla ice cream the dessert; in between, try maybe rabbit *merguez* with *harissa* (Moroccan spicy sausage with hot sauce).... *Tel 0171/727–3184. 201 Kensington Church St. W8, Notting Hill Gate tube stop. AE, DC not accepted. £££*

Khan's. Most agree this institution—a very downmarket, Indian version of Kensington Place (see above)—fails to deserve its popularity, what with barely civil waiters and only so-so curry. But it's still fun, huge, cheap, and goodlooking, and noncurry experts will be happy with the food.... *Tel 0171/ 727–5420. 13–15 Westbourne Grove W11, Bayswater tube stop. £*

Lauderdale House. An exquisitely situated park cafe, with crafts stalls, an aviary, and braille-labelled fragrance garden, and Highgate Cemetery next door. There's more big food here than is usual in such places—lasagna, homemade quiches, and so on.... *Tel 0181/341–4807. Waterlow Park, Highgate Hill N6, Archway tube stop. No credit cards. £*

Lemonia. A big, beautiful, plant-filled, friendly pseudo-taverna on the street where the local well-heeled go to get well-fed. London Greeks are usually from Cyprus, and the personnel here are no exception. *Meze* (a succession of dishes to sample) is good, as is the chargrilled souvlakia and the *kleftiko* (marinated, baked lamb).... *Tel 0171/586–7454. 89 Regent's Park Rd. NW1, Chalk Farm tube stop. AE, DC not accepted. ££.*

Louis Patisserie. Hampstead's traditional Sunday pastime is standing on line for the Hungarian pastries Louis Gat's been baking for 40 years. Poppyseed cake, baked cheesecake, brioches, and Danish; lousy coffee.... *Tel 0171/435–9908. 32 Heath St. NW3, Hampstead tube stop. No credit cards. £*

Maison Bertaux. A little old Soho salon, where you pick your pastry and have it brought to the plain upstairs room. It's in friendly rivalry with Patisserie Valerie (see below).... *Tel 0171/437–6007. 28 Greek St. W1, Leicester Sq. tube stop. No credit cards. £*

Manze's. The other most unspoiled pie and mash shop (see F Cooke & Sons, above) belongs to the other eel dynasty. You won't notice the difference, but this is easier to find (call for other branches).... *Tel 0171/407–2985. 87 Tower Bridge Rd. SE1, London Bridge tube stop. No credit cards. £.*

Marco Pierre White: The Restaurant. The place that loves itself. When chef Marco Pierre White is in, excitement flickers uncoolly around the plush, serious, deep carpeted, all-but-soundproof room—he is all charisma and fame. His cuisine is based on what he learned from his mentor, Michel Roux (of Le Gavroche—see above), but has since gone stellar on its own.

LONDON | DINING

Signature dishes include a pear tarte tatin and White's version of Pierre Koffman's signature dish (of La Tante Claire—see above), pig's trotter stuffed with sweetbreads and wild mushrooms.... *Tel 0171/259–5380. Hyde Park Hotel, 66 Knightsbridge SW1, Knightsbridge tube stop. £££££*

Marine Ices. Many flavors of ice cream and gelato are dispensed, along with sundaes and bombes, but you can also get a proper meal in this tiled and mirrored clean-cut parlor close by Camden Lock market.... *Tel 0171/485–3132. 8 Haverstock Hill NW3, Chalk Farm tube stop. No credit cards. £.*

Maxwell's. This place practically introduced the all-beef patty with correct fixings to London nearly a quarter century ago. See the mural of Martin Luther King, Mick Jagger, the Queen, and others sharing lurid cocktails; avoid the Reuben sandwich.... *Tel 0171/836–0303. 8–9 James St. WC2, Covent Garden tube stop. DC not accepted, ££*

Mega-Kalamaras. A rare non-Cypriot taverna in London, this place serves mainland and other island Greek food, which is slightly less meat-obsessed than the food of Cyprus. It looks like a big 1960s sauna, all pine panelled. Its little sibling, Micro-Kalamaras, a few doors away, has a smaller menu (and check) and a BYOB policy.... *Tel 0171/727–9122. 76 Inverness Mews W2, Bayswater tube stop. £££*

Melati. Pine-lined and brightly lit, this Indonesian is always full, as if everyone in London returns over and over, trying eventually to reach the bottom of the endless menu. *Tahu-telor* (bean curd omelet) is juicy, savory, chewy; the bizarre desserts of avocado, colored syrup, fruit, beans, and ice are an acquired taste.... *Tel 0171/734–6964. 21 Great Windmill St. W1, Piccadilly Circus tube stop. ££*

Moshi Moshi Sushi. A small train delivers color-coded plates of maki and sushi to the counter at this Japanese canteen above Platform One, Liverpool Street Station. Eat, drink, count your plates, hand over the cash.... *Tel 0171/247–3227. Unit 24, Liverpool St. Station EC2, Liverpool St. tube stop. No credit cards. £–££*

Nazrul. This very cheap, very basic BYOB Indian caff in the Brick Lane Little Bangladesh is more a cross-cultural thrill than a gastronomic one. But generations of students have loved it—join them if you're game.... *Tel 0171/247–2505. 130 Brick Lane, E1, Aldgate East tube stop. No credit cards. £*

Neal's Yard Dining Room. A burgeoning enclave of herbalists, masseurs, wholefood shops, and witchcraft accessory stores, Neal's Yard is a Covent Garden must-see. This second floor veggie cafe is a highlight, serving sampling platters of different world cuisines—African stews, Turkish mezze, Indian Thali.... *Tel 0171/379–0298. 14 Neal's Yard WC2, Covent Garden tube stop. No credit cards. £*

New World. Cantonese dim sum are best in this gigantic place where trolleys whizz by. At peak times, about 700 people may be at their tables, clamoring for various little dishes of steamed goodies.... *Tel 0171/734–0396. 1 Gerrard Place W1, Leicester Sq. tube stop. £*

192. A never-ending trend in Notting Hillbilly circles, this color-washed wine bar/restaurant has a long and interesting wine list, fashionable salad ingredients (gremolata, Jerusalem artichokes), appetizers that are more enticing than entrées, and a high-decibel crush of cuties hurling gossip at each other.... *Tel 0171/229–0482. 192 Kensington Park Rd. W11, Ladbroke Grove tube stop. ££–£££*

Orso. Just as he did with his eponymous place, Joe Allen duplicated his Italian joint, Orso, from Restaurant Row, NYC. It opened here to rave reviews—the glossy magazine and theater clientele don't mind the pools of olive oil on the arugula and parmesan, pastas, little pizzas, grilled meat and fish, nor the lightless basement, which looks a bit like the Medici family dungeon.... *Tel 0171/240–5269. 27 Wellington St. WC2, Covent Garden tube stop. No credit cards. £££*

Patisserie Valerie. The other essential Soho pastry shop, Valerie is older than Maison Bertaux (see above), and bigger, with many rather dark tables in back. Choosing the better *pain au chocolat* of the two is a toss-up.... *Tel 0171/ 437–3466. 44 Old Compton St. W1, Leicester Sq. tube stop. No credit cards. £*

Palais du Jardin. Wood-floored, halogen spotlit, this big brasserie is forever full because it's priced a notch below what it's worth. Volume can mar the service, and bits of the large and likeably hokey menu (coq au vin; fish soup; fric-assee of lobster and chicken) don't work, but there's always the shellfish stand.... *Tel 0171/379–5353. 136 Long Acre WC2, Covent Garden tube stop. ££*

Pizza Express. London's favorite chain serves thin-crusted, always good pies, with no surprises on top. The 10 Dean Street branch becomes a major jazz venue most evenings; this one is a former Victorian dairy, with its ceramic tiles intact. Nothing else on the menu is worth eating.... *Tel 0171/636–3232. 30 Coptic St. WC1, Holborn tube stop. DC not accepted. £*

The Place Below. A useful lunching place in the City, in the pretty crypt below a Wren church, complete with courtyard; it becomes a gourmet garage Thursday and Friday nights. Its chefs are inventive enough to cause carnivores never to notice the absence of meat or fish.... *Tel 0171/329–0789. St. Mary-le-Bow, Cheapside EC5, St. Paul's tube stop. Reservations for dinner. No credit cards. £–££*

Pollo. In central Soho on the Compton strip, here's another hangout for every student and clubgoer, and one they may never outgrow. Good pasta, nothing fancy, long lines, shared formica tables, great hubbub—this is Pollo.... *Tel 0171/734–5917. 20 Old Compton St. W1, Leicester Sq. tube stop. No reservations, no credit cards. £*

La Pomme d'Amour. As the name suggests (though it means "tomato", it's literally "love apple"), the ambience here is tooth-achingly, sweetly romantic. The interior is all Provençal, with a conservatory in back; the French food is classical-lite.... *Tel 0171/229–8532. 128 Holland Park Avenue W11, Holland Park tube stop. Reservations on weekends. £££*

Le Pont de la Tour. In Sir Terence Conran's "Gastrodrome" of converted-warehouse food emporia, on the south bank just downstream from Tower Bridge (the restaurant's name, translated into French—too cute), this is the best entry, as long as your plastic is healthy. Salade niçoise or scallops with pancetta and hollandaise in the less swanky bar/grill is a relative bargain, but the shellfish is hard to resist. Kill for a terrace table in summer.... *Tel 0171/403–8403 (restau-*

rant), 403–9403 (bar). 36D Shad Thames, Butlers Wharf
SE1, Tower Hill tube stop. £££ (bar/grill), £££££(restaurant)

Quaglino's. The first flush of its celebrity is past, but you still feel
like you're being filmed when you sashay down the sweeping
staircase into this ocean liner of a restaurant, with its
sequoia-sized, artist-daubed pillars and "Crustacea Altar."
Most of the food's just fine, too—saffron crab tart, rosemary-
crusted rabbit with polenta; good desserts.... Tel 0171/
930–6767. 16 Bury St. SW1, Green Park tube stop. £££

Rebato's. In Vauxhall, south of the river, where no tourist has
ever been, is this long-running real Spanish tapas bar and
restaurant. The tapas bar has a rotation of about 20 dishes
(the *pulpo*—octopus—is essential), while the restaurant
serves Catalan and other regional dishes. Music on Friday
and Saturday swells the crowd to fiesta proportions.... Tel
0171/735–6388. 169 South Lambeth Rd. SW8, Vauxhall
tube stop. Reservations on weekends. £–££

The Ritz. The bemirrored, be-muraled rococo Louis XVI room is
heart-rendingly beautiful, overlooking the hotel's formal
Italian garden by day, lit rosily to flatter by night. Order apt
crab Antoinette—an artist's impression of shellfish salad,
with only the best crustacean parts. Like most everything on
the menu, it's exquisite, and royal rich. Chefs have come
and gone a lot, but things seem to have settled down now,
and the food is a treat with a warranty.... Tel 0171/493–
8181. Piccadilly W1, Green Park tube stop. Jacket and tie
required for men. ££££

River Café. This exceptional über-Italian salon began life as the
staff canteen for Richard Rogers' architectural firm, run by
his wife, Ruth, and her pal Rose Grey. They still run it, but
it's become the style-setting place to go for the city slicker's
version of rustic regional meals.... Tel 0171/381–8824.
Thames Wharf, Rainville Rd. W6, Hammersmith tube stop
and bus #11. AE, DC not accepted. ££££

The Room at the Halcyon. An exquisite little hotel by pretty
Holland Park has a sun-filled blue-and-gold basement
restaurant, with chairs dressed in straight jackets, and an
atmosphere half genteel, half louche. Martin Hadden's fash-
ion-plate food has been widely praised—hare on celeriac

puree with morel essence, or lobster in a cumin and cinna-mon sauce, are typical of his considerable style.... *Tel 0171/221–5411. 129 Holland Park Ave. W11, Holland Park tube stop. £££*

Rules. London's oldest restaurant looks Edwardian, though it was founded in the Georgian age and renovated a moment ago. Most customers are, predictably, doing busi-ness, or else are the sort of tourists who count this as a must-see sight: being served pretty good deer (that's venison) from Rules' Scottish estate, by waiters in long white aprons.... *Tel 0171/836–5314. 35 Maiden Lane WC2, Covent Garden tube stop. Jacket and tie required for men. DC not accepted. £££*

Savoy Grill. The most obvious power lunch in town is staged every weekday, starring newspaper editors, City guys, tycoons, and bigshots. Beef Wellington appears on Tuesday; omelette Arnold Bennett (with cheese and smoked fish) was invented here for that novelist, peach Melba for the turn-of-the-century soprano Nellie Melba. Service is avuncular and discreet; everyone has his own teal-upholstered banquette on the yew-paneled perimeter, while nobodies are plunked in the center, looking at them. It's gentle and touristy by night.... *Tel 0171/836–4343. Strand WC2, Aldwych tube stop. Jacket and tie required for men. £££££*

Shaw's. Frances Atkins brings a Yorkshire no-nonsense ethic to fancy food at this serious establishment, done in neutral buff, sand, and manila colors, hushed in atmosphere if not decibel. She cooks only with what's in season, and all her game is wild game (stuffed rabbit with ham, armagnac prunes, leeks, mustard sauce). Dressed-up patrons in their prime enjoy particularly conscientious service.... *Tel 0171/ 373–7774. 119 Old Brompton Rd. SW7, Gloucester Road tube stop. ££££*

Simpsons-in-the-Strand. The Grand Divan Tavern, to give it its full title, prides itself on not having changed—from the heaviest of oak paneling downstairs and Edwardian glitz on the second floor to the roasted animals circulating on silver trolleys, ready to be carved onto your plate. It's like eating on the set of a Merchant-Ivory movie.... *Tel 0171/836–*

9112. 100 Strand WC2, Aldwych tube stop. Jacket and tie required for men. £££

Soho Soho. The useful parts of this successful tri-level operation are the bar and the rotisserie, where an unpretentious lineup of bistro food (chargrilled chicken; omelets; calves' liver; fruit tartes) takes second place to the hubbub and hanging out. Plate glass doors open and spill people onto the sidewalk in summer; inside is Provençal-tiled. Don't bother with the dull and overpriced second-floor restaurant.... *Tel 0171/494–3491. 11–13 Frith St. W1, Leicester Sq. tube stop. No reservations in rotisserie. ££ (rotisserie), £££ (restaurant)*

The Square. Philip Howard's inspired food is reason enough to book a table, but the big, white room, punctuated with deep-pigmented and gold (what else) squares, and the perfect pitch of the service don't exactly mar this awesome operation. High-but-fair prix fixes deter the young and bohemian, leaving more saddle of rabbit, with tarte fine of onions (an appetizer!); ragout of turbot, leeks and mussels; vanilla cream, red fruit compote for the suit and tie, pearls and heels set.... *Tel 0171/839–8787. 32 King St. SW1, Green Park tube stop. Reservations required. DC not accepted. ££££*

St. John. The hippest place in town as soon as it opened, this amusingly spartan refectory (metal-shaded bulbs suspended from soaring ceiling, iron rails, concrete floor, WHITE) may never lose favor. While getting noisily pissed on French wine, *Guardian* journalists and architects (dressed in suits, Arran sweaters, Armani) devour Fergus Henderson's in-your-face food: salted duck breast and red cabbage; deep-fried lambs' brains; smoked haddock and fennel; roast lamb and parsnip; treacle tart. A motto on the menu calls this "nose to tail eating".... *Tel 0171/251–0848. 26 St. John St. EC1, Farringdon tube stop. ££–£££*

St. Quentin. Knightsbridge's long-running informal, classy French place is so Parisian you feel you should get your passport stamped at the door. Eat Gallic standards from *escargots* to *poulet au vinaigre* (chicken braised in wine), cassoulet to chateaubriand, in two floors of unnoticeable, high-ceilinged nondecor, served by polite young French

LONDON | DINING

persons. Prix fixes at both lunch and dinner are a great deal.... *Tel 0171/589–8005. 243 Brompton Rd. SW3, Knightsbridge tube stop. ££–£££*

Surinder's. Bargain old-fashioned French food is served smilingly from a partly-exposed kitchen to loud tables (a birthday party every night) and lovers' tables, in a living room atmosphere. Seasonal prix-fixe menus offer scant choice — spinach roulade, *crabe en cocotte* (crab meat potted with cheese), saddle of lamb, poached salmon; chocolate mousse—but are proficiently despatched. Unlike most things near Portobello, this is not trendy.... *Tel 0171/229–8968. 109 Westbourne Park Rd. W2, Westbourne Park tube stop. Reservations required on weekends. ££*

La Tante Claire. Of all London's famous chefs, Gascon native Pierre Koffman is probably the most dedicated to his art; he's certainly the least publicity-courting, and is nearly always at his stove, here in Chelsea, which can't necessarily be said for, say, Marco Pierre White. If you're serious about food, and wish to put your money where your mouth is, this is the place to choose. The salon is suitably padded and bouqueted, though the yellow-and-blue color scheme is a surprise.... *Tel 0171/352–6045. 68 Royal Hospital Rd. SW3, Sloane Sq. tube stop. Jacket and tie required for men. £££££*

Tootsies. Burgers in two sizes, with fixings (mushroom, egg, bacon, cheese, blue cheese, baked beans, etc.) are served along with crinkle-cut fries, big salads, chips 'n' dip, bottomless pan chili, then banoffi pie and ice cream. Fairly cheerful service in a place with tiled floors, round tables, and vintage ads on brick walls.... *Tel 0171/229–8567. 120 Holland Park Ave. W11, Holland Park tube stop. No reservations. AE, DC not accepted. £*

Wagamama. Japanese ramen and other noodly-soupy dishes, along with "health dishes" and sake and beer, are dished out in vast quantity at high speed, with the aid of high-tech, hand-held computer order pads. At this screamingly successful Bloomsbury spot, there's always a line for the shared tables, but it moves fast, and spirits always seem high.... *Tel 0171/323–9223. 4 Streatham St. WC1, Tottenham Court Rd. tube stop. No reservations. No credit cards. £*

Wódka. Frequented—heavily—by beau monde types who think this place is still their secret, this minimalist-looking but warm-feeling restaurant has founded a new genre: modern Polish. Blinis are daubed with eggplant-olive mousse or Osetra caviar; pierogi (similar to ravioli) are fancily stuffed with veal and wild mushrooms. UnBalkan white-chocolate cheesecake finishes off anyone not already slayed by the vodka, which is handsteeped in maraschinos by the *echt* Polish Prince patron.... *Tel 0171/937–6513. 12 St Alban's Grove W8, Gloucester Rd. tube stop. £££*

The Wren at St. James's. It's just a cafe, and an early (7pm) closing one at that, but the churchyard tables at this Piccadilly place are so very pretty and useful. Hot dishes are simple, vegetarian, and cheap, while the fabulous cakes and pastries are worth breaking your day or your diet for.... *Tel 0171/437–9419. 35 Jermyn St. SW1, Piccadilly Circus tube stop. No reservations. No credit cards. £*

Zoe. There isn't a whole lot in the few blocks surrounding this Anthony Worrall Thompson place behind Oxford Street, which makes it very useful, indeed, for lunch. There's a bustling horseshoe-shaped first floor cafe/bar and a clashingly-colored basement restaurant, serving Med-Brit dishes of a hundred clamoring elements, divided into "Country" (robust) and "City" (refined) sections. The cafe has irresistible sandwiches.... *Tel 0171/224–1122. 3–5 St. Christopher's Place W1, Bond St. tube stop. No reservations upstairs. £–££ (cafe/bar), £££ (restaurant)*

LONDON | DINING

Central London Dining

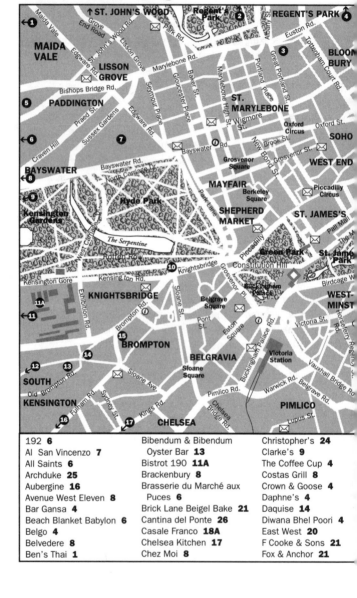

SHOREDITCH

CLERKENWELL
Clerkenwell Rd.

HOLBORN

BARBICAN

Liverpool St. Station

CITY

Cannon St. Station

STRAND
Charing Cross Station

Blackfriars Station

SOUTHWARK

London Bridge Station

Waterloo Station

Westminster Bridge

LAMBETH

ELEPHANT & CASTLE
New Kent Rd.

VAUXHALL

WALWORTH

1 km
0.6 mi

Information ⓘ

Post Office ⊠

Galicia **6**	Marco Pierre White **10**	River Café **9**
Geales **8**	Marine Ices **2**	The Room at the
Gracelands Palace **28**	Mega-Kalamaras **6**	Halcyon **8**
Indian YMCA **3**	Moshi Moshi Sushi **22**	Shaw's **12**
Joe Allen **24**	Nazrul **21**	St. John **19**
Kensington Place **9**	Orso **23A**	St. Quentin **15**
Khan's **5**	Pizza Express **18**	Surinder's **6**
Lauderdale House **4**	The Place Below **23**	La Tante Claire **6**
Lemonia **2**	La Pomme d'Amour **8**	Tootsies **17**
Louis Pâtisserie **2**	Le Pont de la Tour **26**	Wódka **11**
Manze's **26**	Rebato's **27**	

Mayfair, St. James's & Piccadilly Dining

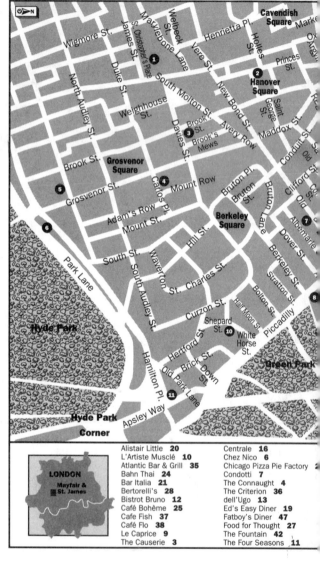

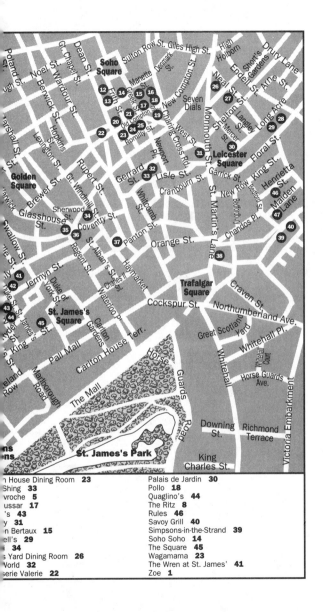

3

sions

As with any big
city vacation, a
London visit
demands a
strategy—maybe
more so than
most, because

this city's so big and sprawling, and there's so much to see. Decide what your priorities are. Does history turn you on? Is art your interest, or are you happiest just hanging? Time spent here is weather-dependent, too, since everything from the mood on the streets to the choice of activities changes in the rain. Fortunately, since rain can set in for three weeks without respite, there's plenty of scope for lousy weather.

Getting Your Bearings

The most important thing to do is to buy a copy of the pocket street atlas *London A to Z* (called simply "the A to Zed"— Londoners themselves always have one on hand). Buy one at the airport (every news agent in town sells it) and navigating the city will become much easier. What follows here is a potted geography of London, containing the only parts of the *A to Z* you need to know. **West End**: the center—you'd call this downtown. It's the younger of the two historic centers that London grew from, dating from 1050, when Edward the Confessor moved his court here and founded an abbey at… **Westminster** (SW1), where the Houses of Parliament are. **St. James's** (SW1), now a posh area of shops and hotels, is named after the (Tudor) Court of St. James's; dignitaries are still said to be ambassadors to St. James.

Mayfair (W1) includes Bond Street and Oxford Street and most of the really grand hotels. **Soho** (W1), east of Mayfair, is a small quadrilateral packed with restaurants. **Covent Garden** (WC2) is the easternmost part of the West End, a target zone for shopping, museums, and restaurants. **The City** (EC2, EC4): the far older, Roman-founded center of town, dating from the first century A.D., it's still the financial center and still an autonomous entity. It is the City of London, with a capital *C*, a.k.a. "the Square Mile," although it isn't square. The Tower of London is here, also the Barbican and the Museum of London. In between Covent Garden and the City is the legal district, with…. **The Inns of Court** (WC2), the historic barristers' quarters and courts. **Holborn** ("Hoe-bn") borders this, an in-between area; **Bloomsbury** (WC1) is also here, with the British Museum and the University of London.

West London: not West End. You'll spend a lot of time in neighborhoods like **Knightsbridge** (SW3), for Harrods, shopping, ladies lunching, and Hyde Park; adjacent **South Kensington** (SW5), for the big museums; residential **Kensington** (W8); and **Chelsea** (SW3, SW10), for King's Road shopping, riverside walks, and residential streetscapes.

Notting Hill (W11) is the hip place for restaurants and Portobello Market; it's bordered by residential **Holland Park** (W11), which has a park and restaurants. **Hammersmith** (W6) offers pleasant Thames-side walks and some restaurants.

The East End: where cockneys come from (which makes it the true center, some say), it's rough-and-tumble, with gentrified bits, and is definitely not touristy. Neighborhoods here include **Whitechapel** (EC1) and **Spitalfields** (E1), where you'll find an art gallery, Georgian houses, and Petticoat Lane market. **Clerkenwell** (EC1) and **Farringdon** (EC4) are not really East End—they're trendy, with restaurants. The **Docklands** (E14) is not really East End either, not now—London's newest section, it was reclaimed from industrial wasteland. A weird place. **Canary Wharf** (E19) is also not East End—not nowhere. It's a megabucks postmodern fake town containing Europe's tallest office tower, shops, and a concert hall.

North London: here you'll find **Regents Park** (NW1), which is not only a big green park that contains the zoo, but also the bordering streets, including Marylebone, with Madame Tussaud's. **Camden Town** (NW1) has the vast Camden Lock market; it's a grungy youth mecca. Mainly residential

The Thames's turbid waters

Many of England's most hallowed sporting events take place on the Thames, though few foreigners know of them. Who has ever heard of **Dogget's Coat and Badge Race**, *for instance? It's a 280-year-old July boat race from Chelsea to London Bridge (to the pub of the same name), and it's actually the oldest event in British sport. English social calendars have* **The Henley Royal Regatta** *in Oxfordshire inked in for late June, as well as the* **Oxford and Cambridge Boat Race** *on the first Saturday in April. In the latter, the two ancient Ivy League of England universities send their best rowing eights to do battle on the Thames for what is nowadays known as the gin-sponsored* **Beefeater Cup**. *The Hammersmith Mall is a good vantage point for the race. The previous Saturday, there's a far lesser-known, far more spectacular professional version of this, when about 420 eights row the* **Head of the River Race**. *Another water event, held a couple of weeks after that, which, despite being the world's toughest canoe race, is even more obscure, the three-day, 125-mile* **Devizes to Westminster International Canoe Race**. *Devizes is a cute town in Wiltshire. The race ends up at Westminster's County Hall at around 9am Monday.*

LONDON | DIVERSIONS

Islington (N1), which borders on Clerkenwell, has restaurants and the Almeida Theatre. **Hampstead** (NW3) is a quaint, expensive hilltop village, hemming a vast heath.

South of the River: this evolving area first attracted Londoners to the **South Bank** (SEI), an arts complex that includes the National Theatre, etc. Great views. **Bankside** (SE1) comes next, site of the new Tate Gallery and Globe Theatre.... **Butler's Wharf** (SE1) has the Design Museum, "Gastrodrome," and Tower Bridge; **Brixton** (SW2) is a funky neighborhood for West Indian culture, youth, and some drugs.

Getting from Here to There

London is usually described as being a good walking city, but you must add a coda to that: It's great to walk from, say, St. James's up Bond Street and across Regent Street to Soho, but it's a day's hike to go on foot from Chelsea to Regent's Park. It's a very big place. Also, the climate has not been exaggerated in folklore: you may find your entire stay is too damp and chilly to enjoy even a window-shopping stroll. However, using your trusty *A to Z*, walking is still the best way to see the details that make London a fun city.

Taking a bus costs the same as the tube in money, but it can cost you much more time, especially during rush hour. The scarlet double-decker bus, however, is one of those features that scream "London," and when you're not in a hurry, the top deck provides the cheapest and best tour, especially for seeing residential nontourist neighborhoods. All you need to do is stay on the bus and when you've had enough, cross the street and take the same route back to where you started. Bus routes, of which there are some 300, are somewhat tough to decipher (pick up free maps at Travel Information Centres). The stops are marked by concrete posts, each with a white or red sign on top and a rectangular one at eye level. A white sign means the bus stops automatically; at a red "Request" stop, you have to stick out your arm to flag a bus down. The rectangular sign shows the major stops on the route. Pay the conductor, or (usually) the driver/conductor, as you board; tell him or her where you're going and you'll be told how much to pay.

The tube, a.k.a. the underground (but never called "the subway" by locals), is far easier than the buses to negotiate—once you've decoded the system's rather beautiful, stylized map (unchanged since Harry Beck designed it in 1933), usually posted on station walls at just the points where you need to consult it. Get your own free map from any station, along with a booklet that explains the ticket price system. As with buses, you can buy tickets for individual journeys, but you'll spend as much (£1–3.10) making one round trip—or "return"—as you would buying a **Travelcard**. The card works for buses and tubes (after 9:30am weekdays), and costs £2.80–3.80 for a day. At £3.90–6.50, the **LT Card** is good for early risers, because it's valid as long as the tubes are running—which is from 5am to about midnight. You can also get weekly and monthly Travelcards, and the **Visitor's Travelcard**, which you can buy only in the U.S. or Canada, for three, four, or seven days ($25, $32, and $49 respectively). Basically it's the same as the LT Card, with a booklet of discount vouchers thrown in. Get it at your travel agent or at BritRail Travel International (1500 Broadway, New York, NY 10036, tel. 212/382–3737).

You have to take a taxi (a.k.a. "black cabs," although they're not always black) at least once during your stay in London, just for the experience. Unlike taxi drivers in most cities, London cabbies have "The Knowledge"—they must pass an exhaustive exam to get their license, for which they memorize every single cul-de-sac, one-way system, and clever backstreet route in the entire metropolitan area. Many are immensely proud of their encyclopedic memories and will regale you with information about the sights you pass. Taxis have chuggy diesel-powered motors, doctored-up steering that enables them to make U-turns on a dime, and signs that say

Pomp and Circumstance

Your basic London ceremony is the Changing of the Guard at Buckingham Palace, which gets really busy, even though they do it every day in summer at 11:30am (September through March, it's every other day, and heavy rain stops play). It may be a tourist cliché, but you cannot see a busby (the guards' fetching fur hats) anywhere else in the world. Another cliché of royal London is the Crown Jewels, housed in the Tower of London. Also at the Tower, and free, though you have to plan ahead, is the Ceremony of the Keys, a hilarious 10pm locking-up ritual that has used the same script and costumes every night for 700 years (for tickets, write in advance with a stamped, self-addressed envelope, preferred dates, and number in your party to: The Resident Governor and Keeper of the Jewel House, Queen's House, HM Tower of London EC3). "Halt! Who comes there?" demands the Sentry. "The Keys," answers the Chief Yeoman Warder. "Whose keys?" asks the Sentry. "Queen Elizabeth's keys," answers the CYW, whereupon the Sentry dispenses with grammar and announces: "Pass. Queen Elizabeth's keys and all's well."

LONDON | DIVERSIONS

"Sit well back in your seat for safety and comfort." They cost £1 for the first 582 yards, then 20p per 291 yards or 60 seconds, with surcharges of 40p to £2. A short ride—say from Harrods to the Dorchester—costs about £3, plus (15%) tip; something longer—say the Savoy to the V&A—will be at least double and is very dependent on London's erratic traffic flow. A taxi is available when the yellow For Hire sign on the roof is lit—though try an unlit one when desperate; sometimes they cruise without the light to skip drunks. Taxis have a way of not being there when you need them. When that happens, unlicensed **minicabs** come in handy. Minicabs belong to privately owned car services and must be ordered by phone or by stopping in at the office, since they can't be hailed on the street. Restaurants will usually call their pet service for you; fares are about 20 percent lower than black cabs.

The Lowdown

Is this your first time?... Which are the sights to see even though you hate sightseeing? Where should you point your camera so that everyone knows you were in London? These places may be corny and crammed with visitors, but they are essential London sights. Start with the **Tower of London,** and to get an idea of the sheer age of this city, ogle the Beefeaters and the Crown Jewels. Next to that is the familiar silhouette of **Tower Bridge,** clad in Portland stone to make it seem as old as the neighboring Tower, though it is several centuries younger. Three more of the big sights are also strung along the banks of the Thames: **St. Paul's Cathedral, Westminster Abbey,** and the **Houses of Parliament.** The latter includes probably the most famous thing of all, the Clock Tower, better known as **Big Ben.** The adjacent Westminster Abbey was founded by Edward the Confessor in 1052 and was the structure around which London grew. St. Paul's, with its distinctive dome, is the great architect Sir Christopher Wren's masterpiece. If you had to choose only one museum, one art collection, and one park, you should make it the **British Museum,** the **National Gallery,** and **Hyde Park,** although you ought to also throw in one of the great Victorian museums of South Kensington—probably the **V&A,** which is almost never given its full title, the Victoria & Albert. It's not very cool to be fascinated by royalty, but, let's face it, we all are. Therefore you must look at the not especially beautiful **Buckingham Palace** (now actually open sometimes for limited tours) and catch the Changing of the Guard. Also, you'd better see **Trafalgar Square**, another of those London landmarks you've seen in a million establishing shots in movies and on TV.

London's special moments... It's small things and details that arrest the attention and take the breath away, and these have done it for us: The **Holland Park** peacocks' bedtime, when the big blue birds flap into the trees, screeching in their special way, while the sun sets over the ruins of the Jacobean mansion. Sneaking in to swim the **Serpentine** after midnight during a heatwave. Pacing the Glass Gallery walkway at the **V&A** on a day without school parties, or looking down on Waterhouse Way—the great hall at the **Natural History Museum**—when it's swarming with children. **Trafalgar Square** at 2am in December (when the giant Danish fir tree's up and lit), waiting for a night bus. The romantic bleakness of the **Thames** during misty gray weather, preferably far downstream. London's lovely when new segues into old, especially if you come upon an ancient thing when you weren't looking for it—like the **Temple of Mithras**, or parts of the **Roman walls** near the Museum of London, or the (not ancient) ghost of the rose window of **Winchester House**, on Clink Street by St. Mary Overie Dock. The very best London moments come out of just happening on odd little lanes and garden squares, mewses and mansions, noticing details and watching life go on. If time is limited and you want the picturesque highly concentrated, try the **Inns of Court** and **Hampstead**.

Only in London... The most screamingly London activities have history, a special relationship with the weather, and are taken for granted by the locals. Qualifying on all counts is a **trip down the Thames**, starting at Westminster Pier, passing St. Paul's and the Tower on the left, the South Bank Centre on the right, and going under Tower Bridge to **Greenwich**. Disembark there and see the one and only **Prime Meridian**—the line which the whole world uses without a thought—from which all time is measured. Parks exist elsewhere, but few cities have

LONDON | DIVERSIONS

palaces across the lawn. **St. James's Park** has two—the Buckingham Palace façade and the back of St. James's, while **Kensington Gardens** and **Kew Gardens** have an eponymous palace apiece. For assessing the current state of eccentric English behavior, **Speaker's Corner** is the lodestone, though a visit to **Sir John Soane's Museum** illustrates how London-style unconventionality looks when taken to its natural conclusion. **18 Folgate Street** shows the same thing, but being the brainchild of an American, suggests that London may be more a state of mind than a collection of historic buildings.

What if it's raining?... And it probably is raining (nobody lives in England for the climate). Museums are the obvious thing to do, and the **British Museum** (often known as the BM) is big enough—it has about 100 galleries—to keep you indoors all day. So is the **V&A**, but here you can do more than just look—this enterprising museum of decorative arts runs short drawing and painting courses attended by everyone from total beginners to art-school professors. Or you could just pig out at the V&A's Sunday morning jazz brunch and read the papers. Take in the Glass Gallery first, because it's so full of reflected light, you'll forget the awful weather. At the other end of town, the **Saatchi Gallery** is a good rainy-day place, since its acres of white space and red-hot contemporary works form their own micro-environment. After that, the **Louis Patisserie** (see Dining) isn't too far away. Two art-laden houses in which to forget the gray clouds are that eccentric wonderland, **Sir John Soane's Museum**, and the 18th-century version, the **Wallace Collection**. Satisfy a different sense during lunchtime concerts at the churches of **St. John's Smith Square** and **St. Martin-in-the-Fields**. (At the latter, descend to the crypt for the **London Brass Rubbing Centre** and make your own rainy-day souvenir.) For some unpredictable and occasionally ghoulish live theater, drop in on a trial at the **Old Bailey**, the principal criminal courts of the land. Visiting the **Commonwealth Institute** is like fantasizing a round-the-world trip—the 51 independent members of the Commonwealth run from Vanuatu to Tuvalu, Kiribati to the Solomon Islands, and here they all are in hand-painted dioramas and displays of grocery packets and car tires representing exports. This sweet museum never got out of the sixties—catch it before they renovate. If you must shop, the department stores are obviously good, but better still are the **Piccadilly Arcades** (see Shopping), which predate the oldest mall by about 150 years and are rather more posh. Have afternoon tea nearby (at the **Ritz**, perhaps—see Dining), because it's best in the rain.

When the sun shines... Anything you do in London on a warm sunny day is enhanced at least 100 percent, since everyone's idiotically happy (this doesn't apply to heat-waves, when complaints soon set in), but a **Thames boat trip** is the best of all. Take one downriver from West-minster to the Tower, or to Greenwich, but think twice before committing to a long (about three-hour) upstream trip—to **Hampton Court** or **Richmond**—since there are great stretches of nothing to look at. The **Regent's Canal** is fun, whether on foot or by canal barge; the prettiest parts are between **Camden Lock** (by the markets) and **Regent's Park**, and at **Little Venice**—an expensive, little-visited area of big white houses. The Canal Café Theatre (see Entertainment) can be your destination—or maybe you're here on the first weekend in May for the water fes-tival, the **Canalway Cavalcade**, a celebration with boat pageants, craft stalls, and a teddy bear's picnic (Blomfield Road, Little Venice, W9). The **London Zoo** is where everyone with children congregates on sunny days. Avoid it. Go to the recently renovated **Ham House** in Richmond instead, with its great 17th-century gardens, or to the exquisite **Chelsea Physic Garden**, both in neigh-borhoods that cry out for aimless strolling. Or stay in **Regent's Park** and buy tickets for Shakespeare (usually one of the comedies) at the open-air theater. Another open-air theater is secreted in exquisite **Holland Park**, on a stage fashioned from the ruins of a Jacobean mansion blitzed in the Blitz. It stages opera and dance, all to the sound of peacocks screeching. For a theatrical experience without script, go to **Speaker's Corner**, by Marble Arch, where anyone is welcome to stand on a soapbox and hold forth. You may be lucky enough to catch a memorable loony—sunny days attract them.

The oldest things... London's very oldest thing has noth-ing to do with London, or with the person it's named after. It is the Egyptian obelisk by Victoria Embankment,

Cleopatra's Needle, and it's around 3,500 years old. Younger, but still ancient, are two of the **British Museum**'s best treasures, the 4th-century **Mausoleum of Helicarnassus**, one of the Wonders of the Ancient World, and the controversial **Elgin Marbles**, carved on the Parthenon frieze in Athens in about 440 B.C. and named after the English earl who saved them from ruin in the early 19th century. They should now go back to Greece, say the Greeks—and many Brits. Only about 200 years younger than Cleopatra's Needle is the **Sarcophagus of Seti I**, which the fun-loving architect of the Bank of England, Sir John Soane, bought for a song and installed in his basement. His house, now **Sir John Soane's Museum**, outdoes the sculpture. As for indigenous things, you can see parts of London's Roman walls in and around the **Museum of London**, as well as the 3rd-century **Temple of Mithras**, which was unearthed about 50 years ago. It's a little strip of history, although there's nothing but a boring set of foundations to look at. A better example of ancient/modern juxtaposition is the rose window of **Winchester House**, palace of the Bishops of Winchester until 1626, built into the St. Mary Overie Dock development adjacent to the bishops' old jail, now a museum called **The Clink**. Down in the law enclave, on High Holburn, you'll find London's oldest (1586) Elizabethan black-and-white half-timbered building, the **Staple Inn**, where wool traders were lodged and their commodity weighed and traded. Times have changed; now it's Ye Olde Smoke Shoppe. The oldest part of the famously old **Tower of London** is the **White Tower**, which was the tallest building in London on its completion in 1097.

The newest... The tallest building now is Cesar Pelli's 50-story tower at 1 Canada Square, the centerpiece of London's weirdest square mile, **Canary Wharf**. Modeled on an American downtown, this business district was reclaimed from slums as part of the 1980s redevelopment of the Docklands, but it never really fit in or took off; it makes for a really offbeat outing, from deserted mall to riverside pub. The newest train line in town, **Docklands Light Railway**, is the way to see it all. **Shakespeare's Globe Museum** is, in one sense, so new it's not finished yet, but it's also London's oldest stage: a reconstruction of the Bard's "wooden O" on its original site (give or take a few yards), using original materials and building techniques. This great and slightly moonstruck idea of American film director Sam Wanamaker's has—incredibly—now become reality. Though it's far from complete, the main structure's in place, there's a fine exhibit, and there will be summer productions. Go see them. Also unfinished is the new **British Library**, which was supposed to open in 1991; until they solve some major design traumas enough to decant 18-million-odd books into it, this orange-brick ghost library by King's Cross Station could become an antitourist attraction. Nobody likes the building. A new(ish) building that everyone does like is the **Lloyd's Building**, most dramatic when seen at night. Its architect, Sir Richard Rogers, was also responsible for the Centre Georges Pompidou in Paris; he's adored in England.

Don't bother... Although it is an essential building to see from the outside, there's no reason to shell out close to a tenner to go inside **Buckingham Palace**. Since the Queen now has to pay taxes and Windsor Castle (which she much prefers) nearly burned down, she's opened her London digs to the public, though they've been a little cheap with the room selection—all you see are the most public of the public chambers: the State Dining Room, the Throne Room, the White Drawing Room (where the family firm congregates before appearing in public). Not the prettiest of palaces or the oldest (it dates from 1703), Buckingham Palace has been heavily remodeled, and has only housed the monarch since Victoria moved in in 1837. **Madame Tussaud's** consistently appears on the top visitor volume list at about number 3, and there's a permanent line outside. This is a complete mystery. Inside are lifesized wax models of famous people and historic figures wearing their own clothes—which could be cute if this place didn't charge the greediest admission in all of London. Admittedly, Tussaud's also offers the Spirit of London animatronic "time taxi" ride, which isn't bad, and the Chamber of Horrors murderers' gallery is always a laugh. Also charging a high admission, and only intermittently worthwhile, is the **London Zoo**. We don't want to be mean to the dear zoo, which nearly had to close because of falling ratings, but things are a little tired in Regent's Park. The famous Elephant Pavilion, Penguin Pool, and Aviary are not as arresting as in their 1960s prime; there's no giant panda anymore; the new Children's Zoo's pathetic; and we're still waiting for the rest of the promised new stuff (a rain forest with tropical storms, for instance). However, when you yearn to look a gorilla in the eye, and want to be inches from a Bengal tiger's fangs (behind glass), the zoo is still great. Do go if you're here with young kids. Finally, **Harrods** as a tourist destination is overrated. Harrods is a shop. (See Shopping.)

Go out of your way for... If it's royal residences you're after, you can't get a better one than **Hampton Court Palace,** closely associated with our most colorful king— 'Enery the Eighth, of the six wives and the weight problem, who moved in in 1525. The last monarch to call it home was poor George III, who decamped to Kew to go mad in relative peace. See one of the world's best privet mazes, the just-restored Tudor kitchens, the Great Hall, the Banqueting House, and—what you can't see at Buckingham Palace—the State Apartments, all in a beauteous Thames setting. It'll take the whole day, being 20 miles out of London, further still than Richmond. Ah, Richmond. **Richmond Park** is quite the wildest in London (well, near London), complete with herds of deer; you can go horseback riding here, or biking, or use it as an excuse for a few pints at the Cricketers, which is like a real village pub. Here also are two stately homes almost facing each other on opposite banks of the Thames: **Ham House** and **Marble Hill House**. At the opposite end of town, and not too much of a trek if you're staying in the West End, is **Hampstead**, a pricey village (think Marie Antoinette) high on a hill, with quaint cottages and Georgian mansions, expensive boutiques, **Keats House** and the Everyman Cinema (see Entertainment), branches of the Gap and McDonald's (how the residents hate that), and surprisingly bad restaurants. Hampsteadites are represented in Parliament by the former actress Glenda Jackson, which should give you an idea of the tone up here. Some best things are the other wild park, **Hampstead Heath**, all rolling hills and dells and ancient woods, which leads to **Kenwood House**, worth seeing for two reasons: the Iveagh Bequest of paintings (Gainsborough, Rembrandt, Turner, Van Dyck, and Vermeer) and summer concerts at the open-air bowl—with tea at the café an important adjunct. There's another, far less known, much smaller park up here, too, **Lauderdale Park**, which segues into **Highgate Cemetery**. The Victorian side is pretty; Karl Marx's black basalt bust on the new side is a place of postmortem pilgrimage, though far outstripped by Jim Morrison's grave at Paris's Père Lachaise. But the best and oldest necropolis in London is barely known by Londoners themselves: It's the 77-acre **Kensal Green Cemetery**, best seen on the first Sunday of the month, when you can descend to the catacombs, guided by fanatic local historians dressed in black, who also point out the last resting places of novelists Thackeray, Trollope, and Wilkie Collins.

Inspiring spires... You don't have to be a believer to love London's churches. Many of the most loved are the work of the great architect so closely associated with London, Sir Christopher Wren, who rebuilt 51 of the 87 churches destroyed in the Great Fire of 1666. Twenty-five remain, plus of course his masterpiece, **St. Paul's Cathedral**. We'll leave it to other guides to do the exhaustive Wren tour, but here are a couple from the Wren stable. The usefully central **St. James's Piccadilly** was his last (1684) and his favorite; its spire, blitzed by the WWII Blitz, is now fiberglass. Learn to read the tarot, or hear a Handel recital here—the accoustics are angelic. **St. James's Garlickhythe** (with St. Michael Queenhithe and Holy Trinity-the-Less, to give it its full name) also has recitals, Tuesday lunchtimes, under Wren's highest ceiling (apart from St. Paul's). It's a handy stop en route to Shakespeare's Globe across the river and the adjacent **Southwark Cathedral** (more recitals here). A lesser building than Westminster Abbey, it's London's second oldest church, with parts of its 12th-century self still intact. Shakespeare worshiped here, his brother Edmund is buried here, and there's a memorial to Sam Wanamaker, who did so much to bring the Bard back to life at the Globe. It's also the only church with its own pizza café. The Café-in-the-Crypt at **St. Martin-in-the-Fields** is pretty good, too, and the church itself is fab. This one will look familiar to New Englanders, since James Gibbs's 1726 design—a sort of classical temple with a spire appended—was taken and run with by the early colonists; there are clapboard versions of it from Connecticut to Maine. The music program here is the best, apart from the June music festival at an exquisite church hardly anyone visits: Sir Nicholas Hawksmoor's 1728 **Christ Church Spitalfields**. Admittedly, it will hardly ever be open, until restoration is finished in about 1998, but go see the gorgeous colonnaded portico on a Brick Lane outing.

Who lived here?... The Bloomsbury Group still haunts London and exerts permanent fascination over the London intelligentsia. Virginia Woolf, the Bells and Dora Carrington, T. S. Eliot and E. M. Forster, John Maynard Keynes, Lytton Strachey et alia lived, wrote, and regarded themselves highly in Bloomsbury. See the group plaque in, yes, **Bloomsbury Square**, and individual residences all over—e.g., **46** (Woolf, the Bells, Keynes) and **51** (Strachey) **Gordon Square**; and **52 Tavistock Square** (the Woolfs). All over town you'll see these blue plaques— cerulean ceramic disks that enable you to do your own dead-celeb spotting, and the "Blue Plaque Guide" is worth getting if you're serious about this. There are about 400 stuck on the house fronts of those who "enhanced human welfare or happiness." Some enjoy more than a plaque—like Charles Dickens, who lived in almost as many houses as he drank in (every London pub claims his patronage), though only one survived to become the official **Dickens House**. On the way to **Keats House** in Hampstead (where the young poet wrote "Ode to a Nightingale," only to expire two years later), you can visit with the Couch of Couches, behind which the father of psychoanalysis practiced, at the **Sigmund Freud Museum**. At **221B Baker Street**, Sherlock Holmes didn't ever actually live—it's the Abbey National Building Society's offices now—but there is a hokey **Sherlock Holmes Museum** that has appropriated the famous address, though it's really at number 237. The best former residence in all of London belonged to somebody you've probably never heard of, but don't miss **Sir John Soane's Museum**. The architect of the Bank of England, among other buildings, Soane had a wacky sense of humor, perfect taste in art, and the sensibility of a fairground proprietor. His house is full of higgledy-piggledy crazy perspectives, thousands of pieces of statuary, an ancient sarcophagus in the basement (for which he once threw a two-day party), an art gallery with fold-back walls, stained glass, and a joyous atmosphere. It simply must be seen.

Their Majesties live here... We've already accused **Buckingham Palace** of being the most boring of royal residences, but if by some miracle you manage to wangle an invitation to one of HRH's garden parties, you'd see it differently—these are the best gardens in London. The Queen is in, by the way, when the royal standard is hoisted, and is never there when the place is open to tourists. Previous palaces are much more fun: We've already mentioned the **Tower of London** and **Hampton Court**, but we've not said a word about another piece of Henry VIII's real estate, **St. James's Palace**, the sweetest and smallest of all, and the one to which visiting dignitaries are still sent. The catch is that it's a completely private palace—all you can see is its redbrick Tudor facade and some side views. You can, however, roam over a great deal of Princess Margaret's home, **Kensington Palace**—or you will be able to once they've finished renovating. Victoria decamped from here to Buckingham Palace at her accession (1837), ending K.P.'s none-too-successful run as primary royal residence, which started with the Bill and Hill of English monarchs, William and Mary (1689–1702). William fell off his horse and died of pleurisy; Mary succumbed to smallpox; Queen Anne suffered a fatal apoplectic fit due to overeating; so did George I (he ODed on melons); and poor George II met the most ignominious Kensington Palace end—he burst a blood vessel while on the royal commode. But by far the most embarrassing monarch was "Farmer George," George III, the mad one. He succumbed to lunacy and died at **Kew Palace**, the most intimate and domestic, and the least visited of all, though lots of visitors stroll around its gardens. If you can't see the current HRH's gardens, then see her horses and coaches at the **Royal Mews**, and some of her priceless and extensive art collection (this is why she's the world's richest woman) at the **Queen's Gallery**. This is not related to the **Queen's House** in Greenwich, which was designed by the great Inigo Jones for James I's queen, Anne of Denmark. The first Classical building in Britain, it is important and exquisite. Inigo Jones was also responsible for all that remains of yet another of Henry VIII's palaces—the one he died in—**Banqueting House**, the only surviving bit of the labyrinthine Whitehall Palace, which burned to the ground in 1698. **Windsor Castle** nearly burned down, too, in 1992. You'll need an entire

LONDON | DIVERSIONS

day for the excursion to this place, reputed to be Elizabeth II's favorite of her modest homes. You can still see most of the public rooms here, despite the restoration and repair program, which also covers various improvements the Royals wanted anyway (and it's all funded by…you).

Modern art… Art lives. It starts in the national collections, continues in galleries mounting exhibitions of new work, and culminates in commercial spaces, avant garde *boîtes*, and independent dealerships. The **Tate Gallery** holds by far the most important and extensive modern collection in London, with far too much art to be on display at one time—they're constantly rehanging the stuff to give it all a fair show. This is where you'll find the most famous works. The **Hayward Gallery** in the South Bank Centre is also a major public space, with changing shows favoring sculpture and installation. Neither is especially known for taking risks, though the Tate causes an occasional outcry when it buys a controversial work (most infamously when it invested in Carl André's *Bricks*—a block of bricks). The **ICA** and the smaller but creatively curated **Serpentine Gallery** are nearer the cutting edge, but to see what's being produced by the latest generation of British artists, go to the **Saatchi Gallery**, whose advertising maven founders were early champions of Damien Hirst and Rachel Whiteread, among other near household names. Ditto the East End **Whitechapel Gallery**, always worth the trek, with major shows and lecture series and a good café. Among newer outlying spaces, the **South London Gallery** and **gasworks** are worth checking out for exciting artists not yet sanctified by the establishment, especially the former. But if you want one neighborhood for unplanned, aimless gallery-hopping, then head to Notting Hill, where many tiny independent galleries around the Portobello and Goldborne Roads have led to a little scene like New York's SoHo. Way the hell out in the East End (combine it with the Whitechapel!), the radical **Camerawork** is a standout for photography. Convenient to Covent Garden is the consistently excellent **Photographers' Gallery**, while the **Barbican**, the **National Portrait Gallery**, and the foyer of the **Royal Festival Hall** often feature photography exhibits.

The old masters… The world does not need another guide to the **National Gallery**, so we'll just point you in that direction and leave you to it. The adjacent **National Portrait Gallery** is not to be sniffed at, though it's smaller and has many obscure faces among the familiar figures. In this museum, who is represented is of more interest than how, and so some of the work is egregiously bad. That can't be said for the **Royal Academy**, housed in the imposing Burlington House, and center of the British art establishment—except during the annual Summer Exhibition, which consists of thousands of works, many unsolicited and chosen by committee in "auditions." The **Courtauld Institute** has the most impressive Impressionists and Post-Impressionists, plus the odd Rubens—talking of which, don't miss the Rubens ceiling at **Banqueting House**. For viewing pleasure and fewer crowds, try the exquisite **Wallace Collection**, where the Fragonards, Bouchers, and Canalettos are displayed *in situ*, as if the Marquesses of Hertford who collected them were about to stroll by. Ditto the small, eccentric collection of paintings, starring several from Hogarth's Rake's Progress series, at **Sir John Soane's Museum**, with countless statues and architectural fragments and *objets* bursting the walls of this amazing house. Soane also designed what was London's first public art gallery, the practically perfect **Dulwich Picture Gallery**, little changed since its 1811 opening, right down to its parkland surroundings—a mere 12-minute train ride from Victoria for Tiepolo, Canaletto, Gainsborough, Rembrandt, Van Dyck, Poussin… and all for free on Fridays.

Art al fresco… Avert your eyes when passing the paintings hung along the sidewalks on Sundays at Green Park's Piccadilly border and the Bayswater Road edge of Hyde Park, unless you like paintings on velvet and watercolors of big-eyed kittens. But do keep an eye out for the ubiquitous statues on London streets. A random sampling: Hubert le Sueur's equestrian *Charles I* (on Trafalgar Square near Whitehall), re-erected by his son, Charles II, nearly on the spot of his father's execution; *Oliver Cromwell*, who was responsible for that execution, close by *Winston Churchill* and *Abraham Lincoln* (all in bronze on Parliament Square); Rodin's *The Burghers of Calais* (nearby, in the Victoria Tower Gardens); and a 600-year-old *Alfred the Great* (though nobody's quite sure of the exact date—Trinity Church Square SE1). Kensington Gardens has three famous sculptures: a rather splendid bronze horse and rider

LONDON | DIVERSIONS

titled *Physical Energy;* a whimsical bronze *Peter Pan,* near the home of his creator, J. M. Barrie; and another children's favorite, the *Elfin Oak,* carved from a tree. The following are more obscure: the hulking vampiric *St. Volodymyr the Great,* a gift of the Russian Orthodox church (opposite Holland Park tube); *William Huskisson,* the first man to be killed by a train, confusingly dressed in a toga (Pimlico Gardens); the pretty blue column of the *Thames Water Surge Shaft* kinetic water barometer—functional art at its finest and funnest (Shepherd's Bush Roundabout, W11); the granite bedouin tent *Tomb of Sir Richard Burton* (the Victorian explorer, not the actor); the *mausoleum art* in St. Mary Magdalen church.

Won't bore the kids... That *Elfin Oak* statue stands just outside a much-loved playground in **Kensington Gardens.** You'll find a similar one in most parks, but the appropriately named **Holland Park Adventure Playground** is among the best. An indoor **Discovery Zone** version is found across the river in Clapham junction. More touristy things that children like include the **London Zoo,** though it isn't much different from any other zoo; the **Royal Mews** with all its ornate coaches; and the **Tower of London,** especially the gory parts. An expensive ticket, but worth the investment for older or tougher children, is the **London Dungeon,** a sort of extrapolation of the Tower's aforementioned gory bits crossed with Madame Tussaud's. Give overpriced **Madame Tussaud's** a miss, skipping next door instead into the **Planetarium,** with its laser shows and brand-new star projector. You'll think it better than the **Trocadero Center**'s plasticky high-tech shows; the kids may disagree. The museums to pick are: the **Museum of the Moving Image** (fly like Superman! take a screen test!), the **Natural History Museum** (especially the Creepy-Crawlies Gallery, the animatronic deinonychus, and the rainforest), and the next-door **Science Museum** (the computer and outer-space stuff is genius). Also a hit are the **London Transport Museum,** where you can climb all over old double-deckers and tube cars, and the far-off **Horniman Museum,** with its bee colony and musical instrument collection. Smaller kids will prefer the V&A's **Bethnal Green Museum of Childhood,** way out in the East End but so worth the trek—it has the world's biggest toy collection, including loads of fabulous dollhouses. If that's too far for you, try the quirky, labyrinthine **Pollocks Toy Museum**. Greenwich makes a great day out—arrive by boat, and save the **Cutty Sark** for last, because it's the children's favorite, though kids also like seeing the Prime Meridian, from which the world's time is measured, at the **Old Royal Observatory**—you can stand with one foot in each hemisphere. You can do a canal day, too, taking a **canal barge trip** from Little Venice to the zoo. You may be in luck and find the **Puppet Theatre Barge** is in town.

Photo ops... Essential tourist shots start with Trafalgar Square's **Nelson's Column**, which is the official center of London, or at least of the tourists mobbed by pigeons around its base. The rest of the shots you'd expect—Horse Guard sentries, Buckingham Palace guards, Beefeaters at the Tower of London, Tower Bridge, Big Ben (or the Clock Tower), Westminster Abbey, and Westminster Bridge (if its repairs are finally finished, which is unlikely)—you can buy on postcards. Why not look for something more subtle? The Chelsea Pensioners who live in Wren's stunning Palladian **Royal Hospital**, a retirement home for ex-soldiers, are just as picturesque as the beefeaters, in their red-and-gold frock coats. In late May, bring lots of color stock to capture the great tumbling banks of rhododendrons in **Kensington Gardens**, **Holland Park**, and **Kew Gardens**. Get out a zoom lens for the facade of the **Natural History Museum**, with its intricate arches of fauna—extinct creatures to the right, living ones to the left. If, like John Lennon, you've wondered how many holes it takes to fill the **Albert Hall**, take a shot of this curious circular, domed Victorian building just off Kensington Gardens, then point your camera across the street toward the **Albert Memorial**, that ridiculously ornate love token from Victoria to her prematurely dead consort. Doomed to at least a decade of restoration, it's clothed in the world's tallest free-standing scaffolding. Forget nearby Harrods—go instead to **Fortnum & Mason** (see Shopping) and get a shot of one of the city's sweetest clocks, featuring automata of the founders shaking hands on the hour.

A day of grunge... The **Thames Barrier** almost qualifies as part of this day, but we're looking more for the disreputable here. These are things to do when it's raining

LONDON | DIVERSIONS

relentlessly, or for any day if you're under twenty. **Camden Lock** is the Seattle-in-the-late-1980s of London: It's a flea market that ate a neighborhood. On weekends, the High Street's crawling with whatever that slacker demographic's called now; other days, you can still get tattooed or drunk or buy a pair of cheap boots, before installing yourselves in a smoke-hazed former Irish pub with a pool table. The other youth-centric neighborhood is in and around the **Portobello Market** in Notting Hill. More multicultural and cultural than Camden, it has small art galleries, ceramics, and ethnic artifact shops interspersed with vintage clothing and antiques. If you want true sleaze, then **King's Cross** is the seediest part of town—prostitution, drug dealing, the lot. The nasty stuff happens around the British Rail Station, but there's another scene emerging behind it in the warehouses—a youthful, artsy one. Check listings for the current state of play. This day must end with a gig, for which you should consult the Night Life chapter.

A day of romance... Whatever else you do, you must take tea, and no ritual is more genteel than the **Waldorf Tea Dance**. If performing the tango and the quickstep between scones hasn't yet become the fashion again, it soon will. You must also take a walk—perhaps along the **banks of the Thames** around Embankment, or on the south side along Bankside, going as far east as Tower Bridge and timing things to end up at **Le Pont de la Tour** (see Dining) for cocktail hour and oysters from the raw bar. Any park is also good, especially in summer after dark, and there's something very appealing about London's squares, with trees in the middle and maybe a row of Georgian houses around it. Try 18th-century **Kensington Square** (take Derry or Young Streets off Kensington High Street), or the even older—laid out around 1670—**St. James's Square**, from which you could explore the wonderful perfumers and shaving accoutrement emporia and shirt shops of Jermyn Street. Drop into the **National Gallery** and restrict yourself to the romantic works, like Velasquez's *The Toilet of Venus* (you'll recognize her when you see her), Constable's *The Hay Wain* (so bucolic), and perhaps some Canalettos, then on to the **Tate Gallery** for the splendid Turners in the Clore Wing. An evening stroll in **Hampstead** might segue into a show at the Everyman—one of London's last repertory cinemas, and a sweet old-fashioned place (see Entertainment). Alternatively, spend all day at the **Porchester Baths** (see Getting Outside), having massages and sweating in the steam rooms.

For gardeners... Serious horticulturalists should seriously consider coming to London in late May for the **Chelsea Flower Show**, one of the world's foremost flower shows. Failing that, try to be here in summer, when all the parks have flowerbeds stuffed full of color. In **Regent's Park**, St. Mary's Rose Garden is scented and formal, while **Holland Park** has its Dutch Garden, where the first dahlias in England grew in the late 18th century. With 60,000 plant species, **Kew Gardens** has something flowering in every season, and it also has the pair of spectacular 19th-century greenhouses, the Palm House and its corollary the Temperate House, which boasts the world's biggest greenhouse plant—a Chilean wine palm rooted in 1846. An even bigger greenhouse than those two is the 1987 Princess of Wales Conservatory with its 10 separate climates. **Columbia Road Market** (see Shopping) has just the one English climate, but you can fantasize planting your ideal English garden among the overflowing, blooming stalls here and buy horticultural accoutrements to take home. Garden historians should under no circumstances miss **Ham House**, with its meticulously restored 17th-century grounds; they should also allow time to get to **Hampton Court** for the Elizabethan Knot Garden, the Great Vine, the maze, and the topiary—not to mention the only show that rivals Chelsea. Talking of Chelsea, the **Chelsea Physic Garden** is exquisite and educational in equal measure—medicinal plants are grown here alongside the country's oldest rock garden. There's one more stop on the itinerary: the **Museum of Garden History**, housed in a deconsecrated church and featuring another 17th-century knot garden for those who failed to get to Hampton Court.

For the impecunious... Get on a bus, climb the stairs to the top deck, show your Travelcard, and sit back for the least expensive grandstand tour in the land. Good bus routes include the **94** or **12**, for Hyde Park on the north side, Oxford and Regent Streets, Piccadilly Circus, Trafalgar Square, and more; the **11** for Chelsea through to Knightsbridge, the City via Westminster; the **74** for the

South Ken museums through Hyde Park corner past Lord's cricket ground to the zoo; and the **29** from Victoria or Piccadilly Circus through Bloomsbury and the British Museum to Camden Lock. Bus maps are free from major tube stations. Or else you could splash out and board an **LT bus** (0171/828-6449), which is a good buy—they travel around The Sights, allowing you to hop on and off at will. You must be sure to have a **White Card** if you're going in anywhere—it entitles you to three or seven days of unlimited museum and gallery hopping, good at the following: Barbican, Courtauld, RA, and Hayward galleries, and at least eight museums, including Design, Imperial War, London Transport, London, Moving Image, Natural History, V&A, Science, and the museums of Greenwich. Pick one up at any of the above or at Tourist Info centers. They cost £14 for three days, £23 for seven days; family cards (two adults and four kids under 17) cost £29 for three days, £50 for seven days. Some of the best museums in town are free, too: the **British Museum**, the **National Gallery**, and the **Tate** charge no entrance fees, and there are always exhibitions up in the foyers of the **Royal Festival Hall** and the **National Theatre**, too (see Entertainment). Cutting-edge art is viewable gratis in the small galleries around Portobello (the **Todd Gallery**, 1 Needham Rd., is especially well regarded) and in the tonier salons of Cork Street and environs, or check out any of the galleries described above under Art (Modern). If it's late June, look in *Time Out* magazine for news of the student degree shows, where you get the chance to buy work straight from the hands of art-schoolers at ridiculously low rates—the **RCA** (Royal College of Art, next to the Royal Albert Hall) is especially recommended. Lunchtime classical recitals in churches are another great delight of London to look up in the listings, and most are free or bargains. Hang around **Covent Garden** to see the buskers perform, too—if it's summer, the Piazza may even feature a particularly juicy Pavarotti- or Domingo-laden opera production beamed onto giant screens, courtesy of the Royal Opera House. **Street markets** (see Shopping) are probably the best free shows of all, though; those and just walking. Traveling by foot is especially entertaining because you will get lost and you will find yourself in the mewses and alleys and streetlets with which London is crammed.

Go east... There's a strong argument that the East End is the true London, following the truism that a real cockney must be born within the sound of Bow Bells (at St. Mary-le-Bow church). The *Melrose Place* of England, *Eastenders*—a cult in certain Stateside circles—is set here in the fictional, but recognizable, Albert Square. And this is Jack the Ripper land (take a Ripper walking tour if you must—there are loads of them). The neighborhoods of the east are gritty, so don't expect a smooth tourist patina. The major museum, the **Bethnal Green Museum of Childhood**, an outpost of the V&A, is a good excuse to head east, especially with kids in tow. There are several city farms nearby for them, too—**Spitalfields City Farm** has the works: sheep, goats, cows, horses, pony rides, and summer barbecues. Ask about the horse-and-cart local history tour. Instead of Tobacco Dock, which sounds fab with its pirate ships and crafts fairs, but turns out to be one of the most depressing malls you've ever seen, go to **Spitalfields Market** (see Shopping), where there are great sports facilities and a little opera house, a farmer's market and good crafts shops. It's near Hawksmoor's **Christ Church**, which you should probably not make a special trip to see, since it's usually closed, but do check the concert schedule—this is a treat. Last but not least is one of London's most surprising and evocative museums, the **Geffrye Museum**, which contains a series of period rooms done with a Hollywood movie-scale attention to detail and authenticity. Unlike the stately homes you normally have access to, these interiors are domestic, so you get a powerful sense of how people lived. It's really out of the way but worth it if your interests tend at all toward popular and cultural history. Easier to reach (right next to the tube) is the **Whitechapel Gallery**, most certainly worth a special trip for anyone with an eye for the big-name and up-and-coming artists of now (plus it's got a pretty good café). From there, stroll down to the **Whitechapel Bell Foundry** to see the birthplace of the Liberty Bell (yes, that one) and Big Ben. Or nearly see—you can't go into the actual foundry, but you can buy a handbell and look at a cute little exhibit. The classic thing to do around here is to spend Sunday at the markets. Chief among them are **Brick Lane** and **Petticoat Lane**—which are adjacent to each other—and **Columbia Road Flower Market** (see Shopping for details). The last one is not much use for souvenirs, but it's full of local color and then

LONDON | DIVERSIONS

some. **18 Folgate Street** is the home of eccentric California-born Denis Sever, who shares it with a ghostly fictional family named Jervis; three times a week he (they?) enact a kind of philosophical three-hour *son et lumière* in which the audience follows several generations of invisible Jervises through the house. The Georgian house is in perfect period style, outdoing the Geffrye Museum in authenticity, since Sever actually lives there, without electricity but with a butler in 18th-century livery.

The wild west... There's nothing wild about west London, actually, except for the neighborhood known as Notting Hill, which denotes the square mile or so around Portobello Road, the hippest part of the whole city. There is, however, plenty to keep you occupied in this quadrant, with many parks, great big beautiful (mostly Victorian) covetable houses, and shopping. The shopping is concentrated in expensive **Knightsbridge**, where **Harrods** is, and on into the Brompton Cross area of South Ken. (See Shopping for more on Knightsbridge's stores.) Walking around here will make you feel un-put-together unless you dress for it. You can enter **Hyde Park** from here, to visit the **Serpentine Gallery** or take a rowboat out on the Serpentine Lake. Heading west, the park becomes **Kensington Gardens**; **Kensington Palace** is off-limits until mid-1997, but nearby Round Pond is a magnet for model-boat enthusiasts. Stay on the Knightsbridge (south) side of the park, walk it west, and you reach the road called **Kensington Gore** (which is what fake blood is called on British movie sets); turn south off it down Exhibition Road, and you're in what Albert, consort-of-Victoria, hoped would be a cultural fairyland, an Albertopolis of erudition and edification. His schemes were never fully realized—this boulevard down to the **Natural History** and **Science Museums**, and the later **V&A**, is something of a wasted opportunity (try to get a coffee here and you'll understand). The Millennium Fund just might change all this. (See You Probably Didn't Know) There's more shopping to be had on the formerly famous **King's Road**, the main drag of Chelsea, but it's long lost its glamorous edge. Chelsea today is best for strolling around, noticing all those north-facing over-sized picture windows—the studios of the original bohemian artists who put Chelsea on the map late last century. These are now among the most expensive pieces of real estate in town. Visit **Carlyle's House** if you want to see how literary Victorians lived. Also here are the **Chelsea Physic Garden** and Wren's **Royal Hospital**. Way west off the tourist route, but worth it if you're in the mood, is the **Kensal Green Cemetery**.

Northern lights... The rival to that older necropolis is **Highgate Cemetery**, which is about as far north as you can go without leaving London. You've also heard a lot about Hampstead, which is joined to it at the hip, and has the edge for quaintness. Both are wonderful wandering neighborhoods, and there is, of course, **Hampstead Heath** to complete the package. Also there's Waterlow Park bordering on Highgate Cemetery, **Kenwood House**, **Keats House**, and much shopping in Hampstead village. Going down south—literally down the hill—you reach Camden Town, that youth mecca of markets and pubs and cheap leather jacket shops, which borders on **Regent's Park** (see Getting Outside), where **London Zoo** is. In Camden is a recently relocated museum we haven't yet mentioned, the **Jewish Museum**, where, as you'd imagine, the history of the Jewish in Britain is illustrated. From **Camden Lock** (see Shopping), you can walk along the canal towpath in either direction—west to Little Venice (and the zoo), or east to King's Cross. There's the little **London Canal Museum** down that way if you want to know more about the rather fascinating British waterways and the way of life they support.

The deep south... Ignore any South of the River snobbery and lame jokes you encounter (don't forget your passport, etc.)—there really is life across the Thames. **Shakespeare's Globe Museum** is such a very exciting project, and one that, if you hurry, you can see in its formative stages. Catch one of the first productions on the open-air stage, or help them out and immortalize your name on a flagstone for £300. Eventually, the new **Tate Gallery**, replacing the one in Pimlico, will be its neighbor. There's a rather vibrant putative art scene emerging in the cheaper, bigger spaces south of the river—the **South London Gallery** could be called its hub, but check others listed in *Time Out* under "Alternative Spaces." After gallery-hopping, you could head to **Tower Bridge**, or lunch in one of the "Gastrodrome" restaurants (see Dining), or visit the **Design Museum**. Back upstream, the **South Bank Centre** is still vibrant and fun, fun, fun, after all these years—London's biggest arts complex, housed in a set of Brutalist-style buildings by Denis Lasdun (about to be covered in Richard Rogers's glass canopy, if the funding comes through) that have weathered into classic London landmarks. Between the Globe and the Olivier theaters, don't ignore **Southwark Cathedral**, as most people do. And **Battersea Park** is a charmingly different place for a visitor to visit—a place that will show you the echt atmosphere of South London like no museum can.

Street scenes... **Brixton** is the nearest thing to Caribbean culture in London, a magnet for the young and hip, though it helps to have a local show you around. **Notting Hill** is the posher version, and even hipper. It's THE place—here are galleries, restaurants, gewgaw shops, antiques shops, clothes shops, all clustered around the hub of **Portobello Market** (see Shopping) and the formerly rasta ganja-dealing, now restaurant- and café-laden **All Saints Road**. You may hear people refer to this area as West Eleven, which is simply its post code. The three-day **Notting Hill Carnival**, held over the August Bank Holiday weekend, is the ultimate London street party; West Indian culture rules here, but it's eclectic. It once had a reputation for trouble, but the worst you'll have to deal with anymore is the crush of thousands of revelers. **Camden Town** is less groovy and cool, being more populated with high school kids and wannabes than are the Portobello environs, but it's not dissimilar. A million miles more touristy, and also dead central, is **Covent Garden**. Every single visitor to London swarms to the piazza, especially in summer, and actually, it's not too bad there—with its cobbled streets and picturesque converted market building, it's just a big ole mall. Nearby is **Leicester Square**, home of large movie houses and a backpackers' mecca. In London, which tends to close down early, it's nice to see so much life at night, and Leicester Square never gets too quiet. Next to that is **Soho** (see Nightlife).

Working up a sweat... Two Turkish baths, dating from Edwardian times (though they've been renovated), are sybaritic places to spend a few restorative hours. The

Porchester Baths in Bayswater, just north of Hyde Park, are lovely and atmospheric, with three steam rooms going from hot to hell, a plunge pool, saunas, and so on, plus a relaxation and tea lounge straight out of a '30s ocean liner and a swimming pool adjacent. Call to check whether it's women's, men's, or mixed (coed, with bathing suit) day. It's near the Whiteleys center, for your movie convenience. **Ironmonger Row**, just north of the Barbican in a section of the city rarely penetrated by tourists, is not as delightfully period-looking as Porchester but has far more sports facilities attached, including about ten squash courts and another pool. Men and women are separated here, too.

Unwinding... When it's all been too much, try these. London's best and finest-looking yoga school is the **Notting Hill Gate Life Centre**, where very bendy Godfrey Devereux and staff teach various levels mainly of the energetic Vinyasa technique. Meanwhile, in the City, **All Hallows House** (tel 0171/283–8908, Idol Lane EC3) specializes in Hatha yoga, taught by an ex-footballer—yes that's football, not soccer. If Kundalini is your preference, go for the **Breath of Life Yoga Centre** (tel 0181/964–5255, Unit 57 Pall Mall Deposit, 124—126 Barlby Rd. W10), which has daily lunchtime classes; while Iyengar devotees should try the **Maida Vale Institute of Iyengar Yoga** (tel 0171/624–3080, 223a Randolph Ave. W9). Go to **Bodywise** (tel 0181/981–6938, 119 Roman Rd. E2) for a one-on-one refresher if you're already started on the Alexander Technique—others can get massaged (Reiki-ed, Shiatsu-ed, Cranio-sacral-ed) at this East End holistic health center. If you're a fan of that other conscious body-realignment therapy, Pilates, the **Belsize Studio** (tel 0171/431–6223, 74a Belsize Lane NW3) won't disappoint.

Pearlies

After a big shipment of Japanese pearl buttons arrived in London in the late 18th century, street vendors from this area began sewing them onto their clothes. Fashion became identity in the early 19th century, when the vendors formed the Pearly Kings and Queens Association to meet the challenges they faced from those who would have them put off the streets. The original Kings were elected to help protect the vendors. The Kings and Queens still exist, as do the pearlies, but their roles are more ceremonial now, acting more as a loose charity than as a sort of street vendors' union.

LONDON | DIVERSIONS

The Index

All Hallows House. Hatha yoga devotees come here for classes... *Tel 0171/283–8908. Idol Lane EC3, Monument tube stop.*

Banqueting House. Inigo Jones (1573–1652) designed this Palladian hall, all that remains of Henry VIII's Whitehall Palace, which burned down in 1698. Charles II commissioned the Rubens ceiling in tribute to his father, Charles I, who was beheaded here.... *Tel 0171/930–4179. Whitehall, Charing Cross tube stop. Open Mon–Sat 10–5. Closed Easter, Christmas, and for banquets (call first). Admission charged.*

Barbican. This mega–arts complex is famed for being ugly and labyrinthine, but it's useful for the gallery, the theaters—this is home to the Royal Shakespeare Company—and the concert halls. There's also a vast conservatory secreted inside.... *Tel 0171/638–4141. Silk St., Moorgate/Barbican tube stop. Open Mon–Sat 9am–11pm, Sun noon–7:30pm. Admission free; charges for gallery and conservatory.*

Belsize Studio. The Pilates body-alignment therapy is taught and practiced here.... *Tel 0171/431–6223. 74a Belsize Lane NW3, Belsize Park tube stop.*

Bethnal Green Museum of Childhood. The V&A's outpost focuses on all things small—dollhouses to teddy bears—illustrating the history of play.... *Tel 0181/980–2415. Cambridge Heath Rd., Bethnal Green tube stop. Open Mon–Thur and Sat 10–5:50, Sun 2:30–5:30; closed May 1, Christmas, Jan 1. Admission free.*

Big Ben. The nickname for the bell contained in the Clock Tower of the Houses of Parliament, often applied to the clock and tower as well. The clock face now looks greenish at night, thanks to its new energy-efficient lighting.... *At the Houses of Parliament, Westminster tube stop.*

Bloom's. Venerable purveyor of lokschen and latkes and center of East End Jewish life.... *Tel 0171/247–6001. 90 White-chapel High St., Aldgate East tube stop. Open Mon–Thur and Sun 11–9, Fri 11–2.*

Bodywise. A holistic health center in the East End offers various massages and classes in the Alexander Technique.... *Tel 0181/981–6938. 119 Roman Rd. E2, Dalston BR.*

Breath of Life Yoga Centre. Kundalini yoga classes are the specialty here..... *Tel 0181/964–5255. Unit 57 Pall Mall Deposit, 124–126 Barlby Rd. W10, Latimer Road.*

British Museum. The national collection of man-made objects from all over the world—some as old as humankind—fills 2.5 miles of galleries. Highlights are the Egyptian Rooms, including the Rosetta Stone and many mummies, and the Elgin Marbles.... *Tel 0171/636–1555. Great Russell St., Russell Sq. tube stop. Open Mon–Sat 10–5, Sun 2:30–6pm. Closed May 1, Christmas, Jan 1. Admission free.*

Buckingham Palace. The Queen's London home has a limited opening for visitors, with the State Rooms open a couple months a year. Get in line early.... *Tel 0171/839–1377. Buckingham Palace Rd., Green Park tube stop. Open Aug–Sept daily 9:30–5:30 (ticket office opens 9am). Admission charged.*

Camerawork. An East End gallery with a political conscience, it shows the latest in photographic art.... *Tel 0181/980–6256. 121 Roman Rd. E2, Bethnal Green tube stop. Open Tue–Sat 1–6pm. Admission free.*

Canal barge trips. Cruise the Grand Union and Regent's Canals by barge, from Little Venice or Camden Lock to the zoo.... *Jason's Trip, tel 0171/286–3428, and London Waterbus Co., tel 0171/482–2550. Operates Apr–Sept; call for details.*

Canary Wharf. Futuristic new business district fashioned from a once-decrepit loop of the Thames called the Isle of Dogs....

Tel 0171/418–2000. Visitor Center, Cabot Place E14, Canary Wharf tube stop. Admission free.

Carlyle's House. This pretty Queen Anne house, home of 19th-century author Thomas Carlyle and his witty poet wife, Jane, was a hub of Victorian literary life.... Tel 0171/352–7087. 24 Cheyne Row, SW3; Sloane Sq. tube stop, and bus #11, 19, or 22. Open Apr–Oct Wed–Sun and bank holidays 11–5. Closed Good Friday. Admission charged.

Chelsea Physic Garden. An exquisite and educational garden of medicinal plants, herbs, shrubs, and flowers including England's first rock garden, dating from 1673.... Tel 0171/352–5646. Swan Walk, 66 Royal Hospital Rd. SW3, Sloane Sq. tube stop, and bus #11, 19, or 22. Open Apr–Oct, Sun and Wed 2–5 (during Chelsea Flower Show, daily noon–5). Admission charged.

Christ Church Spitalfields. Nicholas Hawksmoor's 1729 masterpiece is one of only six London churches by the great associate of Wren's. Currently under renovation, but there are frequent classical concerts, and a music festival in June.... Tel 0171/377–0287. Commercial St. E1, Shoreditch tube stop. Call for opening times, which are limited during renovations. Admission free.

Cleopatra's Needle. This granite obelisk, dating from about 1475 B.C., was given to the British by the viceroy of Egypt (named Mohammed Ali) in 1819.... Victoria Embankment Gardens, Embankment tube stop.

The Clink. The jail of the Bishops of Winchester's palace is now a black-walled dungeon museum, including an R-rated room illustrating the history of prostitution in the "Southwark Stews" here.... Tel 0171/403–6515. 1 Clink St., London Bridge tube stop. Open 10–6. Closed Christmas, Jan 1. Admission charged.

Commonwealth Institute. Dioramas create a lovable anachronistic tour around the 51 Commonwealth countries, with added arts events, in a wacky blue copper-roofed building. It's about to be totally renovated.... Tel 0171/603–4535. Kensington High St. W8, High St. Kensington tube stop. Open Mon–Sat 10–5, Sun 2–5. Closed Easter, Christmas, Jan 1. Admission charged.

Courtauld Institute. Impressionists and Post-Impressionists star in Somerset House, with plenty of Old Masters to back them up.... *Tel 0171/873–2526. Strand WC2, Holborn tube stop. Open Mon–Sat 10–6, Sun 2–6; closed Easter, Christmas, Jan 1. Admission charged.*

Cutty Sark. One of the Greenwich delights, this handsome tea clipper is evocative of the seafaring life and has a wicked collection of figureheads.... *Tel 0181/858–3445. Island Gardens station, Docklands Light Railway. Open Apr–Sept Mon–Sat 10–6, Sun noon–6; Oct–Mar Mon–Sat 10–5, Sun noon–5. Closed Easter, Christmas, Jan 1. Admission charged.*

Design Museum. A temple to domestic and small-scale commercial design, from Corbusier chairs to the Coke bottle, this south-of-the-river museum (across Tower Bridge) always has special exhibitions on tap.... *Tel 0171/403–6933. Butler's Wharf, Tower Hill tube stop. Open daily 10:30–5:30. Admission charged.*

Dickens House Museum. The house where he wrote *Nicholas Nickleby* and *Oliver Twist* and finished *Pickwick Papers* is a shrine to the great novelist.... *Tel 0171/405–2127. 48 Doughty St. WC1, Russell Sq. tube stop. Open Mon–Sat 10–5. Closed Christmas. Admission charged.*

Discovery Zone. Small kids can be completely indulged here, with slides and swings, ball pools and tunnels. Under-12s only, and they must be accompanied.... *Tel 0171/223–1717. The Junction Shopping Centre, Clapham Junction SW11, Clapham Junction BR. Open 10–8. Admission charged.*

Dulwich Picture Gallery. London's first purposefully-built art gallery, designed by Sir John Soane, has some 300 works, including many Old Masters.... *Tel 0181/693–5254. College Rd. SE21, West or North Dulwich BR. Open Tue–Fri 10–5, Sat 11–5, Sun 2–5. Admission charged, free on Friday.*

18 Folgate Street. In a meticulously authentic early-18th century house, Denis Severs leads a small audience on a time-traveling odyssey.... *Tel 0171/247–4013. 18 Folgate St., Liverpool St. tube stop. Three performances a week,*

7:30–10:30pm; house alone open first Sunday of month 2–5pm. Reservations necessary. Admission charged.

gasworks. One of South London's alternative gallery spaces.... *Tel 0171/735–3445. 155 Vauxhall St. SE11, Vauxhall tube stop. Open Thu–Sun 11–6. Admission free.*

Geffrye Museum. In a row of 18th-century almshouses, this perfect museum re-creates the sitting room of England from 1600 to 1950.... *Tel 0171/739–9893. Kingsland Rd. E2, Liverpool St. tube stop. Open Tue–Sat 10–5, Sun and bank holidays 2–5. Admission free.*

Greenwich. This riverside town has many attractions—the *Cutty Sark* (see above), the Royal Naval College, and the Royal Observatory (see below). Get there via boat (see Thames boat trips, below) or the Docklands Light Railway.... *Island Station DLR.*

Ham House. This Stuart stately home, dating from about 1610, has 17th-century furniture and gardens; it's just been restored.... *Tel 0181/940–1950. Ham St., Richmond, Richmond tube stop. Open Apr–Oct Mon–Wed 1–5, Sat 1–5:30, Sun 11:30–5:30. Admission charged.*

Hampton Court Palace. Henry VIII's stunning Thames-side palace satisfies every royal fantasy—see everything from the King's Apartments to the Tudor kitchens, and maybe a royal ghost. The 1714 yew maze is famous.... *Tel 0181/781–9500. East Molesey, Surrey, Hampton Court BR. Open Mar–Oct daily 9:30–6, Oct–Mar daily 9:30–4:30 (except opens at 10:15 Mon). Closed Christmas, Jan 1. Admission charged.*

Hayward Gallery. The art department of the South Bank Centre stages about five exhibitions of modern work per year.... *Tel 0171/261–0127. Belvedere Rd. SE1, Waterloo tube stop. Open 10–6 (until 8pm Tue–Wed). Closed between exhibitions. Admission charged.*

Highgate Cemetery. This atmospheric early-Victorian grave-yard is the last resting place of Karl Marx and George Eliot.... *Tel 0181/340–1834. Swains Lane, Highgate tube. East side open daily Apr–Oct 10–4:45, Oct–Mar 10–3:45.*

Closed Christmas. West side tours only, call for times. Admission charged.

Horniman Museum. An anthropological museum of great charm, best known for its bee colony and its 1,500 musical instruments.... *Tel 0181/699–2339. 100 London Rd. SE23, Forest Hill BR. Open Mon–Sat 10:30–5:30, Sun 2–5:30. Admission free.*

Houses of Parliament. "The mother of all parliaments" takes place in Charles Barry and Augustus Pugin's mid-19th-century neo-Gothic pile, complete with the famous Clock Tower (Big Ben). It's possible to visit both the House of Commons and the House of Lords in session, but the lines are long.... *Tel 0171/219–3000. St. Margaret St. SW1, Westminster tube stop. Commons open Mon–Thu 2:30–10pm, Fri 9:30–3; Lords open Mon–Thu 2:30–10. Closed Easter week, May 1, Jul–Oct, 3 weeks at Christmas. Admission free.*

ICA. The Institute of Contemporary Arts is secreted in a Nash terrace on the pink road and houses much arts action, with galleries, two small movie theaters, and a theater.... *Tel 0171/930–3647. The Mall, SW1, Charing Cross tube stop. Gallery open noon–7:30 (Fri until 9pm). Admission charged.*

Inns of Court. Legal London is still centered around the four Inns of Court: Gray's Inn, Lincoln's Inn, Middle Temple, and Inner Temple, the earliest part of which is the 12th-century Temple Church. The name stuck from when 14th-century lawyers lodged together here, and the labyrinth is centered around the country's principal law courts, the Royal Courts of Justice.... *Tel 0171/936–6000. The Strand, Temple, Chancery Lane, Aldwych tube stop. (Law courts) Mon–Fri 9–4:30. Admission free.*

Ironmonger Row. These public baths offer swimming, sweating, and various other pleasures, in Edwardian surroundings.... *Tel 0171/253–4011. Ironmonger Row EC1, Old Street tube stop. Admission charged.*

Keats House. The poet lived two years of his short life here in handsome Hampstead; today it also houses the Keats archives.... *Tel 0171/435–2062. Wentworth Place NW3, Hampstead tube stop. Open Mon–Fri 10–6, Sat 10–5, Sun*

124

and holidays 2–5 (Nov–Mar, opens at 1pm weekdays). Closed 1 hr at lunch; closed Easter, Christmas, Jan 1. Admission free.

Kensal Green Cemetery. "London's oldest necropolis" (from 1832) is atmospheric and beautiful to behold; it contains the remains of Wilkie Collins, Thackeray, Trollope, and other great Victorians.... *Tel 0181/969–0152. Harrow Rd. W10, Kensal Green tube stop. Open Mon–Sat 9–5:30, Sun 10–5:30; tours Mar–Oct Sat and Sun 2:30, Oct–Feb Sun 2PM; catacomb tours first Sunday of month. Donation requested.*

Kensington Palace. The state apartments contain the possessions of the Stuart and Hanoverian monarchs who called it home and the Court Dress Collection. Currently closed for renovation into a re-creation of Victoria's childhood home.... *Tel 0171/937–9561. Kensington Gardens W8, High St. Kensington tube stop. Closed for renovations.*

Kenwood House. A Robert Adam masterpiece, this neo-classical villa on a heavenly hillside near Hampstead Heath holds the Iveagh Bequest, which has some important paintings, and the Hull Grundy Jewelry Collection. The lakeside concert bowl opens summertime.... *Tel 0181/348–1286. Hampstead Lane NW3, Archway tube stop, and bus #210. Open daily Apr–Oct 10–6, Nov–Mar 10–4. Closed Christmas. Admission free.*

Kew Gardens. The 300-acre Royal Botanic Gardens grow 40,000 kinds of plants, art galleries, a visitors' center, and—especially—the Victorian crystal-palace glasshouses make this a perfect day trip.... *Tel 0181/940–1171. Kew, Richmond, Surrey, Kew Gardens tube stop. Open daily 9:30–dusk. Admission charged.*

Kew Palace. There's even a royal palace in the gardens—the littlest and most picturesque one of all, where King George III lost his marbles.... *Tel 0181/332–5189. Kew, Richmond, Surrey, Kew Gardens tube stop. Open Apr–Oct 11–5:30. Admission charged.*

Lloyd's Building. One of London's few amazing modern buildings, this 1986 inside-out glass and steel tower, headquar-

LONDON | DIVERSIONS

ters of the venerable Lloyd's of London, is recognizably Richard Rogers's (Paris's Pompidou center architect).... *Tel 0171/623–7100. 1 Lime St., Monument tube stop. Closed to visitors.*

London Brass Rubbing Centre. The crypt of St. Martin-in-the-Fields provides paper, metallic waxes, and instructions on how to rub your own replica of historic brasses.... *Tel 0171/437–6023. Trafalgar Sq. W1, Charing Cross or Leicester Sq. tube stop. Open Mon–Sat 10–6, Sun noon–6. Closed Easter, Christmas, Jan 1. Charge for rubbing.*

London Canal Museum. This small museum in a former ice-storage house illustrates the life of the waterways of England.... *Tel 0171/713–0836. 12 New Wharf Rd. N1; King's Cross tube stop. Open Apr–Sept Tue–Sun 10–4. Closed Easter, Christmas, Jan 1. Admission charged.*

London Dungeon. Ghastly and gory exhibits of torture and treachery, mostly from the Middle Ages, appeal greatly to horrid children. Complete with the "Jack the Ripper Experience".... *Tel 0171/403–0606. 28–34 Tooley St SE1, London Bridge tube stop. Open daily Apr–Sept 10–6, Oct–Mar 10–5:30. Closed Christmas. Admission charged.*

London Transport Museum. Better than it sounds, this has lots of hands-on stuff that kids like, with climb-aboard vehicles, plus actors role-playing and interactive exhibits.... *Tel 0171/379–6344. 39 Wellington St. WC2, Covent Garden tube stop. Open 10–6. Closed Christmas. Admission charged.*

London Zoo. About 8,000 creatures call this home. You can get real close to the big cats, watch the penguin feeding, and ride a camel—all the usual stuff, but in a pretty setting.... *Tel 0171/722–3333. Regent's Park NW1, Camden Town tube stop. Open daily Mar–Sept 10–5:30, Oct–Feb 10–4. Closed Christmas. Admission charged.*

Madame Tussaud's. A Frenchwoman learned to make waxwork people by fashioning death masks of aristocrats during the French Revolution, then inflicted this museum of the frozen famous on London. Expect to stand in line forever to see the

Superstars, Grand Hall, Chamber of Horrors (homegrown murderers), and the "time taxi trip," the Spirit of London.... *Tel 0171/935–6861. Marylebone Rd. NW1, Baker St. tube stop. Open Mon–Fri 10–5:30, Sat–Sun 9:30–5:30. Closed Christmas. Admission charged.*

Maida Vale Institute of Iyengar Yoga. For Iyengar yoga classes, just as the name promises.... *Tel 0171/624–3080. 223a Randolph Ave. W9, Maida Vale tube stop.*

Marble Hill House. Built in the Palladian style for George II's mistress, Henrietta Howard, this Thames-side villa, nearly opposite Ham House, offers summertime concerts and teas in the Coach House.... *Tel 0181/892–5115. Richmond Rd., Twickenham, Richmond tube stop. Open daily, Apr–Oct 10–6, Nov–Mar 10–4. Closed Christmas. Admission free.*

Monument. Christopher Wren's tower commemorates the terrible destruction wrought by the Great Fire of 1666. Climb the 311 steps for an iron-caged view of the City.... *Tel 0171/626–2717. Monument St., Monument tube stop. Open Apr–Sept Mon–Fri 9–5:30, Sat–Sun 2–5:30; Oct–Mar Mon–Sat 9–3:30. Admission charged.*

Museum of Garden History. The Tradescant Trust, named after great botanist John Tradescant (1575–1638), runs this museum in a deconsecrated church, complete with a 17th-century knot garden and the grave of Captain Bligh of the *Bounty*.... *Tel 0171/261–1891. Lambeth Palace Rd. SE1, Waterloo tube stop. Open Mar–Dec Mon–Fri 11–3, Sun 10:30–5. Admission free.*

Museum of London. This chronologically arranged museum gives the background to what you've seen outside. Highlights include a street of Victorian shops in the basement and a Great Fire diorama.... *Tel 0171/600–3699. 150 London Wall EC2, St. Paul's tube stop. Open Tue–Sat 10–5:30, Sun noon–5:30. Closed Christmas. Admission charged.*

Museum of the Moving Image. MOMI features hands-on fun exhibits, like a Superman flight simulator and a mock interview setup, plus hundreds of clips and some actors, illustrating the history of film and TV.... *Tel 0171/928–3535. South Bank SE1, Waterloo tube. Open 10–6. Closed Christmas. Admission charged.*

National Gallery. The national collection of art is suitably impressive, full of familiar masterpieces. The Sainsbury Wing contains the early Renaissance collection, but the whole place spans 700 years, up to 1920. Get oriented and print out a personal map at the Micro Gallery.... *Tel 0171/839–3321. Trafalgar Sq. WC2, Charing Cross tube stop. Open Mon–Sat 10–6, Sun 2–6. Closed Easter, May 1, Christmas, Jan 1. Admission free.*

National Portrait Gallery. Next to the National Gallery, this intimate and likeable museum, recently renovated, features portraits of the famous—and the forgotten—from medieval times to now.... *Tel 0171/306–0055. St. Martin's Place WC2, Charing Cross tube stop. Open Mon–Sat 10–6, Sun 2–6. Closed Easter, May 1, Christmas, Jan 1. Admission free.*

Natural History Museum. Almost as big as the world it depicts, this is one of the best museums around, with its many renovated galleries. The insects, dinosaurs, and ecology ones are especially fine, but the older stuffed-mammal rooms also have their charms.... *Tel 0171/938–9123. Cromwell Rd. SW7 South Kensington tube stop. Open Mon–Sat 10–5:50, Sun and holidays 11–5:50. Closed Dec 23–26. Admission charged.*

Nelson's Column. The geographical center of London is this 145-foot granite column from which E. H. Baily's 1843 Admiral Lord Nelson keeps watch.... *Trafalgar Sq., Charing Cross tube stop.*

Notting Hill Gate Life Centre. Classes in Vinyasa yoga offer a way to relax here.... *Tel 0171/221–4602. 15 Edge St. W8, Notting Hill Gate tube stop.*

Old Bailey. Crowned by a gilded statue of Justice, this incarnation of England's Central Criminal Court was built in 1907 on the site of notorious Newgate Prison.... *Public gallery entrance at Newgate St., St. Paul's tube stop. Public gallery open Mon–Fri 10–1 and 2–4. Admission free.*

Old Royal Observatory. This 1675 Wren-designed museum calls itself "the place where time begins," and it does not exaggerate. Here's where Greenwich Mean Time is measured from, and here's the Prime Meridian, which bisects the world.... *Tel 0181/858–4422. Greenwich Park SE10, Island Gardens DLR. Open Mon–Sat 10–5, Sun noon–5 (2–5 Oct–Mar). Closed Christmas. Admission charged.*

Photographers' Gallery. Conveniently central place to see top shows of 20th-century photographic art.... *Tel 0171/831–1772. 5 Great Newport St. WC2, Leicester Sq. tube stop. Open Mon–Sat 11–6. Admission free.*

Planetarium. See the Star Show under this recently refreshed dome in tandem with its neighbor, Madame Tussaud's, or on its own. There are outer-space exhibits too.... *Tel 0171/486–1121. Marylebone Rd. NW1, Baker St. tube stop. Shows every 40 mins, Mon–Fri 12:20–4, Sat–Sun 10:20–5. Closed Christmas. Admission charged.*

Pollocks Toy Museum. A pair of 19th-century houses are crammed to the beams with every conceivable Victorian toy.... *Tel 0171/636–3452. 1 Scala St. W1, Goodge St. tube stop. Open Mon–Sat 10–5. Admission charged.*

Porchester Baths. Splendid Edwardian facilities for soaking and steaming.... *Tel 0171/229–9950. Queensway W2, Queensway or Bayswater tube stop. Admission charged.*

Puppet Theatre Barge. When it's open, this Little Venice floating marionette show is a treat for toddlers, with fairy tales, rhymes, and songs.... *Tel 0171/249–6876. Blomfield Rd. W9, Warwick Ave. tube stop. Call for times. Admission charged.*

Queen's Gallery. Some of HRH's countless, priceless canvases are on show here in Buckingham Palace's former chapel.... *Tel 0171/799–2331. Buckingham Palace Rd. SW1, Victoria tube stop. Open Tue–Sat 10–5, Sun 2–5. Closed Easter, Dec 24–Mar 4. Admission charged.*

Queen's House. The first Classical house in England, designed by Inigo Jones for the Stuart Queen Anne of Denmark, is one of the delights of Greenwich.... *Tel 0181/858–4422. Romney Rd., Greenwich, Island Gardens BR. Open Apr–Sept Mon–Sat*

10–5, Sun noon–5; Oct–Mar Mon–Sat 10:30–5:30, Sun 2:15–4. Closed Christmas, Jan. Admission charged.

Royal Academy. Eighteenth-century Burlington House is the venue for whichever major art show is in town, plus the vast and unruly Summer Exhibition.... *Tel 0171/439–7438. Piccadilly W1, Piccadilly Circus tube stop. Open 10–6. Admission charged.*

Royal Hospital. The retirement home Charles II founded for his best soldiers, designed by Wren, still houses some 400 quaintly costumed ex-servicemen, "Chelsea Pensioners." Parts are open to the public; more when it's Chelsea Flower Show time.... *Tel 0171/730–0161. Royal Hospital Rd. SW3, Sloane Sq. tube stop, and bus #11 or 22. Open Mon–Sat 10–1 and 2–4, Sun 2–4 (closed Sun Oct–Mar). Closed national holidays. Admission free.*

Royal Mews. Not all the Queen's horses are here, but many are, alongside her ceremonial fairy-tale coaches and carriages.... *Tel 0171/799–2331. Buckingham Palace Rd. SW1, Victoria tube stop. Open Apr–Oct Tue–Thur noon–4, Oct–Mar Wed noon–4. Closed Mar 25–29, Oct 1–5, Dec 23–Jan 5. Admission charged.*

Saatchi Gallery. All the young turks of the British art scene are snapped up by the older turk advertising and media maven, Charles Saatchi, to be shown off in this glorious white-on-white space.... *Tel 0171/624–8299. 98a Boundary Rd. NW8, Swiss Cottage tube stop. Open Thur–Sun noon–6. Admission charged.*

St. James's Garlickhythe. One of Wren's City churches, notable for its concerts.... *Tel 0171/236–1719, Garlick Hill EC4, Mansion House tube stop. Concerts Tue 1:10pm, but call to confirm. Admission free.*

St. James's Piccadilly. Another Wren church with a concert program, this one is improbably supplemented by various new-agey events, plus a crafts market and a café.... *Tel 0171/437–5053. Piccadilly, Piccadilly Circus tube stop. Call for hours. Admission free; charged for some events.*

St. John's Smith Square. Yet another church with concerts, this one deconsecrated and next to Conservative Party headquarters.... *Tel 0171/222–1061. Smith Sq., West-minster tube stop. Admission charged.*

St. Martin-in-the-Fields. Not another one? Yes, another one, albeit the daddy of all churches-with-music, being the home of the famous gothic music combo, the Academy of St. Martin-in-the-Fields. The James Gibbs church is well worth visiting in its own right.... *Tel 0171/437–6023. Trafalgar Sq. W1, Charing Cross tube stop. Open Mon–Sat 10–6, Sun noon–6. Admission free.*

St. Paul's Cathedral. Wren's undoubted masterpiece is instantly recognizable as one of the defining buildings of the London skyline and should not be missed. Bribe the kids with the Whispering Gallery and its magic acoustics.... *Tel 0171/248–2705. EC4, St. Paul's tube stop. Open for sightseeing Mon–Sat 8:30–4, for worship Mon–Sat 7:15–6 and Sun 7:45–5. Admission charged.*

Science Museum. Neighbor of the Natural History Museum, this is similarly popular with kids who love the interactive stuff and the cool Space Gallery and Flight Lab.... *Tel 0171/938–8000. Exhibition Rd. SW7, South Kensington tube stop. Open Mon–Sat 10–6, Sun 11–6. Closed Christmas. Admission charged.*

Serpentine Gallery. In the middle of Kensington Gardens is this space for avant-garde, modern shows.... *Tel 0171/402–6075. Lancaster Gate tube stop. Open 10–6. Closed between exhibitions. Admission free.*

Shakespeare's Globe Museum. The late American film director Sam Wanamaker brought into being this ambitious project to re-create Shakespeare's original theater and add an over-due London center for Bard worship and study. Events and performances supplement the exhibition.... *Tel 0171/928–6406. New Globe Walk, Bankside SE1, Mansion House tube stop. Open 10–5. Closed Christmas. Admission charged.*

Sherlock Holmes Museum. A hokey tourist trap cashes in on the fictional detective, but it's probably magnetic to addicts for the address alone.... *Tel 0171/935–8866. "221B" Baker St., Baker St. tube stop. Open 10–6. Closed Christmas, Jan 1. Admission charged.*

Sigmund Freud Museum. Where the father of analysis spent his final months—see The Couch, personal paraphernalia, and Freud events.... *Tel 0171/435–2002. 20 Maresfield Gardens NW3, Belsize Park tube stop. Open Wed–Sun noon–5; closed Easter, Christmas, Jan 1. Admission charged.*

Sir John Soane's Museum. One of London's most wonderful museum experiences, the architect of the Bank of England's house is full of ancient sculpture, mad perspectives, juicy colors, and art, art, art. It makes you smile.... *Tel 0171/405–2107. 13 Lincoln's Inn Fields, Chancery Lane tube stop. Open Tue–Sat 10–5. Closed Christmas, Jan 1. Admission free.*

South Bank Centre. Home of the Royal National Theatre, the National Film Theatre, MOMI, the Hayward Gallery, Royal Festival Hall, and other concert halls... You're bound to end up here at least once. See Entertainment for more details.... *Tel 0171/928–2252. South Bank SE1, Embankment tube stop.*

South London Gallery. Hip youngsters show art here.... *Tel 0171/703–6120. 65 Peckham Rd. SE5, Bus #2, 36, or 171. Open Tue–Fri 11–6 (until 7pm Thur), Sat–Sun 2–6. Admission free.*

Southwark Cathedral. London's second-oldest church, after Westminster Abbey, is where Shakespeare worshiped, his brother Edmund is buried, and the founder of Harvard College was baptized. Look out for concerts.... *Tel 0171/407–2939. Winchester Walk, London Bridge tube stop.*

Speaker's Corner. Sunday afternoons, the northeast corner of Hyde Park welcomes anyone with anything to say in public and a soapbox to stand on.... *Marble Arch tube stop.*

Spitalfields City Farm. As it sounds, this is a farm in the middle of the East End, complete with cows, sheep, goats, and ducks, pony rides for kids, summer barbecues, and horse-drawn cart tours.... *Tel 0171/247–8762. Pedley St., Spitalfields tube stop. Open Tue–Sun 9:30–5:30. Call for tour information and closing times. Admission free; charged for tours.*

LONDON | DIVERSIONS

Staple Inn. Central London's oldest surviving Tudor (1586) half-timbered house was once the wool staple, where that commodity was weighed and traded.... *High Holborn. Holborn tube stop.*

Tate Gallery. Britain's modern collections are vast, and not all on show at once—not until the new Tate is completed in 2000. More than just modern work is here: the Tate holds the national collection of British painting from 1500 to now, plus the Turner collection, housed in the separate Clore Gallery.... *Tel 0171/887–8000. Millbank SW1, Pimlico tube stop. Open 10–5:50 (Sun opens at 2). Closed Easter, May 1, Christmas, Jan 1. Admission free; charged for special exhibitions.*

Temple of Mithras. Mithraists preferred Christ's 3rd- and 4th-century rival, the Persian god of light, Mithras, though it took archaeologists a while to figure that out from the foundations they unearthed here in 1954.... *Queen Victoria St., Mansion House tube stop.*

Thames Barrier. Resembling a silver stretched-out version of the Sydney Opera House, the world's largest moveable flood barrier will rise when needed to protect the city—the exhibition here tells how. There are riverside walkways.... *Tel 0181/854–1373. Unity Way, Woolwich SE18, Charlton BR. Open Mon–Fri 10–5, Sat–Sun 10:30–5:30. Closed Christmas. Admission charged.*

Thames Boat Trips. From April to October, many boats ply the Thames, most departing from Westminster Pier or Charing Cross Pier. Destinations downstream are the Tower, Greenwich, and the Thames Barrier, while the longer upstream trips end up at Richmond, Kew, and Hampton Court.... *Call for schedules: Westminster Pier, tel 0171/930–4097, or Charing Cross Pier, tel 0171/ 839–3312.*

Tower Bridge. "Harry," an animatronic Victorian bridge worker, tells the story of the famous drawbridge, complete with the architect's ghost and a miniature music-hall show. Fab walkway views, too.... *Tel 0171/403–3761. Tower Bridge SE1, Tower Hill tube stop. Open daily Apr–Oct 10–6:30, Nov–Mar 10–5:15. Closed Christmas. Admission charged.*

LONDON | DIVERSIONS

Tower of London. A prime sight, where London's history is oldest and bloodiest. The 900-year-old palace has the Beefeaters, countless firearms and suits of armor, and, of course, the Crown Jewels.... *Tel 0171/709–0765. Tower Hill EC3, Tower Hill tube stop. Open Mon–Sat 9–6, Sun 10–6 (closes 5pm Nov–Feb). Closed Christmas, Jan 1. Admission charged.*

Trafalgar Square. The geographical center of London has Nelson's Column and the National Gallery, and is also the hub for night buses and pigeons.... *Charing Cross tube stop.*

Victoria and Albert Museum. The V&A is the national shrine of the decorative arts, with everything from the Shakespeare-immortalized Great Bed of Ware to last year's Lacroix and Comme outfits in the famous dress collection. Don't miss the glittering new Glass Gallery.... *Tel 0171/938–8500. Cromwell Rd. SW7, South Kensington tube stop. Open Tue–Sun 10–5:50, Mon noon–5:50. Closed Christmas, Jan 1. Admission charged (by voluntary donation).*

Waldorf Tea Dance. Nothing is more bizarrely British than a five-course afternoon tea with a fox-trot on the side. Even more bizarrely, it's not touristy. Jacket and tie must be worn by the gentlemen.... *Tel 0171/836–2400. Waldorf Hotel, Aldwych WC2, Aldwych tube stop. Open Sat–Sun 3:30–6. Admission free; tea costs £19.50.*

Wallace Collection. Four generations of Marquesses of Hertford assembled this exquisite collection of European paintings (much Fragonard and Boucher; Canaletto, Van Dyck, Rubens...), Sèvres porcelain, Italian majolica, and Renaissance gold, all housed in a late 18th-century mansion. Don't miss Frans Hals's *Laughing Cavalier*.... *Tel 0171/935–0687. Hertford House, Manchester Sq. W1, Bond St. tube stop. Open Mon–Sat 10–5, Sun 2–5. Closed Easter, May 1, Christmas, Jan 1. Admission free.*

Westminster Abbey. London's other ur-sight (along with the Tower), this Gothic church was founded by Edward the Confessor in 1040, on the site of a Saxon church. Inside are the Coronation Chair, on which six centuries of monarchs have been crowned, Poets' Corner, and many beautiful chapels, tombs, and monuments. Prepare to queue.... *Tel*

0171/222–5152. *Parliament Sq. SW1, Westminster tube stop. Open 8–6 (nave & cloisters); royal chapels open Mon–Fri 9:20–4, Sat 9:20–2:45 and 4–6. Admission to chapels charged.*

Whitechapel Bell Foundry. The place where Big Ben and the Liberty Bell (yes, the cracked one) were forged, this working foundry has a little exhibition, but the foundry itself is off-limits.... *Tel 0171/247–2599. 34 Whitechapel Rd. E1, Aldgate East tube stop. Open Mon–Fri 8:30–5:30. Closed public holidays. Admission free.*

Whitechapel Gallery. An excitingly curated space where group and solo shows of notable contemporary work are mounted in an Art Nouveau building.... *Tel 0171/377–0107. Whitechapel High St. E1, Aldgate East tube stop. Open Tue–Sun 11–5 (Wed until 8pm). Closed Christmas, Jan 1, between exhibitions. Admission free.*

Windsor Castle. The Queen's favorite weekend home—and the world's largest inhabited castle—makes for a classy day trip. See the State Apartments, St. George's Chapel (restored after the fire of 1992), royal carriages, and Queen Mary's Doll's House. The town of Windsor is cute, too. By the way, oil was struck here in 1994, and HRH has granted permission to drill, thus making the British royal family more like soap-opera characters than ever.... *Tel 0175/383–1118. Windsor, Berkshire, Windsor & Eton Central BR. Open 10–5. Closed for some state visits (call first). Admission charged.*

Diversions in and Near the City

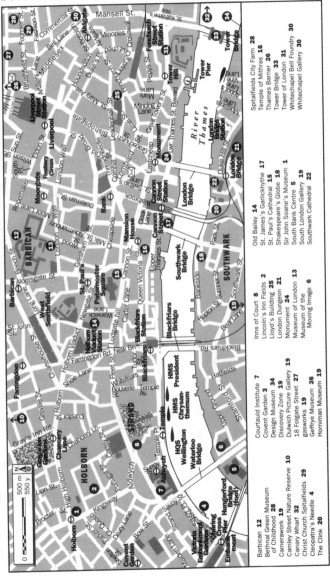

Barbican **12**
Bethnal Green Museum of Childhood **28**
Camerawork **19**
Camley Street Nature Reserve **10**
Canary Wharf **32**
Christ Church Spitalfields **29**
Cleopatra's Needle **4**
The Clink **20**

Courtauld Institute **7**
Covent Garden **3**
Design Museum **34**
Discovery Zone **19**
Dulwich Picture Gallery **19**
18 Folgate Street **27**
gasworks **19**
Geffrye Museum **26**
Horniman Museum **19**

Inns of Court **8**
Lincoln's Inn Fields **2**
Lloyd's Building **21**
London Dungeon **22**
Monument **24**
Museum of London **13**
Museum of the Moving Image **6**

Old Bailey **14**
St. James's Garlickhythe **17**
St. Paul's Cathedral **15**
Shakespeare's Globe **18**
Sir John Soane's Museum **1**
South Bank Centre **5**
South London Gallery **19**
Southwark Cathedral **22**

Spitalfields City Farm **28**
Temple of Mithras **16**
Thames Barrier **26**
Tower Bridge **33**
Tower of London **31**
Whitechapel Bell Foundry **30**
Whitechapel Gallery **30**

Information ⓘ   Tube Station ⊖

Central London Diversions

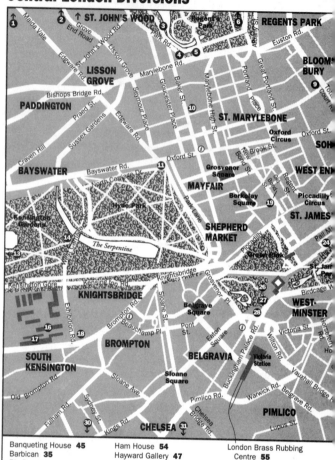

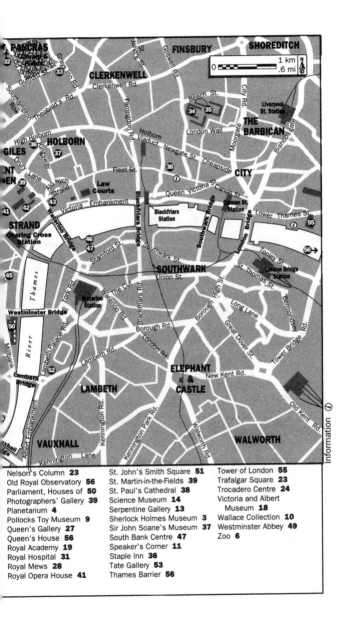

Nelson's Column **23**
Old Royal Observatory **56**
Parliament, Houses of **50**
Photographers' Gallery **39**
Planetarium **4**
Pollocks Toy Museum **9**
Queen's Gallery **27**
Queen's House **56**
Royal Academy **19**
Royal Hospital **31**
Royal Mews **28**
Royal Opera House **41**

St. John's Smith Square **51**
St. Martin-in-the-Fields **39**
St. Paul's Cathedral **38**
Science Museum **14**
Serpentine Gallery **13**
Sherlock Holmes Museum **3**
Sir John Soane's Museum **37**
South Bank Centre **47**
Speaker's Corner **11**
Staple Inn **36**
Tate Gallery **53**
Thames Barrier **56**

Tower of London **55**
Trafalgar Square **23**
Trocadero Centre **24**
Victoria and Albert
  Museum **18**
Wallace Collection **10**
Westminster Abbey **49**
Zoo **6**

getting

4

outside

If a Londoner
claims not to
work out at all,
believe it. The
aerobic eighties
did hit town, but
now regular

vigorous exercise has regained its former English image of
being punitive and faintly embarrassing. Games are another
matter (you'd call them "sports"), but although many
Londoners indulge in tennis, squash, cycling, golf, etc., they
do try not to wear the right clothes. Horse pursuits, cricket,
and the burgeoning American sports—especially softball—
are exceptions, where the correct kit is key. Of course, many
people do work out, and quite seriously, too, but you'll be surprised by the dearth of physical activity in all those acres of
park. You'll see a trickle of joggers and bladers, miniature
packs of cyclists, and few team games (many more on summer
weekends), but even in those parks most conducive to sportif
fun, the players amount to a mere fraction of the volume in,
say, Central Park. This does mean more space for you....

The Lowdown

Parks to get lost in... The biggest by far are outlying
Richmond Park and **Hampstead Heath**. Wild
Richmond Park, in the upriver town of Richmond (reachable by British Rail or riverboat; see Diversions), even has
a herd of deer, but its sports appeal is limited to horseback
riding and biking; outside of Regent's Park, this is true of
most of London's parks. Hampstead Heath, in the upscale
north London neighborhood of the same name
(Hampstead tube stop), is all rolling hills and dells and
ancient woods, good for long contemplative walks. On
summer evenings, you can pretend you're the poet Keats,
who lived nearby, and sit under a tree listening for a
nightingale's liquid warbling. In the center of town, **Hyde
Park** and its neighbor (there's no dividing line),
Kensington Gardens, are not at all small, and include
Kensington Palace (though it's closed for renovations)
and the Serpentine Gallery, as well as lesser sights like the
Italian Gardens and the Round Pond and a living grotto
of green that turns shrieking yellow in laburnum season
(near the Palace). Farther out, but still central, is **Regent's
Park**, medium-sized (for London—that's huge for elsewhere) but impossible to get lost in, because it's encircled
by a road and has a vast open space in the middle that
makes it prime for sport. The London Central Mosque,
due West, is an ever-visible navigation aid: See the sunset
over its golden dome. The most heavenly of the heavily

planted, landscaped, and manicured parks is **Kew Gardens,** far upstream (reachable via British Rail or river-boat—see Diversions). Wander through its great Victorian conservatories and their micro-environments from desert to rainforest, have a brush with the tropics under the palm trees or spend an hour waiting for a fly to land in one of the carnivorous plants.

Perfect petite parks... Locals will swear their own green patch is the best, but they're lying unless they're from **Holland Park.** These grounds of a ruined Jacobean mansion are crammed with goodies, viz: an open-air theater mounting full-scale operas; a restaurant; a youth hostel; tennis courts; an adventure playground for kids; flocks of peacocks, guinea fowl, and Canadian geese; a Japanese water garden; a cricket pitch; a café; an art gallery; rose gardens and rhododendrons; and the Commonwealth Institute. It's really pretty, too. If you're hitting the tourist trail in town and need respite, **St. James's Park** and, across The Mall, **Green Park,** are the obvious solutions, with the former winning hands down for scenery (lake, ducks, bandstand), and the latter having nothing but a weird new Canadian Air Force WWII memorial (southeast corner by Constitution Hill) and nice daffodils. The **Chelsea Physic Garden,** with its antique rock garden and medicinal herbs, is gorgeous. Be sure to get afternoon tea from the lovely volunteer ladies, then go say hi to the nattily dressed Chelsea Pensioners in the Royal Hospital grounds. Up north, between Regent's Park and the Heath is pretty **Primrose Hill,** with panoramic skyline views, while even farther north is a bizarre slice of countryside, in the shadow of gasometers, on a street that's half light-industrial and half red-light, called **Camley Street Nature Reserve.** It's only worth visiting if you're at Camden Lock or doing a canalside walk, but it's guaranteed never to have appeared in a previous guidebook. This disreputable (and then some) neighborhood was going to be Europe's biggest building site until the plans fell through, and now it's spawning ever more interesting arts activity. It was the site of many a legendary "warehouse party" of the Ecstasy-enhanced late 1980s.

Green escapes from tourism... Vest-pocket-sized, but useful for the West End, are the squares **Berkeley,** where the nightingale sang, and **Grosvenor**, where the U.S. Embassy stands. From Trafalgar Square, head to the Thames for **Embankment Gardens,** or nip across the Hungerford Bridge (for trains and people only) to **Jubilee Gardens** for a peerless view, and summer events. From Westminster Abbey, visit Rodin's "Burghers of Calais" at **Victoria Tower Gardens**, on the riverbank just south of the Houses of Parliament. For a quick fix of green during a South Ken museum marathon, penetrate the heart of the **V&A**, where there's a surprising cloister garden. If you're not doing the museum, tell the ticket sellers and they should waive the donation "fee"—or you can walk brazenly past them. If you're at the British Museum, you're near the best hidden park of all: **Lincoln's Inn Fields** (if you're at Sir John Soane's Museum, you're in it), surrounded by the beautiful 17th-century courts of law. Further north is the 7-acre **Coram's Fields**, next to which Charles Dickens lived (see his house at 48 Doughty Street) and drank (try the Lamb on Lamb's Conduit Street). **Covent Garden** is dense and annoying, but find escape in the secret garden behind the "actors' church," St. Paul's.

Best central jogging... Any Park Lane, Piccadilly, or St. James's hotel has **St. James's** and **Green Parks** on the doorstep, which together provide one of the most scenic running tracks there are. A Green Park perimeter run is 1 mile, or you can start on Piccadilly, cross Green Park due south, and then run all around the St. James's lake and north back across Green Park for a 2-mile run. You'll pass the back door of St. James's Palace and the front gates of Buckingham Palace, and meet many species of ducks. If you're staying, say, at the Lanesborough or the Halkin, **Hyde Park** is your locale, as it is from any of the Knightsbridge hotels; starting from Hyde Park Corner, you'll find a loop right around the Serpentine, crossing its bridge and returning on the south shore, 2.5 miles long. Extend that into **Kensington Gardens** to circle around the northern section of the lake called the Long Water and you've clocked 3 miles. To run the entire 4.5-mile perimeter of both parks, follow the east and west paths, both called Broad Walk, the Carriage Drives on the north side, and the riding path, Rotten Row, on the south. Increase the cardio-intensity by running on the sandy horsetrack, but don't do this early in the morning when the Household Cavalry exercise their hundreds of steeds. For an unusual and scenic 1-mile route, head out to Hammersmith to run from Hammersmith Bridge along the Upper, Lower, and Chiswick Malls (nothing to do with shopping—rhymes with "pals")…. If you'll never run alone, London's several running clubs welcome visitors, especially the long-established **Hash House Harriers**.

Balls… You're not going to be able to participate in the British national sports, **cricket** and **football**. ("Football" means soccer, but nobody calls it that. What Americans call football is known here as American football.) Both sports are played weekends in Regent's Park by teams of varying levels of seriousness; football's played in fall and winter, cricket starts in late spring. Cricket is relaxing to watch, however, even if you can't make head or tail of its rules; watch amateur games in Regent's Park, or more picturesquely in Holland Park, where there's a designated Cricket Lawn, with a tea room adjacent. Professional cricket is played at Lord's and the Oval (see Entertainment). In Regent's Park and also in Hyde Park, each spring you'll find a phenomenon of the last eight years or so—a ballgame you'll be far more familiar with: **softball**. Teams are organized, but bring your mitt and you'll probably be able to pick up a game, especially Sundays in the middle of Regent's Park. Other softball parks include **Battersea** and **Clapham Common**. The standard's getting pretty good, especially since most serious teams include American expat ringers, who imported skills that have now been thoroughly absorbed. *Time Out* lists finals in the various leagues; the men's fast-pitch team the **Zoo Crew** and the coed slow-pitch London **New Zealand** are worth catching. The **Seymour Leisure Centre** (tel 0171/402–5795, Seymour Place W2) has a hall that accommodates many sports, from badminton to five-a-side football, from circuit training to, yes, basketball; there's also a serious amateur b-ball league sponsored by Budweiser. The games are played indoors, and though you're welcome to watch, you can probably see better at your local college gym. **Baseball** is played in Britain, but really badly. If you're any good, you'll probably be a welcome ringer, but you'd have to be desperate, because most teams are based in the suburbs. Two sports you can play here, and not at home, are **Australian**

Rules Football and Camogie. The rules in the former are apparently very loose—this is like gridiron crossed with mud wrestling (call the West London Wildcats for information, tel 0181/896–1458). Camogie (call the Islington Camogie Club, tel 0171/272–1374) is the most Irish of sports, somewhere between hurling, lacrosse, and field hockey. Field hockey is called hockey here, and hockey is called ice hockey; on Hampstead Heath, there's a high-standard hockey pickup game you're welcome to join that's been going on every Sunday since WWII (about 300 yards past Whitestone Ponds; to the right, near the TV antenna. Bully-off at 3pm).

Horsing around... The English really like messing around with large quadrupeds, and you can do it with them, either in the center of town or, in a bigger way, by taking a tube to the end of a line. In Hyde Park is Rotten Row, a sand-track artery with various sand track arterioles, which has been handy for showing off an equestrian wardrobe and a perfect seat (that's your form on horseback) since Charles II laid it down. The name Rotten Row is probably a corruption of *route du roi*, in reference to that same king. Both Ross Nye (tel 0171/262–3791, 8 Bathurst Mews W2) and Hyde Park Riding Stables (tel 0171/723–2813, 63 Bathurst Mews W2) can mount you and send you off into the park, albeit not unaccompanied, not dressed in jeans, not Western style, and not at a gallop. It's a pretty formal affair, riding in London, and if you've never ridden English saddle, be prepared for a shock—it's utterly different and far more complex than Western saddle, though experienced wranglers should get the hang of the basics pretty fast. The London Equestrian Centre (tel 0181/349–1345, Frith Manor Farm, Lullington Garth N12) is a good place, even for beginners; all new riders get a half-hour assessment lesson before heading out on a hack (a trail ride). Trent Park Stables (tel 0181/363–8630, East Pole Farm, Bramley Rd. N14) has the dual advantages of being on the end of a tube line (get the Piccadilly at Oakwood) and having acres of "green belt" protected countryside to ride around in. You'll leave the city far behind. Hard hats and shoes with heels are a requirement to ride in the U.K.; stables can usually furnish you with a riding helmet.

Teeing off... There are many fine courses in England, and world-class ones in Scotland; in London itself, however, the pickings are slimmer. Next door to Trent Park Stables is **Trent Park Golf Club** (tel 0181/366–7432, Bramley Rd., Southgate N14, Oakwood tube), about the only full-scale 18-hole round of golf so accessible to downtown. It is a club, and you do have to join, but you can do so on the spot for around £50, rent sets of clubs, and so on. There are also two 18-hole public courses that are reputed to be quite good a bit farther out at **Richmond Park** (tel 0181/876–1795, Roehampton Gate SW15), which you don't have to join, but which do get mobbed with all London's golfers. Just to keep your hand in and pacify your addiction, try **Regent's Park Golf School** (tel 0171/724–0643, in Regent's Park, near the zoo), where you can schedule a lesson or just putt around on the small greens or drive in the ranges.

On the water... You can watch rowing on a stretch of the Thames from Hammersmith to Putney, but you can't easily do it yourself—real Oxford and Cambridge Boat Race–style rowing and sculling clubs are exclusively members-only. From a hut on the Lido, you can take out a recreational rowboat on the Serpentine during the months of April through September. Though it's a bargain (around £5 an hour to rent a boat), it is really just a pale imitation of river sculling. Sailing, believe it or not, is available in London on the Thames—at **Westminster Boating Base** (tel 0171/821–7389, 136 Grosvenor Rd. SW1) and in the 'burbs on a big lake in the 23-acre **Lee Valley Park** (tel 0181/345–6666, Myddleton House, Bulls Cross, Enfield EN2).

In the swim... Thanks to the climate, water is a natural element for the English, and there are consequently loads of public swimming pools in London, though surprisingly few hotels have pools. The best pools among the hotels we list in the Accommodations are at **Grosvenor House** and **Kensington Close**; **Dolphin Square**'s is the most atmospheric, and often the emptiest, while the pool at the **Regent** is small and perfectly formed. Two unlisted (by us) hotels with spectacular pools are the under-brand-new-ownership-at-presstime **Meridien** (tel. 0171/734–8000, Piccadilly, W1), whose megabucks health club is run by

LONDON | GETTING OUTSIDE

the swanky spa Champneys, and the **Knightsbridge Berkeley** (tel. 0171/235–6000, Wilton Place, SW1), with a roof that peels back to expose its elysian pool. If your hotel is poolless, search out a public pool—on the whole, they're well-maintained and sparkling clean, though the chlorine level is high and the changing rooms are communal. The **Oasis** (tel 0171/831–1804, 32 Endell St. WC2) has two pools, including a not particularly beautiful outdoor one, and it couldn't be more central, but every office worker near Covent Garden seems to be there at lunchtime. A better outdoor option is the **Serpentine** Lido pool (tel 0171/262–5484, Hyde Park W2, open May-Sept), with a chlorinated section. Join the mad Serpentine Swimming Club for a dip in the Serpentine itself at 6am every single day of the year; get on TV when they break the ice in the year's first freeze. Of course you don't need to join the club to swim here; it's open all year. As far as public indoor pools go, **Swiss Cottage** pool (tel 0171/586–5989, Winchester Rd. NW3) is one of the biggest (37 yards long) and conveniently next to the Swiss Cottage tube stop, but it gets crowded; the **Chelsea** pool (tel 0171/352–6985, Chelsea Manor St. SW3) is handy for aqua-addicts staying in the west. **Seymour Leisure Centre** (tel 0171/402–5795, Seymour Place W2) has a good, long four-lane lap pool just a fifteen-minute walk from Marble Arch. Watch out for aqua-aerobics times, though—the Seymour Centre is well known for its fitness classes. You can also get your scuba diving certification here. You'd need a good reason to head all the way out to the enormous **Crystal Palace National Sports Centre** (tel 0181/778–0131, Ledrington Rd. SE19), and what better one than a game of underwater hockey? A.k.a. Octopush, this involves teams of six flicking a rubber squid along the pool bottom. It's a serious sport—just ask the reigning Southsea men's team or the sport's development officer (tel 0125/271–2632).

Climbing the walls... London offers no mountains but several opportunities to learn to climb them—rock climbing and mountaineering are popular here, and Brits even win medals at it. Oldest and finest of the climbing centers is indoors at **NLRC** (tel 0181/980–0289, Cordova Rd. Bow E3, Mile End tube), which stands, thrillingly if misleadingly, for "North London Rescue Commando." It's hidden deep in the East End (call for directions) but is worth the trek for rock fans, since there are faces with many features—for bouldering (traverse climbing), competition climbing (with moveable holds), high up, medium, easy, impossible, and completely upside-down climbing. There are lessons, and it's all extremely inexpensive. The newest wall is outdoors at the **Westway Sports Centre** (tel 0181/969–0992, 1 Crowthorne Rd. W10, Latimer Road), with a 15-meter tower, a 12-meter pyramid, and 30 meters of traversing wall. Both cost well under £5 a day and offer lessons. One more wall is the 70-footer at north London's **Sobell Sports Centre** (tel 0171/609–2166, Hornsey Rd. N7, Finsburg Park), an all-around sports facility that offers plenty to do.

Downhill racing... What's that other mountain sport? Skiing! Why on earth would you attempt this in London? Because you can! At the **Hillingdon Ski Centre** (01895/255183, Gatting Way, Uxbridge) there's a 170-meter main slope, floodlit for night skiing. There is no snow.

On ice... Time was, the Thames froze solid enough to situate a fair on top of it for the duration of winter. Even in the 1960s, the winters were reliably cold enough for the Round Pond in Kensington Gardens to be London's unofficial skating rink. Now, however, we must rely on a handful of artificially frozen rinks, of which **Queens Ice Skating Club** (tel 0171/229 0172, Queensway W2) is the largest, most central, and best known. There are disco evenings, classes, skate hire, but no ice hockey—for that you'd have to go way out to the 'burbs for a chance at playing (hockey skates are never allowed on regular rinks). If you're desperate, you can substitute stupid games like brushball (which is just what it sounds like), some of which aren't even played in skates, at the fall and winteronly **Broadgate Arena** (tel 0171/588–6565, 3 Broadgate EC2) in a swanky City business development. Broadgate, London's only outdoor rink, is small—as is the indoor rink at the **Sobell Sports Centre** (tel 0171/609–2166, Hornsey Rd. N7, Finsburg Park).

Getting fit indoors... London's hotels are not necessarily equipped with the kind of gym you expect for the rates they charge; see Accommodations for the few that offer exercise facilities. If a workout is essential to your well-being, try the following multipurpose gyms offering temporary memberships or drop-in rates. The trusty **Central YMCA** (tel 0171/637–8131, 112 Great Russell St. WC1, Holborn), like every Y, is very well equipped, though frill-free; come here also for a wide range of martial-arts classes, which are most popular in the United Kingdom. The bustling **Seymour Leisure Centre** (tel 0171/402–5795, Seymour Place W2, Marble Arch tube) has a gym, badminton, and morning-to-evening classes in the Move It program (the funk class, especially if Julie Corsair is still around, is a party). **Jubilee Hall** (tel 0171/379–0008, 30 the Piazza WC2, Covent Garden tube) actually feels swankier and more expensive than the public facility that it is; you can do tai chi or wu shu (Chinese boxing) before your step class here. The still tonier **The Gym at the Sanctuary** (tel 0171/240–0695, 11 Floral St. WC2, Covent Garden tube), attached to the women-only day spa of the same name but operated separately, is a good place for women to sweat unobserved by Schwarzeneggers. The **Albany Fitness Centre** (tel 0171/383–7131, St. Bede's Church, Albany St. NW1, Great Portland tube) is fun and full of weight-training hardware for would-be Schwarzeneggers, in a deconsecrated church. For dance classes, **Pineapple** (tel 0171/836–4004, 7 Langley St. WC2, Covent Garden tube) tends toward the aerobics, hip hop, jazz side, as well as tai chi, while **Danceworks** (tel 0171/629–6183, 16 Balderton St. W1, Bond Street tube) has everything from ballet to line dancing at all levels from beginner to pro, plus various aerobics innovations, like "Kick-aerobics"; professional dancers who need to take a class might try **The Place** (tel 0171/388–8430, 17 Dukes Rd. WC2, Euston tube), attached to the London Contemporary Dance School. Tennis players should gravitate toward two new indoor tennis centers built for the public, to bring the game out of the posh exclusive clubs: the **Islington Tennis Centre** (tel 0171/700–1370, Market Rd. N7), is a bit remote, though five minutes from the Caledonian Road tube; and the **Westway Sports Centre** (tel 0181/969–0992, 1 Crowthorne Rd. W10), is nearer to downtown and close to the Latimer Road tube. For squash, head for **Ironmonger Row** (tel 0171/253–4011,

Ironmonger Row EC1, near Old Street tube), **Portobello Green** (tel 0181/960–2221, 3–5 Thorpe Close W10, Ladbroke Grove tube), or the **Sobell Sports Centre** (tel 0171/609–2166, Hornsey Rd. N7, Finsbury Park tube). Isola Akay's wonderful west London boxing gym housed in a church, **All Stars Gym** (tel 0181/960–7724, 576 Harrow Rd. W10; call after 5pm) welcomes all contenders to its two-hour, no-contact KO circuit; it's the friendliest (stay for tea and biscuits after) and most challenging workout in town.

shop

5

ping

If you ask us—
and you did—
London is one of
the world's great
shopping cities.
Sure, it's full of
the international

chain stores that make it difficult to discern which country you're in, but there are depths below that scummy surface— and some of the home-grown clothing chains are actually pretty good. Prices aren't the lowest, and the dollar–sterling exchange rate periodically makes shopping London fiendishly expensive, but you make up for that with quality and selection.

What To Buy

Get antiques, or just lust after them. If you're not rich, trawl fleamarkets, street markets, and so-called junk shops for treasure. Stock up on books—antiquarian, out-of-print, and those written by European and British writers without a U.S. publisher—then lug them home. Some of the world's best porcelain and china is indigenous to England—Royal Doulton, Spode and Wedgewood spring to mind—and London's good for rustic European tableware, too. Buy clothes here, really. The big European designers have at least a store each, as do the Americans, but British designers you may not have heard of will surprise you, and they're perfectionists with the finish. Traditional English tailoring is famous, of course. Savile Row (it rhymes with "gravel") is the apogee, but look at the less exorbitant (but still not cheap) huntin', shootin', and fishin' outfits, elements of which work with any wardrobe. Ralph Lauren, eat your heart out. At the other extreme, look for street clothes—London's been famous for funky since the mods put Carnaby Street on the map. The word "crafts" conjures images of crocheted granola Birkenstocks, but really means acres of exciting, handmade design wares that you can only find here. Also buy tea—loose leaf, not bags—and a teapot and strainer. Other food gifts and treats are cheeses, especially whole mini-cheddars and stiltons, and the oatcakes to accompany them (try the Prince of Wales's line); then there are pork pies, Thornton's special toffee, Scottish smoked salmon, and anything from Marks & Spencer, Waitrose, or Sainsbury's (in order of decreasing poshness) for the packaging. This is a nation of gardeners. If you share that obsession, get paraphernalia here.

Target Zones

There are so many shopping districts; here's a whizz through. The **West End**'s artery is the busiest street in town: **Oxford Street**, with chain stores and tacky closeout stores, plus good department stores and two swanky fashion streets on the edge

(**South Molton Street** and **St. Christopher's Place**). Around the corner is **Bond Street** (New, segueing into Old), famous for top-dollar clothes, art, jewelry. **Savile Row, St. James's,** and the arcades of **Piccadilly** (the sine qua non of window shopping) also count as West End, as does **Regent Street** (for big stores **Liberty** and **Hamleys,** and the little streets around **Soho** and **Carnaby Street,** full of t-shirts and sneakers, plus more interesting designer-type boutiques. **Covent Garden** is sort of counted as West End, but is a very fruitful shopping district in its own right. It has all the better clothing chains, plus market stalls, and many little boutiques—mainstream but appealing to all, with the bookstores of **Charing Cross Road** and **Cecil Court** on its border. A 20-minute ride north on the 24 or 29 bus, **Camden Town** has its huge teenage street market, the **Lock,** but also available in its shops are plenty of vintage clothes, Indian brassware, denims, head gear, funky hats and boots, kilims, and silver jewelry. Keep going north and you hit **Hampstead,** which is a picturesque way to shop the best clothing chains, and get some less chain-store-like stuff on the side. You wouldn't make **Upper Street, Islington** your shopping destination, unless you were antiquing in **Camden Passage,** but if you happened to be in the neighborhood at the Almeida Theater, you would find many interesting small shops, mostly clothes and housewares. In the west, **Knightsbridge** is the ultimate destination, with London's most famous store, **Harrods,** plus every European designer represented in shops strung along **Sloane Street** and **Brompton Road.** Keep going, and you reach **Brompton Cross** with its cluster of very fancy fashion and interiors shops. North of Knightsbridge, you'll hear Kensington's main drag shortened to **Ken High Street.** It has most of the chains, plus the interesting curve of **Ken Church Street,** where antiques are expensive, but of museum quality. More egalitarian antiques are found further north, in and around famous **Portobello Road**—not just a market, but a way of life. Explore the entire neighborhood for fashion designers just starting out, stuff for interiors, young artists you can afford, vintage clothes, ceramics.... One more westerly destination is **Chelsea.** The **King's Road** has been past its prime for years, though it's okay for mid-priced antiques and the better clothing chains, and has a **Waitrose** reputed to be a good place to shop for both groceries and for a date. Its nether reaches, around **World's End,** where designer Vivienne Westwood has her shop, are better.

Bargain Hunting

You can make London much less expensive by applying three main strategies: shopping the sales, hitting markets, and (for clothes) seeking out resale stores. The sales seasons are traditionally January and June, although these are moveable feasts which leak further into December and July every year. Lots of shops also have a permanent sale rack. We list resale shops, but look in the *Evening Standard*, and in *Time Out*'s "Sell Out" section for news of designers' "warehouse sales" or showroom clearances. Look below for how to do markets, and what to get there. By the way, here the phrase "it's on sale" doesn't mean the price has been reduced, it just means you can buy it.

Trading with the Natives

Certain rituals familiar to every American shopper are mysteries to Brits. The layaway is not done, for instance (how long are you staying anyway?), and you may find assistants less attentive than you're used to. Londoners don't wish to know how a stranger thinks this looks on them and whether it goes with their new jacket. You won't see "We Ship Anywhere" signs either. Big stores will ship, but otherwise you're usually on your own, though your hotel may help. Places that ship are usually set up for instant VAT refunds, as well (see below). Delivery in London is also the exception rather than the rule, and usually costs extra. As you would expect, bargaining for a lower price is not done in regular shops, though haggling can pay dividends in street markets.

Hours of Business

There is less and less uniformity to the hours a shop keeps, since Sunday trading laws have relaxed, and Londoners are getting more demanding. Traditional opening hours are 9 to 5 or 6, with one half-day closing (almost an extinct practice in London, but still found in the provinces) and one day with extended hours, usually Thursday till 7 or 8pm. Regardless of whether they're allowed to open, most shops stay shut on Sundays, with the odd exception, like Camden, where Sunday is the busiest day.

Sales Tax

England's sales tax is called **Value Added Tax**, or **VAT**, and it runs at a greedy 17.5% on so-called non-essential goods. You can get it refunded by filling out a form at the time of purchase, which you then take, with the goods and receipts, to customs at Heathrow. For this reason, always shop with your passport. Some shops have a minimum (about £30, and up), some don't want to do it at all, and some have big long lines. If you have something shipped, you can get an on-the-spot VAT refund.

The Lowdown

The big stores... Of Oxford Street's three department stores, **Selfridges** is the best, and is getting better, because they're pouring money into a major sprucing-up program. The Food Hall and the fashion departments were first to be throroughly revamped. (By the way, clothing is the core merchandise at all of these stores, unless otherwise indicated.) Still on Oxford Street, pass by **Debenhams**, the K-Mart to Selfridges' Macy's, and head to **John Lewis** (loveable for its motto, "Never Knowingly Undersold") and its excellent fabrics, notions, and haberdashery. Around the corner in Regent Street, **Dickens & Jones** is the flagship of the nationwide **House of Fraser** group, which is not generally known for fashion leadership. This store, however, tries really hard with its prices in the middle range, and its great sales. Nearby is irresistible **Liberty**, which started as an Oriental bazaar, and still maintains an Eastern bias in certain exotic corners of its mahogany and stained-glass interior. Down Bond Street, find slightly odd **Fenwick**, a store that often attempts to be all things to all people but isn't, except in the underwear department. Two other West End stores are in Piccadilly. **Simpson** is worth seeing for its spooky reflectionless windows alone, and is meant for the older and better-heeled dresser, but the lord of department stores is **Fortnum & Mason**. It's the queen's grocer, and you shouldn't pass up the food halls with liveried servers and towers of teas, preserves, handmade chocolates, and cans of turtle soup. But go upstairs, too, for the least frenetic cosmetics counter in town, a general air of anachronistic serenity, and many matronly clothes. Mega-successful nationwide chain, **Marks & Spencer** is the hamburger of shops, universally known and loved. Every Londoner has Marks & Sparks knickers (panties, that is), sweaters, and an addiction to some item from the food ranges. In the west, **Peter Jones**, another House of Fraser number, is more of a sociological phenomenon than a store, the spiritual home of the Sloane Ranger and purveyor of school uniforms. The great store of the west, though, is **Harvey Nichols**, spiritual home to Patsy and Edina of television's *Absolutely Fabulous*, and practically nothing but fashion—but what clothes! And what prices. Nearby is **Harrods**. What do you want us to say? That it's overrated? Overpriced? Over? Well, it isn't, it's wonderful. This London landmark and its 230 departments do attempt to live up to the store motto "Omnia, Omnibus, Ubique" (everything for everyone, everywhere).

Rattling the chains... Instead of the Gap, and other places you can patronize chez vous, sport local styles. Look like a teenage clubber in irridescent minis and dayglo rubber Ts—shop **Top Shop**, **Miss Selfridge**, and (for more formal occasions), **River Island**, the best of the cheapies. Best of the best for the generation formerly known as X, though, is **Warehouse**, where stock moves so fast, it's blurred. Some stuff there suits the older girly too, but better is **Jigsaw**, where things don't fall apart as quickly as at most chains. Everyone goes to **Marks & Spencer** for underwear, but it's an open secret that Marks 'n' Sparks gets fancy designers to consult on bigger garments, and there's much to discover in the formerly frumpy superchain—for men too. A very *short* chain, but best of all for quality, and being on target aesthetically, is **Whistles**.

The big names... The shop with the mostest has to be **Browns**, from which owner Joan Burstein has led London into the appreciation and assimilation of tasty clothes for many years. Here are Galliano, Demeulemeester, Ozbek, Rykiel, Karan, Tyler, Gigli, Sander, Muir, etc., etc. Other places where you can compare and contrast multiple makers include **Pellicano**, a few doors down, for local young turks Bella Freud, Joe Casely-Hayford, and Nicholas Knightly, to name a few; and the tony Knightsbridge **À La Mode**, which favors the Americans and the Belgians. All designers you've ever heard of are in London somewhere, but here are some highlights among those (non-British ones) with whole shops, starting with the gods: it's possible **Prada**'s star may have waned by the time you read this, but Signorina Miuccia opened a shop in 1995 anyway, as did **Dolce & Gabbana**, while **Christian Lacroix** doubled his outlets, with a New Bond Street salon, and Kawakubo expanded **Comme des Garçons**—which now also encompasses all her less pricy lines. **Armani**, predictably, opened another **Emporio** store, tightening his stranglehold on our taste, while **Gianni Versace** displays his lack of same in an over-the-top four-floor roccoco marble folly on Bond Street, where you get sneered at if you dare enter. For less cash outlay than at any of the above, shop **Joseph** for enticing ranges of mostly French-made and monochrome separates.

Homegrown talent... The British Isles once produced great writers, but now it's better at clothes. You may know that her ladyship **Vivienne Westwood** is one of the world's most inventive and most copied designers, but you should see her clothes close up—they're exquisitely tailored, as well. Easier to wear, though, are **Betty Jackson**'s slightly offbeat classics. Also check out this pair of designers who do the riding-clothes–country-tweeds–rumpled-linens look better than anyone: **Margaret Howell**'s clothes last forever; Irishman **Paul Costelloe** does the Irish version with *lots* of linen. Also see **Mulberry** for the most staid versions of this look, and next door to that, the secret of certain well-dressed, anti-fashion mature women, **Paddy Campbell**, who makes timeless fitted suits and separates. **Paul Smith** is the menswear king, for suits with a sense of humor, plus accessories and tons of shirts, with a limited women's range too. The other terribly famous (and deservedly so) menswear man is the clothes **Conran**, Jasper, who also dresses women. **Nicole Farhi**'s another one who swings both ways. She's London's Donna Karan. On the opposite bank, wearing work clothes in denim with something clingy, rhinestoned, and small, and a well-cut jacket, stands **Katharine Hamnett**. In the same wardrobe, but younger and madder, not to mention cheaper, are the clubwear pieces by **Red Or Dead**, which start at the feet, since their shoes were what gave birth to their glitterwear and catsuits in bubblegum colors.

For riot grrls and boys... Streetwear stays out of the limelight and is found, yes, on the street—in market stalls, thrift stores (called charity shops here), and rummage

LONDON | SHOPPING

sales (jumble sales). However, to approximate a London look, try the following: the **Duffer of St. George** has the Chelsea boot-boy kitted out in vaguely threatening style; riot girls wear it too. **The Dispensary** edits other people's lines—some from the U.S.—and makes their own to dress you not too outrageously, while **Johnsons** has been going forever, whether in or out of fashion with its teddy-boy suits and boots. There's a branch in **Kensington Market**, which is one-stop shopping for teenage clubbers, down to the tattoo and haircut. As for fleamarkets, forget **Camden Lock**, and head to the Westway on Friday morning for the clothes part of **Portobello**. Nearby is the number one fetishwear center, **Skin Two**, which specializes in rubber.

Labels for less... We mentioned in the intro how you should check listings in the *Standard* and *Time Out* for warehouse sales, and call the showroom too. Some other sources: **Labels For Less** is **Browns'** outlet store. **Whistles** also has one, not far away. Both **Vivienne Westwood** and **Paul Smith** have permanent sale stores. Find more Westwood, along with Conran, Galliano, and more, at **Venus**, a friendly consignment store with a feel for the street. Of London's collection of more mainstream consignment and used designer clothing shops, the best are Hampstead's **Designs** (for the Escada and Genny type of woman—the German well-pressed look), and **Designer Secondhand Store** (a little hipper, with some Comme des Garçons, Rifat Ozbek, and Paul Smith); the Knightsbridge **Pandora** (big and well known with wodges of Alaïa, Armani, Karan, and even Chanel), and the small and variably stocked Portobello **Designer Sale & Exchange Shop**, which gets showroom samples from some designers, including Patrick Cox, Paddy Campbell, and Pascal Smets. For designers who are no longer designing, there's nowhere better than the incredible **Steinberg & Tolkein**. The basement here is like a funky version of the V&A Dress Collection where everything's for sale with a ton of affordable tat alongside the Jacques Fath and historic Chanel pieces from the days of Coco herself.

For sir, with $$$... The famous tailors of Savile Row are moving with the times... a bit. **Richard James** is a newer face, who cuts with nontraditional cloths like denim, as well as the suitings one would expect. At 1 Savile Row is the quintessential, ultimate bespoke tailor, **Gieves & Hawkes** (that's a hard "G"), who started with Admiral Nelson and graduated to Hugh Grant's Oscar-night suit. Get your shirts made where the Prince of Wales and Warren Christopher get theirs, **Turnbull & Asser**. A Savile Row suit will take maybe six weeks and at least three fittings, will not cost less than £1000, and the tab may be almost double that. A minimum order half-dozen bespoke shirts with shell buttons and collar stays of bone will set you back £600–£900. If you're not in that tax bracket yet, try **Squire**, who resides at the Duffer of St. George, and can do a spivvy whistle (whistle & flute-suit) for around £400 with one fitting only. Finish the look at **Favourbrook** with a brocade weskit, or vest, in one of their many dandy fabrics. Nearly all these tailors will also make to measure for women.

Your own crown jewels... The actual crown jewels are watched over by **Garrard**, where you can order your personal collection any way you like it, or try out the royal-looking work of **Theo Fennell**—his ecclesiastical gold-smithery is quite distinctive. But, let's face it, you're probably looking for something a little less *real*. The most outrageously rhinestoned of **Butler & Wilson**'s wares fool nobody none of the time and are irresistible to human magpies, especially the crown brooches and earrings; there's also great classic French gilt and a lot of jet. If you really do require an actual crown, **Slim Barrett** is your man. His stone-encrusted coronets and tiaras are fashion-victim favorites. But for something to wear on a daily basis, visit with **Dinny Hall** (who works mostly in silver), see the jewelry departments at **Liberty** and **Harvey Nichols**, or check out the score of young designers at **Janet Fitch**.

Gifts that scream London... Janet Fitch is a great gift source for your modern and design-conscious friends, and the diamanté crown pieces from **Butler & Wilson** are cute British gifts, or get a St. Paul's dome in umbrella form from the **Museum Store**. There are racks and racks more of the essential English accessory at the gorgeous Victorian brolly (umbrella to you) emporium **James Smith & Sons**, where you can also get shooting sticks (a portable seat), silver topped canes, Mary Poppins parrot-top umbrellas, and riding crops. Our favorite scarves come from genius **Georgina von Etzdorf**, whose devoré velvets and hand printed silk chiffons and opulent satins are much copied but never equalled. For gifts in quantity, for the entire office, perhaps, get orchid or banana tea from **The Tea House**, or Twining's Earl Gray (the best) from **R. Twining & Co.**, with its little tea museum on the company's original premises; or go for smokey Lapsang Souchong and the New York blend (made to brew with New York water—really) from **Fortnum & Mason**, which is one-stop shopping for the entire gift list. Smellies are not boring gifts when they come from **Penhaligon**'s, where you'll have a blast uncorking crystal flacons and sniffing precious waters. William Penhaligon was Victoria's court barber, and the same Blenheim Bouquet he blended is sold still—it's in the Ritz's bathrooms too.

Guy gifts... For jocks and tomboys (i.e., guys of both genders), London's got every accoutrement—also for Bond, James Bond, who could have bought bugs, counter-bugs, Coke-can safes, and cigarette lighter cameras at **Spycatcher**. Bigger cameras can be drooled over at the self-explanatory **Rare Camera Company**, where Leicas are born again; whereas real cigarette lighters can be picked up at **Davidoff**, which is really more for cigar smokers, with wall-to-wall Havanas in its walk-in humidor. For the pipe man, **Inderwicks** is the place. Those who prefer an indigenous English sports souvenir will fare best at **Lillywhite's**, the amazing sports department store. Football gear, including the jerseys of all London teams, plus those of the glamorous Italian *Serie* A and other Euro footy players, is at **Soccer Scene**, while British boxers (one of the few sports for which we supply stars) get their hands wrapped at **Lonsdale**.

Remarkable markets... **Bermondsey** is for serious antique collectors. It's where dealers buy, but early, very, very early—before dawn. **Camden Passage** has a picturesque setting, with its alleys and little shops, in which the prices are higher than on the stalls. Finds are also still possible among the 2000-odd dealers at the most famous market, **Portobello Road**. The antiques are concentrated at the Notting Hill end; they give way to fruit-and-veg, to the flea under the Westway (great vintage clothes), then into the nether reaches of Goldborne Road, where it's all junk and rummage, character, and the important pitstop, the Lisboa Portuguese bakery. **Brick Lane** has antiques too, but you'll have to sift. It has great atmo, this East End Sunday agglomeration of *stuff*—cassettes, work tools, candies, leather jackets, glasses, wallets—and provides your the best chance of catching old market trader's banter and maybe rhyming slang. For a "real" market bang in the West End, you can't beat the fruit and vegetable traders of Soho's **Berwick Street**, so good that chefs shop there. For the diametric opposite, try **Camden Lock**—heaven to some (most under 20), hell on wheels to others. Another very famous market is **Petticoat Lane**, which is really a lot of tat nowadays and is surpassed by its neighbors **Brick Lane**, and the totally contrasting, covered **Spitalfields Market**, whose Sunday greenmarket is a breath of the country.

Very old things... London has rich antique pickings in shops and at auction, as well as at the markets above. Here is one area where a price tag is a mutable thing, and haggling is advisable. Annual antiques fairs—of which the three biggies are the **Grosvenor House**, the **Chelsea**, and the **British Antique Dealers' Association**—attract international buyers and carriage trade alike. Several collections of stalls under one roof—sort of permananent versions of those—are your best bets for casual purchases,

Cockney Rhyming Slang

If you wander the East End of London, you may hear a few odd word-pairings that are meant to substitute for things related only inasmuch as they rhyme. For example: whistle+flute=suit, or Brahms+Liszt=pissed, or apple+pear=stair. These are sometimes boiled down to just the first word, which then produces sentences such as, "Nice whistle, matey," meaning, "That is an elegant suit." Years of Ealing comedies and "My Fair Lady" have convinced much of the world that these constructions, called Rhyming Slang, are a secret language of the Cockneys. In fact, the rhyming slang used by some Londoners is really a form of wordplay common among traders in the 18th century and found as well in Australia and the United States. Its continued presence on English radio and television shows in this century has given it a prominence based more on regional identity than on actual use, much like the famous Brooklyn accent in New York.

LONDON | SHOPPING

though. In the King's Road are no fewer than three: **Antiquarius**, **Chenil Galleries**, and **Chelsea Antiques Market**. Between those and the West End **Grays**, you'll probably score a hit. If not, try the **London Silver Vaults** for a set of Edwardian fruit knives, **Hope and Glory** for its stock of affordable commemorative china, the wonderful **Gallery of Antique Costume and Textiles**, which also makes its own reproduction 18th-century vests and coats, or **The Button Queen** for something to jazz up your jacket.

Handsome handmade... The acceptibility, and even cachet, of the once-reviled thing made by hand, or "craft" is reflected in the name **Contemporary Applied Arts**, which showcases the work of designer-makers in a half-gallery, half-shop environment. Find the wares of the hippest jewelers, glassblowers, and textile designers in town, but for potters go to **Contemporary Ceramics**. Take in several designer-makers at once at **Gabriel's Wharf**, nicest on a summer Friday because of extra stalls, plus a high probability of live jazz, all near the South Bank Centre. It's better than the **Apple Market** in the Covent Garden Piazza, where there are too many painted wooden clowns and bunny wabbit sweaters for comfort.

Money's no object... A tasteful way to splash some cash around would be to commission one of those British designers to make you the *objet* of your dreams. **Contemporary Applied Arts** operates as a mediator for such transactions, which can be more complex and emotional than even the kind of bespoke Savile Row experience offered by **Gieves and Hawkes**. Speaking of which, only Hong Kong rivals London as a place to achieve perfect head-to-toe tailoring—and Hong Kong lacks the class of the bowler hat capital. **James Lock** is your guy for that hat, except that Mr. Lock himself expired around the early eighteenth century, after making Admiral Lord Nelson's titfers (tit-for-tat hat). Your platinum cards will want to leave St. James's, when they see the beautiful, security-guard-patrolled **Burlington Arcade**, where the **Irish Linen Co.** has some of the world's finest pure white sheets, and which leads to Piccadilly. Show them the bathroom fittings heaven that is **Czech & Speake** before crossing that street to Mayfair, with its Old Masters

(**Marlborough Fine Art**—you don't have to buy), jewelers (**Asprey**), and the finest purveyor of porcelain and crystal, **Thomas Goode & Co.**

Money's too tight to mention... For those without means who yet aspire to the pristine Irish linen sheets and English bone china tea service, **The Linen Cupboard** and **Harrods' Sale** were invented. Alternatively, forget the whole aspirational thing and creatively go to **Neal Street East** for an enormous selection of Oriental imports for the home, to **Columbia Road Market** for stuff to enhance the yard, and to **The Stencil Store** for supplies to do the wall art at which the English are curiously expert. Cheap gifts that look expensive are easy. The **Tea House** supplies tea and "teaphernalia," as they call it; **Marks & Spencer** has good things to wear, and its food department packages so gorgeously, you could make a gift of a TV dinner.

For bookworms... London's literary legacy lives! Bookstores come in all sizes. In the West End resides vast and impossible to understand **Foyles**; its near neighbors **Dillons** and handsome **Hatchards**, where they're really helpful, and the original **Waterstone's**, which cloned itself all over London. Those are the best big ones, but look for the countless little specialty stores. Around book heaven Charing Cross Road, browse several varieties of **Zwemmer** (the art store is especially fine) and the self-explanatory **Dance Books**, among others. There are shops stocked as exhaustively as sections of the British Library, such as **French's Theatre Bookshop**, with every English-language play; beautiful, wood-paneled **Daunt Books** for travel tomes; **Stanford** for the accompanying maps and guides; and **Sportspages** for the obvious. Antiquarian books are a famous commodity of this town, as told to the world by the Helene Hanff novel *84 Charing Cross Road*, though nowadays try **Any Amount of Books** at no. 62 instead of no. 84. If you need a specific out-of-print title, go to **Skoob**; for a rarity or a signed first edition, investigate the world class dealer **Bernard Quaritch**, who quotes prices in dollars.

For aural obsessives... London's been the world's vinyl capital since the Beatles, and now that everyone's got CDs (which are ridiculously expensive here), it still is. If you're looking for records cut in the heyday of those Beatles, **Vinyl Experience** is the be-all and end-all of collectors' shops. For club music that always did and still does hit the streets in 12" single form, this city's number one. Try **Trax**, for Euro dance (trance, house, Ballearic) and **Fat Cat Records** in Covent Garden, for hardcore genres, while the chief place for jungle is Chelsea's **Section 5**. For jazz, the near-legendary **Mole Jazz** is better than it ever was in its new and larger place—it's kept up with the times on the CD front, too. The Portobello **Honest Jon's** has a Blue Note collection that's sublime, plus a good secondhand section, and many new CDs. As you would guess from its name, that other Soho institution, **Reckless Records**, stocks only vinyl, and only secondhand at that, with rock, soul, and jazz the main genres.

For the green thumb... London is frustrating for American gardeners, since you can't take the plants home. Ideas and inspiration, however, are free. **The Chelsea Gardener** and the **Camden Garden Centre** are the city's two best outdoor emporia, with shrubs, climbers, and rosebushes to die for, advice for free, and accessories worth paying excess baggage for. Ditto the pots of **S & B Evans** at the unmissable **Columbia Road Market**, which is itself full of wrought iron, terracotta, and wooden accessories.

Small fry... Convert fractious kids into shopping experts by showing them the five floors of **Hamleys**, the "world's biggest toy store" (or is that Toys R Us?). Down the block is **Humla**, a cult among grandmas, for the gorgeous European garments and wooden toys at remarkably ungreedy prices. Older girls find heaven at **Hennes**, a Scandinavian chain, which does high fashion cheap—and has great young kids' clothes, too. If you forgot to bring something, classy British chain **Mothercare** is fine for baby equipment and toddler stuff. Wooden and traditional toys, teddies, dolls, stationery, and games are London finds. Try well-stocked **Tridias**, or if that isn't enough, take them to nearby **Harrods**, whose fantasmagorical **Toy Kingdom** is the kind where the plush lions are life-sized and roar. Owners of dolls' houses will remember **Kristin Baybars** all their lives, so it's worth the trek.

For gastronomes and epicures... For gifts in bulk, Prince Charles has obligingly done a Paul Newman—he packs of his own brand, the disarmingly delicious Duchy Originals oatcakes and ginger biscuits fill every carry-on bag. The whole baby stilton cheese for the oatcakes should be got from **Paxton & Whitfield**, the cheese shop of cheese shops since 1797 (no Monty Python references please), or the **Neal's Yard Dairy**, in which everything is from the British Isles, or made on the premises, and you can ask for tasters. Neal's Yard products are among the epicurian riches of **Tom's**. This may stretch your credulity, but Tom is yet another Conran: brother of Jasper the clothes designer, and son of Sir Terence, whose "Gastro-drome" by Tower Bridge provides smoked fish and sea-weed bread, French charcuterie, fruit vinegars, Tuscan olive oils, homemade English chutneys, and more in four separate shops. Of these, the **Oils and Spice Shop** is the most things-to-take-home oriented. **Fortnum's**, as you know by now, also fulfills this role. Get cans of brown windsor, mulligatawny, or turtle soup, truffled foie gras, thick-cut marmalade with Scottish whisky, fruit pâtés from Provence, the anchovy paste in decorative ceramic jars called "Patum Peperium Gentleman's Relish," and English mustard, but not, as a persistent myth has it, red ants in chocolate.

For sweet teeth... Almost as exotic as Fortnum's fictional sweetmeat are certain of master chocolatier Gerard Ronay's handmade fillings, like his award-winning smoked lemon. They are available at **Selfridges** and at **Theobroma Chocolates**, which is handy for Camden Lock. Chocoholics dedicated to quality will enjoy **Rococo** on the King's Road, a cocoa paradise run by the founder of the Chocolate Society. Anyone preferring quantity will favor the many branches of **Thorntons**—for Belgian fresh cream truffles, children's novelty shapes in creamy milk and sickly white chocolate, and the aptlty named Special Toffee, which is chewy, buttery caramel, not brittle like the "English toffee" of Heath Bars.

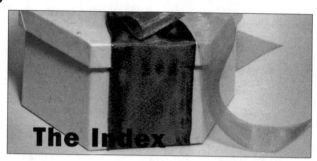

The Index

All shops are closed Sunday, unless otherwise indicated.

À La Mode. Opposite Harrods is this tony *boîte* stocking the hottest designers for wardrobe investments.... *Tel 0171/584–2133. 36 Hans Crescent, SW1. Knightsbridge tube stop.*

Antiquarius. A long-established collection of antique dealers, with art deco especially notable.... *Tel 0171/351–5353. 131–141 King's Rd. SW3. Sloane Square tube stop.*

Any Amount of Books. Take this secondhand (as opposed to antiquarian) store on book row literally.... *Tel 0171/240–8140. 62 Charing Cross Rd. WC2. Leicester Square tube stop. Open Mon–Sat 10:30–9:30, Sun 10:30–7:30.*

Apple Market. In and around the Covent Garden Piazza building are about 40 crafts stalls where you buy direct from the maker—jewelry, leathergoods, sweaters, wooden toys, and more. *The Piazza WC2. Covent Garden tube stop. Open daily 9–5.*

Asprey. Jewelry, silver, leather goods, crystal, and bone china are exquisitely served by this swankiest of traditional gift emporia.... *Tel 0171/493–6767. 165–169 New Bond St. W1. Bond Street tube stop. Open Mon–Fri 9–5:30, Sat 9–1.*

Bermondsey Market. Join the serious antique collectors and trade professionals here at dawn (take a flashlight). If you go later, you miss the choicest pieces, and the best atmosphere. *Bermondsey Square SE1. Borough tube stop. Fri 5am–noon.*

Bernard Quaritch. Quaritch has the finest rare manuscripts and antiquarian volumes, all priced in dollars. You should know what you want before you go–there is no browsing here.... *Tel 0171/734–2983. 5–8 Lower John St. W1. Piccadilly Circus tube stop. Closed Sat.*

Berwick Street Market. Soho's fruit and vegetable market serves local color in every sense; bargain prices too. *Berwick and Rupert Streets W1. Leicester Square tube stop. Open Mon–Sat 9–6.*

Betty Jackson. With her kind cuts, interesting textures, and out-of-the-ordinary color combos, Jackson's women's collection is always a hot seller.... *Tel 0171/589–7884. 311 Brompton Rd. SW3. South Ken tube stop.*

Brick Lane Market. For our money, this is the most fun Sunday market—from bric-a-brac and antiques to bikes and bagels, it's best early. *Brick Lane, east to Cheshire St., north to Club Row. Shoreditch tube stop. Open Sun 6am–1pm.*

British Antique Dealers' Association Fair. The newest of the big fairs happens in early May.... *Tel 0181/948–9802 for information. Oriel House, 26 The Quadrant, Richmond, Surrey, TW9 1DL.*

Browns. One-stop shopping if you live for fashion and have healthy plastic. All known desirable designers live in several connected shops, with Browns' own label providing missing links (white cotton shirt, black wool turtleneck, etc.). Don't forget **Labels For Less** at no. 50.... *Tel 0171/491–7833. 23–27 South Molton St. W1. Bond Street tube stop.*

Butler & Wilson. Come out dripping with diamanté, multicolored rhinestones, gilt, and jet, but still managing to look chic.... *Tel 0171/409–2955, 20 South Molton St. W1. Bond Street tube stop; Tel 0171/352–8255, 189 Fulham Rd. SW3, South Ken tube stop.*

The Button Queen. A comprehensive array of clothes closers–from antique, precious, and collectible to wacky, kitsch, handmade, and plain useful.... *Tel 0171/935–1505. 19 Marylebone Lane W1. Bond Street tube stop. Sat closes 1:30pm.*

Camden Garden Centre. This garden-like outdoor store is a living catalogue for the green-thumbed.... *Tel 0171/485–*

8468. *2 Barker Dr., St. Pancras Way, NW1. Camden Town tube stop. Open Sun 11–5.*

Camden Lock. The labyrinthine 21-year-old maze in warehouse and railway buildings both historic and fake 'round the Regent's Canal gets beyond busy on sunny Sundays. Depending where you stand, it's a trip, an ordeal, or browsing nirvana. *Camden Lock, Chalk Farm Rd., all down Camden High St., NW1. Camden Town, Chalk Farm tube stop. Open Sat, Sun 10–6; limited stalls daily 9:30–5:30.*

Camden Passage. Unrelated to the Lock, and in Islington, not Camden, this twice-a-week antiques market still offers the odd bargain. Shops augment the stalls.... *Tel 0171/359–9969. Camden Passage, Upper St. N1. Open Wed 7am–2pm, Sat 9–3:30.*

Chelsea Antiques Fair. Twice a year (March and September), dealers of pre-1830 pieces congregate at the Old Town Hall, King's Rd.... *Tel 01444/482514 for info. Sloane Square tube stop.*

Chelsea Antiques Market. And here is a permanent, if less exalted, version—an accessible place in every sense.... *Tel 0171/352–5689. 245–253 King's Rd. SW3. Sloane Square tube stop.*

Chelsea Gardener. The toniest of garden stores, with multitudes of ideas to steal, and yard accessories to buy.... *Tel 0171/352–5656. 125 Sydney St. SW3. Sloane Square tube stop. Open Sun 11–5.*

Chenil Galleries. And another! This sister to Antiquarius has higher price tags, perhaps, and more serious pieces than its neighbors.... *Tel 0171/351–5353. 181–183 King's Rd. SW3. Sloane Square tube stop.*

Columbia Road Market. Heaven for flower fans, gardeners, or people with a spare Sunday morning, this is the cut flower, bedding plant, and yard accoutrement bargain center of Europe. *Gosset St. to the Royal Oak pub E2. Old Street tube stop. Sun 8–1.*

Comme des Garçons. Rei Kawakubo's structural, monotone, collectible art clothes are augmented by her more affordable lines.... *Tel 0171/493–1258. 59 Brooke St. W1. Bond Street tube stop.*

Contemporary Applied Arts. A gallery-cum-shop showcasing the best work of designer-makers in many media. Here are also talks and events, and a commissioning service.... *Tel 0171/836–6993. 43 Earlham St. WC2. Covent Garden tube stop.*

Contemporary Ceramics. This is the Craft Potters' Association's showcase, where prices start simple (£25-ish), and rise to art, like the work.... *Tel 0171/437–7605. William Blake House, 7 Marshall St. W1. Oxford Circus tube stop.*

Czech & Speake. Mecca for bathroom hardware fanatics prepared to *invest* in an Italian brushed-steel faucet.... *Tel 0171/439–0216. 39c Jermyn St. SW1. Piccadilly Circus tube stop.*

Dance Books. Also magazines and memorabilia for balletomanes. *Tel 0171/836–2314. 9 Cecil Court WC2. Leicester Square tube stop.*

Daunt Books. This handsome galleried shop covers travel worldwide. *Tel 0171/224–2295. 83 Marylebone High St. W1. Baker Street tube stop.*

Davidoff Cigars. Mainly Davidoff, but all the rare breeds are carried here, plus European packaged varieties in all cigar sizes are sold by appropriately snotty gents.... *Tel 0171/930–3079. 35 St. James's St. SW1. Green Park tube stop.*

Debenhams. Not London's most exciting department store, but this part of the Burton Group empire keeps prices on the low side, and contains a few designer surprises.... *Tel 0171/580–3000. 334–338 Oxford St. W1. Bond Street tube stop. Open until 8pm Wed–Fri.*

Designer Sale & Exchange Shop. A resale and consignment place with its finger on the pulse of its hipper-than-thou Notting Hill neighborhood—meaning trendy clothes, and prices 20–60% of new.... *Tel 0171/243–2396. 61 Lancaster Rd. W11. Ladbroke Grove tube stop.*

Designer Secondhand Store. The Hampstead version of above, straighter of label (Mugler and Muir, not Ozbek and Westwood), and a tad friendlier. (Look for new 132 Long Acre Covent Garden branch.) *Tel 0171/431–8618. 24 Hampstead High St. NW3. Hampstead tube stop.*

Designs. This other Hampstead designer secondhand shop is the most staid of the three (Genny, Saint Laurent, Escada), but everything is scrupulously as-new. Convenient of these to group themselves alphabetically.... *Tel 0171/435–0100. 60 Rosslyn Hill NW3. Hampstead tube stop.*

Dickens & Jones. This department store went from old-fashioned to good on fashion, especially the mid-price lines on the ground (first) floor.... *Tel 0171/734–7070. 224–244 Regent St. W1. Oxford Circus tube stop. Open till 8pm Thur.*

Dillons. A very helpful staff who know the comprehensive stock that characterizes this bookstore by the University of London.... *Tel 0171/636–1577. 82 Gower St. WC1. Goodge Street tube stop. Open Mon, Wed–Fri 9–7; Tue 9:30–7; Sat 9:30–6; Sun noon–6. Branches.*

Dinny Hall. Jeweler Dinny favors silver, turning out wearable, beautifully crafted pieces at reasonable prices.... *Tel 0171/792–3913. 200 Westbourne Grove W11. Notting Hill Gate tube stop.*

The Dispensary. Three branches of this hip clothes emporium serve up the longer-lasting (i.e., well-made) model of street style—Patrick Cox's Wannabes, Schott leathers, Stüssy, and its own label.... *Tel 0171/287–8145, 9 Newburgh St. W1, Oxford Circus tube stop; tel 0171/221–9290, 25 Penbridge Rd. W11, Notting Hill Gate tube stop; tel 0171/727–8797, 200 Kensington Park Rd. W11, Notting Hill Gate tube stop.*

Dolce & Gabbana. We would love to afford the beautifully tailored, sexy clothes of these Italians, like Madonna does.... *Tel 0171/235–0335. 175 Sloane St. SW1. Sloane Square tube stop.*

Duffer of St. George. Perennially hip club garb from this menswear street stylist, with added sports stuff and U.S. labels (Phat Farm, Antoni & Alison).... *Tel 0171/439–0996. 27 D'Arblay St. W1. Oxford Circus tube stop.*

Emporio Armani. Oh, you know what this is like. Here's his newest of three London branches.... *Tel 0171/491–8080. 111 New Bond St. W1. Bond Street tube stop; tel 0171/917–6882. 57 Long Ave. WC2. Leicester Square tube stop; tel 0171/823–8818. 187 Brompton Rd. SW3. Knightsbridge tube stop*

Fat Cat Records. A basement full of club sounds on the cutting edge—trance, techno, jungle.... *Tel 0171/209–1071. 19 Earlham St. WC2. Covent Garden tube stop.*

Favourbrook. Brocades and damasks, silks, velvets and embroidered linens get made into exquisite vests, jackets, and frock coats at this co-ed tailor. Perfect wedding wear.... *Tel 0171/491–2337. 19–21 Piccadilly Arcade. Piccadilly Circus tube stop.*

Fenwick. Four floors of fashion. Standout departments are lingerie, and a designer floor with Betty Jackson, Jean Muir, Paul Costelloe, Jasper Conran, Nicole Farhi, and Georges Rech.... *Tel 0171/629–9161. 63 New Bond St. W1. Bond Street tube stop.*

Fortnum & Mason. The *ne plus ultra* of grocers has the royal warrant for her very majesty, plus gifts for your entire list, and a quaint clock in front. Check out the other lovely, pricey, old-fashioned departments, too.... *Tel 0171/734–8040. 181 Piccadilly W1. Piccadilly Circus/ Green Park tube stop.*

Foyles. The biggest bookstore in town is also the worst organized, but this has its charm, since it's such fun to get lost in the stacks.... *Tel 0171/437–5660. 119 Charing Cross Rd. WC2. Leicester Square tube stop.*

French's Theatre Bookshop. This aims to stock every play in the English language that's in print.... *Tel 0171/ 387–9373. 52 Fitzroy St. W1. Warren Street tube stop. Closed weekends.*

Gabriel's Wharf. This fun enclave of designer-maker-craftspeople, a short stroll from the South Bank Centre, comes into its own on a summer's afternoon when there is live music.... *Tel 0171/ 620–0544. Upper Ground SE1 (east of LWT building). Waterloo tube stop. Closed Mon.*

Gallery of Antique Costumes & Textiles. Another shop you can treat as a museum, except you'll want to walk out with a 1920s tea gown, a chenille throw, or one of the reproduction brocade vests they fashion here.... *Tel 0171/723–9981. 2 Church St. NW8. Marylebone tube stop.*

Garrard. Yet another gallery of a shop, this one studded with precious gems and laden with gold. They polish the crown jewels here.... *Tel 0171/734–7020. 112 Regent St. W1. Oxford Circus tube stop.*

Georgina von Etzdorf. Darling of the fashion pages, Von Etzdorf produces England's most desirably opulent scarves in precious materials. Feel like a million for a hundred or two.... *Tel 0171/409–7789. 50 Burlington Arcade W1. Piccadilly Circus tube stop. Branches.*

Gianni Versace. This vainglorious marble palace with the snootiest staff in the kingdom matches Versace's gaudy, gilt-embossed, dominatrix-wear exactly.... *Tel 0171/499–1862. 34 Old Bond St. W1. Bond Street tube stop.*

Gieves & Hawkes. One of Savile Row's best-known, yet also most approachable, bespoke tailors has fiendish rates, but for the best.... *Tel 0171/434–2001. 1 Savile Row W1. Picadilly Circus tube stop.*

Gray's Antiques Market. One of those collections of collectors, based conveniently downtown, and not overpriced.... *Tel 0171/629–7034. 58 Davies St. W1. Bond Street tube stop. Closed weekends.*

Grosvenor House. For a week in June, the toniest of antiquing opportunities.... *Tel 0171/499–6363. Grosvenor House, Park Lane W1. Marble Arch tube stop.*

Hamleys. The vastest toyshop this side of FAO Schwartz creates similar problems for parents trying to reach the exit.... *Tel 0171/734–3161. 188–196 Regent St. W1. Oxford Circus tube stop. Open Mon–Wed 10–6:30, Thu 10–8, Fri 10–7, Sat 9:30–7, Sun noon–6.*

Harrods. The one and only. Go ogle the food hall, visit the pets, covet stuff in the young designer room, then get an olive green-and-gold logo bag. The sales are essential.... *Tel*

0171/730–1234. 87 Brompton Rd. SW1. Knightsbridge tube stop.

Harvey Nichols. Here are Galliano, Dolce & Gabbana, Rifat Ozbek, Claude Montana, Jil Sander, Moschino, and oh, thousands more, including new young Brits-to-watch, like Pearce Fionda, sweetie darling.... *Tel 0171/235–5000. 109–125 Knightsbridge SW1. Knightsbridge tube stop.*

Hatchards. This wood-panelled store, with its royal warrant and helpful staff, is a most pleasant way to stock up on reading matter.... *Tel 0171/439–9921. 187 Piccadilly W1. Piccadilly Circus/ Green Park tube stop. Branches.*

Hennes. The hottest fashion moments frozen in cheap materials for addicts who need high turnover, which means teenage girls. Mothers also bless the kids' department.... *Tel 0171/493–8557. 481 Oxford St. W1, Oxford Circus tube stop; tel 0171/493–4004, 261 Regent St. W1, Oxford Circus tube stop; tel 0171/937–3329, 123 Kensington High St. W8, Ken High Street tube stop.*

Honest Jon's. A vinyl destination for about three decades, this is black-music central, from jazz and funk to soul and reggae, vintage and rare, plus new CDs.... *Tel 0181/969–9822. 278 Portobello Rd. W10. Ladbroke Grove tube stop. Open Sun 11–5.*

Hope & Glory. Commemorative china is an egalitarian antique, easily within all pockets, as long as you don't mind a mere Liz's Silver Jubilee mug—more exalted anniversaries have higher prices.... *Tel 0171/727–8424. 131 Kensington Church St. W8. Notting Hill Gate tube stop.*

Humla. Under-eights almost welcome clothes gifts when they're colorful fun things from here, especially when backed up by a Humla wooden toy.... *Tel 0171/434–0385. 4 Marlborough Court W1. Oxford Circus tube stop.*

Inderwicks. Makes its own pipes, and sells others as well, plus other smokers' paraphernalia.... *Tel 0171/734–6574. 45 Carnaby St. W1. Oxford Circus tube stop.*

Irish Linen Company. Delicious, pristine bed-linens and home accessories made of that crunchy, rare fabric. Things cost

LONDON | SHOPPING

not a little, but look it.... *Tel 0171/493–8949. 35 Burlington Arcade W1. Piccadilly Circus tube stop.*

James Lock. Hats to the gentry since 1676. A bowler costs from £150, but they also sell more modern headgear, for women too.... *Tel 0171/930–5849. 6 St. James's St. SW1. Green Park tube stop.*

James Smith & Sons. Every umbrella under the sun, or rain. Also riding crops, shooting sticks, walking canes, and other fetishists' dreams sold in handsome Victorian premises.... *Tel 0171/836–4731. 53 New Oxford St. WC1. Tottenham Court Road tube stop.*

Janet Fitch. Jewelry, bags, and *objets* are hand-picked by Ms. Fitch, who's known to have the most perfect taste in town.... *Tel 0171/287–3789. 25 Old Compton St. W1. Leicester Square tube stop. Open Mon–Sat 11–7, Sun 1–6; tel 0171/240–6332, 37 Neal St. WC2.*

Jasper Conran. He's got no store of his own, but find his delicious women's tailored stuff at Harrods, Selfridges, Harvey Nick's, Fenwicks, and À La Mode.

Jigsaw. A superior clothing chain, where the finish is finer, the fabric denser, the style hipper than its competitors in this middle price range (like Benetton, for instance).... *Tel 0171/584–6226. 31 Brompton Rd. SW3. Knightsbridge tube stop. Branches.*

John Lewis. "Never Knowingly Undersold" is a boast not bearing very close scrutiny; nevertheless, this no-frills department store is pretty unbeatable for practical homemaking items, especially textiles and notions.... *Tel 0171/629–7711. 278–306 Oxford St. W1. Oxford Circus tube stop.*

Johnsons. The original source of teddy-boy gear—stovepipes, sharkskin drape jackets, Chelsea boots, at reasonable prices, too.... *Tel 0171/351–3268. 406 King's Rd. SW10. Sloane Square tube stop; branch in Kensington Market.... Tel 0171/937–4711.*

Joseph. Joseph Ettedgui has had a major influence on how London dresses and furnishes for two decades. He doesn't design himself, but has an eye to buy what we want, at mid-

price. Monochrome, youthful, fitted, or knitted is the tone....
*Tel 0171/629–3713. 23 Old Bond St. W1. Bond Street
tube stop. Mon–Wed 10–6:30, Thu 10–7, Sat 9:30–6, Sun
noon–5. Branches.*

Katharine Hamnett. Half bad-girl, half environmental activist,
Hamnett's clothes are similarly schizoid, with spandex and
canvas, nicely cut jackets, and slut dresses, plus the good
Hamnett Active jeans line.... *Tel 0171/823–1002. 20
Sloane St. SW1. Knightsbridge tube stop.*

Kensington Market. This resembles a hipster's mall, with hundreds of stalls and shops for high school kids to pose around
on the weekend.... *Tel 0171/938–4343. 49–53 Kensington High St. W8. High Street Kensington tube stop.*

Kristin Baybars. Everything for the doll's house, including the
doll's house—this tiny place is unrivalled.... *Tel 0171/
267–0934. 7 Mansfield Rd. NW3. Gospel Oak BR. Closed
Sun, Mon.*

Lacroix. Some feel his multi-hued Provençal-print, tarty, dirndl
frocks touch the heavens. *Tel 0171/409–1994. 29 Old
Bond St. W1. Piccadilly Circus tube stop.*

Liberty. What started as an importer of Oriental goods is the
most enticing department store in town, with lovely Liberty
prints, good jewelry, accessories, and fashion housed in
Arts-and-Crafts grandeur.... *Tel 0171/734–1234. Regent
St. W1. Oxford Circus tube stop.*

Lillywhite's. Sports nirvana, with six floors of paraphernalia, kit,
and garb for the usual jock competitions, British games, and
cruel and unusual activities you've never heard of. High ticket,
high quality.... *Tel 0171/930–3181. 24–36 Lower Regent
St. SW1. Piccadilly Circus tube stop. Open Sun 9:30–6.*

The Linen Cupboard. Bargain bedclothes; good things mixed
up with tat in chaotic shop.... *Tel 0171/629–4062. 21
Great Castle St. W1. Oxford Circus tube stop.*

London Silver Vaults. About two-score traders have gathered
under this roof since the mid-19th century. Bargains are
possible.... *Tel 0171/242–3844. Chancery House, 53–63
Chancery Lane WC2. Chancery Lane tube stop.*

Lonsdale. The place for pugilists, and for those who just imitate them—the British answer to Everlast and Reyes does a leisurewear line.... *Tel 0171/437–1526. 21 Beak St. W1. Oxford Circus tube stop.*

Margaret Howell. Unpretentious, tailored English clothes that nod to the equestrian for men and women, from around £100 for a pair of serge or linen pants.... *Tel 0171/495–4888. 24 Brook St. W1. Bond Street tube stop; tel 0171/584–2462, 29 Beauchamp Place SW3.*

Marks & Spencer. Whatever their social stratum, the Londoner shops M&S for underwear and sweaters. Clothes are inexpensive, well made, and getting more exciting by the season. The food department is equally adored.... *Tel 0171/935–7954. 459 Oxford St. W1. Marble Arch tube stop. Open Mon–Wed, Sat 9–7, Thu–Fri 9–8. Branches.*

Marlborough Fine Art. Where to shop for an Old Master—or just look like one.... *Tel 0171/629–5161. 6 Albermarle St. W1. Green Park tube stop.*

Miss Selfridge. Hip high-school girls find constantly metamorphosing clothing here to gratify short attention spans and modest allowances.... *Tel 0171/318–3833. 40 Duke St. W1. Bond Street tube stop. Open Mon–Wed, Fri–Sat 9:30–7, Thu 9:30–8. Branches.*

Mole Jazz. Probably the best of all London's excellent jazz stores, with a load of rare stuff, and comprehensive stacks of new CDs, too.... *Tel 0171/278–0703. 311 Gray's Inn Rd. WC1. King's Cross tube stop.*

Mothercare. One-stop shopping for baby and toddler requirements; low prices, high quality.... *Tel 0171/629–6621. 461 Oxford St. W1. Marble Arch tube stop. Branches.*

Mulberry. Tweed hacking jackets, cord jodhpurs (but not for riding in), leather purses, belts, and wallets, tailored separates and staid frocks—not bargain, but top quality.... *Tel 0171/493–2546. 11 Gees Court W1, Bond Street tube stop; tel 0171/225–0313, 185 Brompton Rd. SW3, Knightsbridge tube stop.*

Museum Store. Collected goodies from museums around the world—reproduction ancient artifacts to arty scarves—last-minute gifts that look like you shopped your heart out.... *Tel 0171/240–5760. 37 The Market, The Piazza WC2. Covent Garden tube stop. Mon–Sat 10:30–6:30, Sun 11–5; tel 0171/581–9255, 50 Beauchamp Place SW3, Knightsbridge tube stop; tel 0171/431–7156, 4 Perrins Court NW3, Hampstead tube stop.*

Neal Street East. Gorgeous gifts on a budget, many penny toys, kitchenware, clothing, and knick-knacks from the Orient make this not indigenous, but long-running store fun.... *Tel 0171/240–5760. 5 Neal St. WC2. Covent Garden tube stop. Mon–Wed 11–7, Thu–Sat 10–7, Sun noon–6.*

Neal's Yard Dairy. All these cheeses are British, and many are from right here. This is in London's best holistic-healing, herbalist, massage therapist, natural-foods, occult-arts center.... *Tel 0171/379–7646. 17 Shorts Gardens WC2. Covent Garden tube stop. Mon–Sat 9–7, Sun 11–5.*

Nicole Farhi. Wearable, well-made suits and separates in muted colors and natural fibers, and at medium fashionability and cost for both male and female grown-ups.... *Tel 0171/499–8368. 158 New Bond St. W1. Bond Street tube stop; tel 0171/497–8713, 11 Floral St. WC2, Covent Garden tube stop; tel 0171/486–3416, 25 St. Christopher's Place W1, Bond Street tube stop; tel 0171/235–0877, 193 Sloane St. SW1, Knightsbridge tube stop.*

Oasis. Inexpensive, reasonably trendy clothes for young career girls. Color is a strong point.... *Tel 0171/240–7445. 13 James St. WC2. Covent Garden tube stop. Open Mon–Sat 10–7 (8pm Thu), Sun noon–7. Branches.*

Oils & Spice Shop. The aromatic entry in the gastro-row of foodie shops in the Conran mall by Tower Bridge.... *Tel 0171/403–3434. Butlers Wharf Building, 36E Shad Thames SE1. Tower Hill tube stop. Open Mon–Fri noon–6, Sat–Sun 10–6.*

Paddy Campbell. Campbell's suits and frocks in natural fabrics and non-hysterical cuts come off as if tailored for you, and swift alterations are indeed offered at her boutique.... *Tel 0171/493–5646. 8 Gees Court W1. Bond Street tube stop.*

LONDON | SHOPPING

Pandora. Here is so much top quality used designer garb that there are entire Armani and Chanel sections. Plenty of other names and lesser labels, too.... *Tel 0171/ 589–5289. 16–22 Cheval Place SW7. Knightsbridge tube stop.*

Paul Costelloe. Best known for his mid-priced Dressage collection of Irish linens and tweed suits, Costelloe also does a more high-fashion line.... *Tel 0171/589–9480. 156 Brompton Rd. SW3. Knightsbridge tube stop.*

Paul Smith. If we read the phrase "classics with a twist" in relation to this loveable retailer one more time, we'll scream. Women are catered to next door.... *Tel 0171/379–7133. 40–44 Floral St. WC2, Covent Garden tube stop;* **Sale Shop**.... *Tel 0171/493–1287. 23 Avery Row W1, Bond Street tube stop.*

Paxton & Whitfield. The cheese shop of your dairy dreams is the oldest in the land, in beautiful period premises.... *Tel 0171/930–0259. 93 Jermyn St. SW1. Green Park tube stop.*

Pellicano. The fast-forward face of fashion, with Prada alongside the grooviest high-end Brits.... *Tel 0171/629–2205. 63 South Molton St. W1. Bond Street tube stop.*

Penhaligon's. Gorgeous glass flacons with classic smells are uncorked here for your delectation. Founded by Victoria's court barber.... *Tel 0171/836–2150. 41 Wellington St. WC2, Covent Garden tube stop; tel 0171/629–1416, 16 Burlington Arcade W1, Picadilly Circus tube stop; tel 0171/493–0002, 20 Brook St. W1. Bond Street tube stop.*

Peter Jones. Where the Sloane Ranger mummy gets the cricket sweater and prep school uniform, plus her own twinset and pearls.... *Tel 0171/730–3434. Sloane Square SW1. Sloane Square tube stop.*

Petticoat Lane Market. Famous streets of cheap leather jackets, underwear, CDs, and old gold stalls amount to London's most famous market. Past its heyday, but you may get what you want very cheap. *Middlesex/Goulston/Old Castle/Cutler Streets, Bell Lane. Liverpool Street tube stop. Open Sun 9–2.*

Portobello Road Market. Several markets in one, from the 2000 antique dealers of the Notting Hill end, past the fruit-and-veg traders, to the trendy stalls of vintage stuff under the Westway, and on into the junk of Goldborne Road. London's best, we think. *Portbello Road W11–W10. Ladbroke Grove or Notting Hill Gate tube stop. Antiques open Sat 7am–5:30pm, general Mon–Sat 9–5; closes 1pm Thu.*

Prada. Every fashion victim's, fashion editor's, fashion publicist's favorite fashion fetish of 1994–95.... *Tel 0171/235–0008. 44 Sloane St. SW1. Sloane Square tube stop.*

Rare Camera Company. Like a Leica? They start at £50.... *Tel 0171/405–8858. 18 Bury Place WC1. Holborn tube stop.*

Reckless Records. Here's another venerable vinyl destination, not genre-specialist, but well stocked with secondhand rock, pop, soul, jazz.... *Tel 0171/437–4271. 30 Berwick St. W1. Oxford Circus tube stop. Open daily 10–7.*

Red Or Dead. Shoes for hyper-hip clubgoers were followed by the entire funloving wardrobe—powder pink fake furs, silver poodle-print spandex hotpants, and such.... *Tel 0171/937–3137, 36 Kensington High St. W8, High Street Kensington tube stop; tel 0171/379–7571, 61 Neal St. WC2. Covent Garden tube stop.*

Richard James. The groovy face of Savile Row. Preview his bespoke style—eye up the waiters at the Atlantic.... *Tel 0171/434–0605. 31 Savile Row W1. Piccadilly Circus tube stop.*

River Island. Trendy, inexpensive fashion from this High Street chain, with the Charlotte Halton line going upmarket in suits and frocks for dressing up.... *Tel 0171/937–0224. 124 Kensington High St. W8. High Street Kensington tube stop. Open Mon–Sat 9–6 (Thu 10–7:30), Sun 11–5. Branches.*

Rococo. Chocoholic heaven, way beyond Hersheys, and even Valrhona—get sophisticated high-cocoa content confections, and funny shape novelties.... *Tel 0171/352–5857. 321 King's Rd. SW3. Sloane Square tube stop.*

S & B Evans. Pots for yards, in the market for gardeners—Columbia Road.... *Tel 0171/729–6635. 7 Ezra St. E2. Old Street tube stop.*

Section 5. Jungle is the hot beat at press time, and here is where to get it for a turntable near you.... *Tel 0171/351–9361. The Common Market, 121 King's Rd. SW3. Sloane Square tube stop.*

Selfridges. A venerable department store, founded by an American, and undergoing a new lease on life with current renovations. Food, fashion, and cosmetics are strong.... *Tel 0171/629–1234. 400 Oxford St. W1. Bond Street tube stop. Open Mon–Sat 9:30–7 (Thu until 8).*

Simpson. Somewhat staid home of the Daks brand of slacks for golfers, with excellent, pricey lines of truly Brit clothes, and Euro designers.... *Tel 0171/734–2002. 203 Piccadilly W1. Piccadilly Circus tube stop.*

Skin Two. Fetishwear, mostly rubber, with authentic Victorian-cut wasp-waist corsets and made-to-measure leather on the side.... *Tel 0181/968–9692. 23 Grand Union Centre, Kensal Rd. W10. Ladbroke Grove tube stop.*

Skoob Books. Well-stocked secondhand book mecca, for when you know what you're after.... *Tel 0171/404–3063. 15 Sicilian Ave. WC1. Holborn tube stop.*

Slim Barrett. This hip metalworker/jeweler makes crowns for our times, and also home accessories.... *Tel 0171/387–6419. 72 Crowndale Rd. NW1. Camden Town tube stop. Open Mon–Fri 10–7, weekends by appointment.*

Soccer Scene. Impress your teammates back home with an Arsenal uniform, or a pair of British spikes.... *Tel 0171/439–0778, 30 Great Marlborough St. W1; tel 0171/437–1966 (the year we won the World Cup), 17 Foubert's Place W1. Oxford Circus tube (both).*

Spitalfields Market. An indoor collection of permanent stalls with a changing center—Sunday is greenmarket and crafts day.... *Tel 0171/247–6590. Commercial/Brushfield St. E1. Liverpool Street tube stop. Mon–Fri, Sun 11–3.*

Spycatcher. Everything for espionage.... *Tel 0171/245–9445. 25G Lowndes St. SW1. Knightsbridge tube stop.*

Squire. The hipster's alternative tailor also does some ready-to-wear modern suits.... *Tel 0171/379–4660. At Duffer of St. George, 29 Shorts Gardens WC2. Covent Garden tube stop.*

Stanford. Maps, travel guides, and even globes in great abundance satisfy wanderlust.... *Tel 0171/836–1915. 12 Long Acre WC2. Leicester Square tube stop.*

Steinberg & Tolkein. Museum-quality pre-1960 clothing in classy thrift-shop ambiance downstairs; mountains of vintage costume jewelry upstairs.... *Tel 0171/376–3660. 193 King's Rd. SW3. Sloane Square tube stop. Open Mon–Sat 10:30–7, Sun 1–6.*

The Stencil Store. Everything for wall art, including inspiration.... *Tel 0171/730–0728. 91 Lower Sloane St. SW1. Sloane Square tube stop.*

The Tea House. More varieties and flavors of tea than you can count, including rarities, plus strainers, trivets, infusers, pots, and cosies—ask for translations.... *Tel 0171/240–7539. 15 Neal St. WC2. Covent Garden tube stop. Open Mon–Sat 10–7, Sun noon–6.*

Theobroma Chocolates. Belgian fresh-cream truffles, and especially Gerard Ronay's handmade über-chocs are the stars here.... *Tel 0171/284–2670. 93 West Yard, Camden Lock Place NW1. Chalk Farm tube stop. Open Wed–Sun 10–6.*

Theo Fennell. Gold ecclesiastical/Renaissance-inspired shapes with cabochon gems, and exquisitely detailed silver miniatures are what Fennell does best. Top dollar.... *Tel 0171/376–4855. 177 Fulham Rd. SW3. South Kensington tube stop.*

Thomas Goode & Co. The ultimate store for bone china and porcelain, crystal glassware, and related costly goods.... *Tel 0171/499–2823. 19 South Audley St. W1. Green Park tube stop.*

Thorntons. The confectioner that took over the U.K. started with Special Toffee (and it is), and progressed to Belgian-style cream truffles, kids' novelties, ice cream, and other goodies.... *Tel 0171/434–2483. 254 Regent St. W1. Oxford Circus tube stop. Open Mon–Sat 9:30–6 (Thu until 7), Sun 11:30–5:30. Branches.*

Tom's. A Conran shop, this one from the food son-of-Terence, and a cornucopian deli it is.... *Tel 0171/221–8818. 226 Westbourne Grove W11. Bayswater tube stop.*

Top Shop. Loud clothes in loud shop, cheap and plentiful, colorful and tight, mostly for teens, who find them stylish.... *Tel 0171/636–7700. 214 Oxford St. W1. Oxford Circus tube stop. Branches.*

Trax. A Soho place for Soho club-type groove music.... *Tel 0171/734–0795. 55 Greek St. W1. Tottenham Court Road tube stop.*

Tridias. Toys tending toward traditional, with science sets, coloring pens, and games galore; near the big museums.... *Tel 0171/584–2330. 25 Bute St. SW7. South Kensington tube stop.*

Turnbull & Asser. The minimum first order for customized shirts is a half dozen, from £100 apiece, but these are the world's *best* shirts. Ready-made also available.... *Tel 0171/930–0502. 71 Jermyn St. SW1. Piccadilly Circus tube stop.*

Twining & Co. Where Twining's tea was brought into the world is still a shop, with a tea museum-ette attached.... *Tel 0171/353–3511. 216 Strand WC2. Temple tube stop. Closed weekends.*

Venus. A consignment store with the most avant-garde names of the lot, and the wilder ends of their lines at that.... *Tel 0171/379–1426, 19 Shorts Gardens WC2, Covent Garden tube stop.*

Vinyl Experience. Of all London's record stores, this is the most serious destination for the collector, with associated memorabilia spread over three floors.... *Tel 0171/636–1281. 18 Hanway St. W1. Tottenham Court Road tube stop.*

Vivienne Westwood. The ultimate style queen who constantly invents fashion movements and is copied by the world about three years later.... *Tel 0171/352–6551. World's End, 430 King's Rd. SW3. Sloane Square tube stop, then 11 or 22 bus.* **Sale Shop**.... *Tel 0171/439–1109. 40 Conduit St. W1. Bond Street tube stop.*

Warehouse. High turnover for high fashion; not top quality in the finish, but far from top prices, Warehouse keeps getting better.... *Tel 0171/734–5096. 19 Argyll St. W1. Oxford Circus tube stop. Branches.*

Waterstones. A terribly successful and likeable chain of bookstores, many of which run readings and signings.... *Tel 0171/434–4291. 121–125 Charing Cross Rd. W1. Leicester Square tube stop. Open Mon–Sat 9:30–8, Sun noon–6. Branches.*

Whistles. The toniest and trendiest of chains racks clothes by shade, has its own label, and sells European designer-wear in bright and spacious shops.... *Tel 0171/487–4484. 12 St. Christopher's Place W1. Bond Street tube stop. Branches.*

Zwemmer. Well-stocked bookstores in two arty varieties: the fine arts and photography/cinema.... *Tel 0171/240–4158, 24 Litchfield St. WC2; tel 0171/240–4157, 80 Charing Cross Rd. WC2. Leicester Square tube (both).*

6

tlife

London used to
go to bed early.
The 11pm curfew
(see below) still
applies, but peo-
ple are finding
more and more

creative ways around the anachronistic restriction on late-night partying. Alcohol is not the only fuel for a good time, of course, but Londoners—well, the British in general—prefer a wet bar to a juice bar, however modish those ginseng-guarana-spirulina cocktails were for five minutes early this decade. God knows—Londoners like to drink. Proof is provided by the ubiquity of the age-old, everlasting great British pub. The full title, public house, describes exactly what a good pub offers—a warm environment where many people feel at home. Music is also important to the London soul. Pop, jazz, indie bands, world music, and the indigenous folk traditions of the British Isles—each comes in its appropriate venue, mosh pit to stadium. As for clubbing and youth culture, fashion worldwide still has an eye to what young London is wearing, what it's saying, how it's dancing in its constantly changing array of "one-nighters," warehouse parties, bars, and restaurants *du moment*, and you can only hope to be hip enough yourself to have a sixth sense about where is best. The Soho gay scene is making London in general friendlier than it's ever been, though, and you should find fewer cold shoulders than of old, and not just if you're gay. The hippest gay clubs here are often the hippest clubs, period. Those legendary "Summer of Love II" warehouse parties, full of "E", technobeat, and Vicks Vaporub-enhanced trance-dancing (skip this if you don't understand) really did exist—a phenomenon yet to be equalled for pure nighttime mayhem and depravity, unless you count Jungle. Mind you, someone's starting something new as you read this.

Sources

For an all-around picture of music, clubs, the student scene, and a few background stories, pick up the weekly (out Wednesday; Tuesday in the city center) institution, *Time Out*, whose tone is irritatingly smug, but which does a grand job of listing nearly everything there is to do. The weekly (out Thursday) music papers, especially the *NME (New Musical Express)* are better if you're hip and young and want insight into the band culture here. The gay scene, for both genders and in between, is conveyed through the monthly *Gay Times* and the weekly *MX (MetroXtra)*. However, the best way to find out what's going down is the same as anywhere—word of mouth.

Liquor Laws and Drinking Hours

A subject dear to the London heart is how ridiculous, how outdated, and how restrictive are its liquor licensing laws.

The part that is hated is the 11pm (10:30 Sundays) pub closing time. If you're British, 11pm becomes engrained in the body as the time when the average evening out winds down. The "last orders" bell, rung in pubs at ten of eleven, and the "time" bell are the drinking-up and getting-out signals respectively, and many drunks have been created by the need to chug-a-lug several pints during the last ten minutes' drinking time. Yet there are finally changes afoot. Late pub-type licenses are becoming more common, with more places enabled to let you drink till midnight, or even later on weekends. The law governing daytime drinking was lifted long ago, so you can get quietly pissed in a pub garden all afternoon if you feel like it—except on Sunday between 3 and 7pm, and this may have changed by now too. Separate laws always did apply to private clubs, restaurants, and places with a cover charge.

Pool

Pool is big in London, but you'll need to learn new rules: You don't call your shots, but if you scratch, you donate two shots to your opponent. Solids are called "spots," snookering happens, and sometimes the game resembles chess. Rules are displayed in all pubs (but all pubs have their own versions, so you'd better just ask)....

The Lowdown

Personality pubs... There used to be a pub for every taste, then the big breweries (landlords of most pubs) suddenly converted every dear old grungy, down-home barroom into a small Edwardian theme park, with antiquarian books by-the-mile, a fake log fire, brass rails, and stuffed owls. It's annoying when what one wants in pubs (and people) is authenticity. The real thing still does exist, although **Ye Olde Cheshire Cheese**, for instance, which is about 330 years olde, is terribly touristy. On the other hand, its sawdust floors, low, wood-beamed ceilings, and 14th-century crypt are just the same as when Dickens drank there. Don't get too excited by that last part: either Dickens drank nearly everywhere in London, or publicans are congenital liars. Some that claim the serial novelist are the **George Inn** south of the Thames, which he featured in *Little Dorritt*, and which is worth patronizing for its gallery and courtyard; **Jack Straw's Castle**, out Hampstead way, where he would stay the night, but you can just enjoy the garden (the reconstructed pub itself isn't much cop); and **The Lamb**, which was actually his local when he lived at what is now the Dickens museum. He didn't go to the **French House**, where the Resistance convened during WWII, and where they still don't serve English pints; instead there's wine, and beer in bottles and half pints. It's been a Soho institution for years.

Picturesque pubs... Two northern locals are especially good for summer al fresco drinking—the **Freemason's Arms**, conveniently Heath-side, with a vast garden; and the **Spaniards Inn**, where the summer crowds are fiercer than the highwaymen who used to frequent it. It's also cozily log-fire-warmed and nook-and-crannied in winter. So is the **Holly Bush**, which is a short hill of cute, million-pound cottages away from Hampstead tube. Behind Notting Hill Gate is another garden worth stopping at, the **Windsor Castle**. The food is pretty good there, too, and there are yet more blackened wooden beams and open fires. Yet, yet more beams are all over the 17th-century, riverside **Mayflower** in distant Rotherhithe, where only history groupies should bother to trek. It's named after *that* Mayflower, and marks a spot from which (somewhere nearby) the Pilgrims set sail.

Beards and real ale... Oh, how the British like their beer. They like it warm, they like it dark, they like it flat, they like it strong—they like it any way but cold and gassy and in a bottle. Well, most of them. In truth, millions of Londoners have acquired an American taste in beer, and Rolling Rock, Bud, et al. are omnipresent, as is Corona with a slice of lime wedged in the neck. But "real ale" is true British beer—similar to U.S. microbrewery output, yet older. Its traditional image is mixed up with men who wear sandals with socks and grow unruly beards, but it will be trendy someday very soon. Try **The Sun** for about 20 microbrews on tap, or go to any of the pubs with **Firkin** (a kind of barrel used in beer making) in their names like the **Pheasant & Firkin**, and have a pint of "rail ale" with medical students in their cups. For the good Irish stout, **Minogues** is more salubrious than echt Irish pubs along the Kilburn High Road, and it usually has live music. Try Murphy's stout—afficionados rate it higher than Guinness.

Cruising, schmoozing, meeting (straight)... A designated singles scene really doesn't exist in London, because the unwritten rules of dating are not the same here. Exactly how, we couldn't say (these are unwritten rules), but see if you notice a difference at **Beach Blanket Babylon**, where the decor is suitably gothic for the throbbing mass of smooth-skinned (i.e., young) humanity convening weekend nights, especially in summer. Its young sibling, entitled **Mwah Mwah** (the sound of an insincere air-kiss) is doing similar trade in Chelsea, where teens have more money, but less style. If you can force someone to get you into the **Groucho**, you'll certainly see chatting-up in progress, though you'll need a strong stomach for elitism. Despite being named after the man who wouldn't join a club that would take him as a member, the most famous media-movie-journo hangout is liable to look down its nose at you unless it knows you. Precisely the opposite is true of London's two best fests: the high-summer, West Indian, **Notting Hill Carnival**; and the Celtic party in Finsbury Park, the **Fleadh**. Whatever you did tonight, whomever you met, wherever (within reason) you are, you'll probably end up having an espresso at **Bar Italia**, scoping, dishing, or comparing notes with the other clubbers. The **Hanover Grand** is where you might have been, if you're young, or the **Gardening Club**.

Cruising, schmoozing, meeting (gay)... The earth revolves around "the Compton"—Soho's always-lively Old Compton Street that underwent metamorphosis sometime this decade, and is now almost New Yorky in its hours and its up-frontness. As we've said, places mostly welcome a mix (permutations of gay-straight-men-women), but men are the target customers of **Crews Bar**. Biggest and busiest is probably **The Yard**, while little **First Out** peacefully purveys caffeine. The dyke scene doesn't really center on Soho, nor on any one place, though you can count on any and every women-only event attracting mostly gay women. The West End arts center, **Drill Hall**, runs loads of these, plus it has a girls' bar-night Mondays. It's a fair bet that that long-running one-night-a-week club will endure, as will everybody's favorite (that includes your straight pals) night of clubbing, "Queer Nation," at the **Gardening Club**. Let's all hope the **Royal Vauxhall Tavern** never closes either. It's just a local, but a faggy, sometimes dykey, one with a great vibe and an amateur drag cabaret dating from way before the Lady Bunny. **Heaven** is heaven for dancing.

Already coupled... There are plenty of romantic restaurants and hotels round town, but what to do between dinner and bed? Going on the assumption that a nice bit of history gets the heart beating, the **George Inn** and the **Mayflower** are the pubs to frequent for your post-prandial snifter, though they're rather far out of town. Even further, but even more quaint, are the **Spaniards Inn** and the **Holly Bush**—both best for summer, when you can stroll on the Heath after closing time. If you're gay and male, strolling on the Heath after closing time is far less—let's say, *soft-focus*, a romantic activity—one that is rife with encoded rules, concerning various sorts of safety. If you already have a paramour, **First Out** is cozy and cute. For any gender, some music might be in order, but not at a frenetic stand up and jiggle—or, God forbid, mosh—place. The **Royal Albert Hall** is civilized, and has the added advantage of Hyde Park across the street, though not every night is music night. The right sort of hotel bar is highly romantic, and has a better class of cocktail snack than the pub's packet of salt'n'vinegar crisps. Try the **Savoy's American Bar** for correct martinis—they're supposed to have been invented here. The **Lanesborough** has leather sofas in **The Library**, where you can go mad and order something from bar manager Salvatore Calabrese's collection of "liquid history"—cognacs from historic years that he'll part with for £50 to £500 a shot.

Late license... The one and only **Atlantic** singlehandedly transformed London's nights, thanks to its revolutionary 3am closing time. Since our crystal ball is a bit cloudy, we're not sure who's going to follow suit with a late alcohol license in the center of town. The divey **Bar Sol Ona** (Barcelona, ha ha), and its neighbor, **Café Bohème** both already have, but they're still only open until midnight, and neither has much else to recommend it, beyond permission to drink. Candidate for most sordid and steamy dive in town is the compulsory stop-in-after-the Forum **Triñanes**, a Spanish restaurant (don't eat here) cater-corner from that Kentish Town hall of rock. Its earlier evening flamenco nights can actually be pretty authentic and fabulous. The most genuine, diviest late-night bar is one you can't really visit without an invitation—it's at Bayswater's **Commodore** hotel, where the hippest not-too-famous bands stay, and drink all night if that's the sort of thing they do.

Two-step, waltz, salsa, and boogie... If you want to make like Fred and Ginger, there aren't that many places to go. All the regular dances are in hotels, and the four best are, unsurprisingly, found in four of the best hotels: **Claridges**, the **Ritz**, the **Savoy**'s River Restaurant, and the Terrace at the **Dorchester**. All have dinner dances with prix-fixe menus, inclusive of cover, and all but the Savoy hold the events on Friday and Saturday nights only (till 1am); the Savoy does it every night but Sunday. Tunes tend to be more Sinatra than Strauss at all of the hotel hops—except the **Waldorf**'s tea dance, but that doesn't belong in a nightlife chapter, since it's over by 6pm. Latin dance is getting all popular, meanwhile. Several places follow the same pattern of an early-evening class for the gringos to prepare for the night of non-stop salsa. You should check the listings for these, though the Islington tapas bar, **La Finca**, and the West End **Bar Rumba** have all been running them for some time. The city's grooviest Latin mix is in Brixton, though, at the incredibly popular Loughborough Hotel's **Mambo Inn**, which bears no relation to places with room service, but which has spawned a London subculture of its own. Teddy boys and girls, ska and rock-steady fans, jivers and rockers have two places to go: **Gaz's Rockin Blues**, which is probably Soho's longest-running "one-nighter" club, or the **100 Club**, which, at press time, was holding its chief R&B night Mondays.

Where to be invited by members... **Groucho** thinks it's the center of the publishing/TV/publicity/literary world, and, unfortunately, it's right. After about ten years, the irreverent club that's secretly establishment still has what it takes, to the extent that if you yourself move in these worlds, you'll find it more challenging to avoid Groucho than to be invited. A place with a rep you'll have more trouble entering is near-legendary **Annabel's**, which is a surreal mix of early Jackie-Collins-novel discotheque and black-tie supper club. Yes, Fergie, Di, and all the rollicking royals really do drop in on occasion, and a glass of champagne costs twenty quid. Less predictable, and even older, is the wonderfully housed **Chelsea Arts Club**, with its gardens, bedchambers, dimly lit dining, and its snooker tables in the bar. It's disreputable by design, but really is often full of pissed sculptors taking their clothes off, having fist fights, or simply falling over. Among newer clubs, the **Soho House** was slated to steal all the neighboring Groucho's members and be queen, but after its 1995 opening, no battle ensued, and the two co-exist, the younger club with a younger crowd of the same species.

Jazz standards... This week's big name in town will be found at **Ronnie Scotts**, where the cover charge seems less exorbitant since everywhere else has caught up. Reserve a place, and bring your gas mask, because London jazz fans still smoke. **Pizza Express** is in a similar mainstream-but-musically-hip vein to Ronnies, but serves far better pizza. Meanwhile, there is no food, little atmosphere, but great music (depending who's on, of course) at the **Queen Elizabeth Hall** and **Purcell Room** at the South Bank, where you'll catch the bigger, or more staid, folk. For the absolute coolness of the cutting edge, you'll need to leave downtown, and go north to the **Jazz Café** in sunny Camden Town, northeast to the city border **Blue Note**, or further northeast to the Stoke Newington **Vortex**. Look in the listings for a wealth of free or cheap lunchtime gigs, especially on weekends, and pubs with jazz rooms. Higher quality than most, though way out in Barnes, is the riverside **Bulls Head**.

Live and loud... Rock venues divide themselves up according to what genre of band plays, so it's easy to decide where to go just from reading listings. You'll soon see that the biggest stadium, where your Madonnas and U2s play, is **Wembley**, of which there are both **Stadium** and smaller **Arena** versions. Very famous people also pack out the Hammersmith **Apollo** and the nearby Shepherds Bush **Empire**, while the **Royal Albert Hall** hosts those who aren't even trying to be alternative—including Eric Clapton, for his traditional 10 days in February known as **the Erics**. Among the medium-to-big venues, the best are the north London **Forum**, and the very central (actually opposite the skyscraper known as Centrepoint) **Astoria**. More hip than those—

although the Astoria has its moments—are the **Brixton Academy** in the wilds of South London, and **Subterania**, ditto in the West.

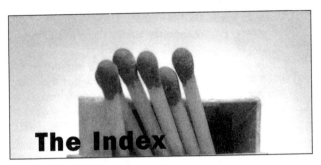

The Index

Annabel's. Whatever the opposite of a dive is, this *strictly* members-only Berkeley Square *boîte* is it. Nobs, snobs, and hoorays (braying, chinless Hooray Henry is the Sloane Ranger's brother) are those members. Surprisingly, it can be a blast.... *Tel 0171/629–3558. 44 Berkeley Sq. W1. Green Park tube stop.*

Apollo Hammersmith. The former Hammersmith Odeon used to be a movie theater, and now hosts biggish rock names, with no dancing at the front, please.... *Tel 0171/416–6080. Queen Caroline St. W6. Hammersmith tube stop. Cover charge.*

Astoria. Very central, at the top of Oxford Street, this big hall on the corner has a pleasantly louche vibe, for wrecks in their twenties to see bands on the up.... *Tel 0171/434–0403. 157 Charing Cross Rd. W1. Tottenham Court Road/Leicester Square tube stop. Late opening. Cover charge.*

Atlantic. See Dining.

Bar Italia. See Dining.

Bar Rumba. A conveniently located West End place that offers a free salsa class before the bargain (at press time, Tuesday night) "Salsa Pa'Ti".... *Tel 0171/287–2715. 36 Shaftsbury Ave. W1. Piccadilly Circus tube stop. Cover charge.*

Bar Sol Ona. A divey Spanish-ish bar with tapas; useful for being Soho central and managing to stay open late.... *Tel*

0171/287–9432. 13 Old Compton St. W1. Leicester Square tube stop.

Beach Blanket Babylon. As a bar and a place to meet fellow twenty–thirties, this gothique Portobello joint rocks on weekends; as a restaurant, see Dinning. *Tel 0171/229–2907. 45 Ledbury Rd. W11. Notting Hill Gate tube stop.*

Blue Note. Past visitors who miss that lovely jazz dive on the city's edge, the **Bass Clef**, should know that this is the very same. It's gone a bit younger and trendier, though, so watch the listings to catch the night you like. There's Latin here, too.... *Tel 0171/729–8440. 1 Hoxton Square. N1. Old Street tube stop. Late opening. Cover charge.*

Brixton Academy. A huge hall in South London's reggae-culture neighborhood tends to be very hip and pretty young, and has bands playing most nights, as well as club events.... *Tel 0171/924–9999. 211 Stockwell Rd. SW2. Brixton tube stop. Late opening. Cover charge.*

Bull's Head. By the Thames in Barnes, this pretty pub has attracted serious jazz buffs (those with beards, who whoop during bass solos) for years and years.... *Tel 0181/876–5241. Barnes Bridge. SW13. Barnes Bridge BR or #9 bus. Cover charge sometimes.*

Café Bohème. This well-bred, Parisian-styled corner bistro-café-bar mutates into a standing-room-only free-for-all when the pubs decant into it at 11pm.... *Tel 0171/734–0623. 13 Old Compton St. W1. Leicester Square tube stop.*

Chelsea Arts Club. Progenitor of the infamous Chelsea Arts Club Ball, wherein artists and artistes pose in small costumes and disgrace themselves, neither Club nor Ball are as naughty as they once were, though an invitation to penetrate the private white walls is still cause for joy.... *Tel 0171/376–3311. 3 Old Church St. SW3. Sloane Square tube stop.*

Claridges. see Accomodations.

Crews Bar. Just a big West End pub tapping into the gay scene with its theme name; a useful rendezvous.... *Tel 0171/379–4880. 14 Upper St. Martin's Lane. WC1. Charing Cross tube stop.*

The Dorcester. see Accomodations.

Drill Hall. This deep-West End, woman-centric arts center runs many a girlish event, and does a women-only bar Mondays.... *Tel 0171/631–1353. 16 Chenies St. W1. Goodge Street tube stop. Cover charge most nights.*

La Finca. This tapas bar/restaurant has salsa classes and dance nights in its upstairs club.... *Tel 0171/837–5387. 96 Pentonville Rd. N1. Angel tube stop. Cover charge; waived for diners.*

First Out. The name is exact—if you're walking into Soho from Oxford Street direction, and are gay, the relaxed and friendly coffee café is the first landmark.... *Tel 0171/240–8042. 52 St. Giles High St. W1. Tottenham Court Road tube stop.*

Fleadh. Finsbury Park's annual Celtic music fest is pronounced "flah," and is practically guaranteed to feature Van Morrison, Sinead O'Connor, and whichever Pogues have still got functioning livers.... *Tel 0181/963–0940. Finsbury Park tube stop. Mid-June. Admission charged.*

Forum. A well-loved and well-frequented former ballroom in the north hosts medium-famous, medium-hip bands, usually for the twenties set, though older performers do attract older kids.... *Tel 0171/284–2200. 9–17 Highgate Rd. NW5. Kentish Town tube stop. Cover charge.*

Freemason's Arms. On the edge of the Heath, this has one of the biggest pub gardens in town, which tends to get overrun with the local, rather wealthy brand of teenager on summer weekends.... *Tel 0171/435–2127. 32 Downshire Hill NW3. Southend Green BR.*

French House. Still flying the *Tricolore*, this wartime hangout of the French Resistance serves *vin ordinaire* and Pernod instead of pints of bitter, has walls crammed with French pugilists, and a bar crammed with arty networkers.... *Tel 0171/437–2799. 49 Dean St. W1. Leicester Square tube stop.*

Gardening Club. Usefully central, this place has shaped up into a long-runner, with the Sunday "Queer Nation" apparently still the place to chill after a hard week's clubbing, gay or

LONDON | NIGHTLIFE

straight. Be young.... *Tel 0171/497–3154. 4 The Piazza. WC2. Covent Garden tube stop. Open late. Cover charge.*

Gaz's Rockin Blues. One of this town's oldest one-night-per-week clubs, Gaz (son of blues man John) Mayall's friendly R&B, ska and rock'n'roll Thursdays are still going strong.... *Tel 0171/437–0525. St Moritz, 159 Wardour St. W1. Tottenham Court Rd. tube stop. Cover charge.*

George Inn. Where Dickens drank, #1. This is London's last galleried inn as well, so maybe worth the trek south.... *Tel 0171/407–2056. 77 Borough High St. London Bridge tube stop.*

Groucho. You can't get in unless you know a member, but this is so integral to the life of the London intelligentsia (drinking division) that it can't be left out.... *Tel 0171/439–4685. 44 Dean St. W1. Leicester Square tube stop.*

Hanover Grand. At press time, very hip, but by now who knows? Another one-nighter host, this one's a West End, two-tier wonderland of swanky decor and heaving dance floor.... *Tel 0171/499–7977. 6 Hanover St. W1. Oxford Circus tube stop. Open late. Cover charge.*

Heaven. A venerable and vast (mostly) gay dance club under the arches behind Charing Cross has the boomingest bass, and laser lights that give you the bends.... *Tel 0171/839–3852. Craven St. WC2. Charing Cross tube stop. Open late. Cover charge.*

Holly Bush. Up a Hampstead back street is the pub you seek—cozy, nook-filled, with open fireplaces and nicotine-stained paintwork.... *Tel 0171/435–2892. 22 Holly Mount. NW3. Hampstead tube stop.*

Jack Straw's Castle. This huge Hampstead landmark, named after the leader of the 1381 Peasant's Revolt, is now only good for the garden, where there are weekend barbecues in summer.... *Tel 0171/435–8885. North End Way. NW3. Hampstead tube stop, then bus.*

Jazz Café. A converted bank in downtown Camden hosts the hottest combos from all over, and consistently swings. It's worth getting tickets in advance, and booking a table if you can (they don't always let you).... *Tel 0171/916–6000. 5 Parkway NW1. Camden Town tube stop. Cover charge.*

Lamb. A Dickens local, #2. This is a pretty, all-around useful pub, slightly off the big tourist route, with drinking on the patio when the weather is kind.... *Tel 0171/405–0713. 94 Lambs Conduit St. WC1. Holborn tube stop.*

Mambo Inn. In deepest Brixton is the happening place to rumba, salsa, merengue and MAMBO. Check the listings for the nights—probably still Friday and Saturday.... *Tel 0171/ 737–2943. Loughborough Hotel, Evandale Rd. SW9. Brixton tube stop. Cover charge.*

Mayflower. From (near to) which the Pilgrims set sail for Plymouth Rock, this cute 18th-century, wood-beamed, riverside pub retains permission to sell U.S. postage stamps.... *Tel 0171/237–4088. 117 Rotherhithe St. SW16. Rotherhithe tube stop.*

Minogues. A rollicking Celtic time is often to be had in this Islington pub with restaurant attached and, often, live Irish music.... *Tel 0171/354–4440. 80 Liverpool Rd. N1. Angel tube stop.*

Mwah Mwah. A Chelsea hangout, young sister of Beach Blanket Babylon, attracts local well-heeled youth.... *Tel 0171/823– 3079. The Queen's Arms, 241 Fulham Rd. SW3. Fulham Broadway tube stop.*

Notting Hill Carnival. A two-day street party of genuine Island vibes, heaving merengue-ing crowds, sound stages, parades, goat curry, Red Stripe and Ganja.... *No phone. August Bank holiday. Centered around the Westway, Portobello Road, Ladbroke Grove tube stop.*

100 Club. A venerable dive that concentrates on rock and jazz, blues and R&B, with live bands and dance nights.... *Tel 0171/636–0933. 100 Oxford St. W1. Oxford Circus tube stop. Cover charge.*

Pheasant and Firkin. One of the pubs bought by a big firm from London's most successful microbrewer, Bruce's. Any Firkin still has a distinct riotous drunken student ambiance—lots

LONDON | NIGHTLIFE

of "firkin" puns, etc.... *Tel 0171/235–7429. 166 Goswell Rd. EC1. Barbican tube stop.*

Pizza Express. A big jazz venue, as well as London's best pizzas. This tends to host mainstream performers.... *Tel 0171/ 437–9595. 10 Dean St. W1. Tottenham Court Rd tube stop. Cover charge.*

The Ritz. See Accomodations.

Ronnie Scotts. London's best-known and most-loved jazz venue is going very strong, still run by saxophonist Ronnie, and still hosting the hottest line-ups, for which you usually must book.... *Tel 0171/439–0747. 47 Frith St. W1. Leicester Square tube stop. Open late. Cover charge.*

Royal Albert Hall. See Entertainment.

Royal Vauxhall Tavern. Just an old south London pub that happens to have hosted drag shows all its life, and still does so.... *Tel 0171/582–0833. 372 Kennington Lane. SW8. Oval tube stop.*

The Savoy. See Accomodations.

Shepherds Bush Empire. A medium-to-big—no, make that a big—venue for bands you've heard of even if you're over forty. Though it's not unhip. Book ahead.... *Tel 0181/740– 7474. Shepherds Bush Green. W10. Shepherds Bush tube stop. Cover charge.*

Soho House. Another members-only Soho haunt of media types. Groucho's much newer rival.... *Tel 0171/734–5188. 40 Greek St. W1. Leicester Square tube stop. Members and guests only.*

Spaniards Inn. Lovely trellised rose gardens get overrun with people as soon as the sun shines, but midweek lunchtimes aren't so mobbed. Inside are blackened oak beams, Dick Turpin's guns (he drank here), and the tea party scene from *Pickwick Papers* (yes, *he* drank here, #3).... *Tel 0171/455– 3276. Spaniards Rd. NW3. Hampstead tube stop, then bus.*

Subterania. A groovy duplex dive beneath the Westway in Notting Hill hosts happening bands, and late-late clubbing for twentysomethings.... *Tel 0181/960–4590. 12 Acklam Rd. W10. Ladbroke Grove tube stop. Open late. Cover charge.*

Sun. A place to do market research on British ale—real ale—in about 20 varieties on tap, no frills.... *Tel 0171/405–8278. 63 Lamb's Conduit St. WC1. Holborn tube stop.*

Triñanes. Where everyone goes when turfed out of the Forum across the street. The tapas—let alone the Spanish entrees—are not why, but the flamenco performers are a weekend plus.... *Tel 0171/482–3616. 298 Kentish Town Rd. NW5. Kentish Town tube stop. Open late.*

Vortex. Serious jazz buffs should make the trek out to Stokey— a residential neighborhood, with Asian/vegetarian restaurants and some good pubs—for the cutting edge of the London scene.... *Tel 0171/254–6516. Stoke Newington Church St. N16. Stoke Newington BR.*

Wembley Arena. A big, big venue for big, big bands, and way the hell out.... *Tel 0181/900–1234. Empire Way, Wembley, Middlesex. Wembley Park tube stop. Admission charge.*

Wembley Stadium. An even bigger venue for even bigger bands.... *Tel 0181/900–1234. Empire Way, Wembley, Middlesex. Wembley Park tube stop. Admission charge.*

Windsor Castle. Not the queen's country cottage, but a li'l old pub down Notting Hill with a sweet garden and good bar food for a sunny afternoon.... *Tel 0171/727–8491. 114 Campden Hill Rd. W11. Notting Hill Gate tube stop.*

The Yard. This gay-oriented Soho café-bar does, indeed, have a little courtyard for coffee or beer, as well as two floors of bars which buzz by night.... *Tel 0171/437–2652. 57 Rupert St. W1. Piccadilly Circus tube stop.*

Ye Olde Cheshire Cheese. Ye original hokey tourist hostelrie, with sawdust-strewn floors and great blackened beams to bang your forehead on, but it's been open over three centuries, so go anyway.... *Tel 0171/353–6170. 145 Fleet St. EC4. Chancery Lane tube stop.*

LONDON | NIGHTLIFE

enterta

7

nment

What London is
most famous for
is theater; known
as "The Theatah"
to distinguish it
from the plebeian
stages of every-

where else in the world. Is its snob reputation deserved? Well, yes, the scope and bravery of the best theater companies here is wide and high, and sometimes innovative, too—although the very newest in physical theater tends to come from elsewhere in Europe. Those European companies visit London, though, so you end up with the best of all worlds: indigenous highbrow, Shakespeare, West End (London's Broadway), homegrown experimental, and imported avant-garde. Look out for the London International Festival of Theatre (LIFT) for concentrated doses of Catalan mimes and French nouvelle clowning. Crossover genres like physical theater (Theatre de Complicité are masters of this), new circus (look for Ra Ra Zoo and Archaos), narrative dance (Yolanda Snaith), and comedic performance (Rose English, for instance) are worth seeking out here if you're a true fan of living theater, and not just worshiping at the shrine of the traditional proscenium arch and three acts. Not that there's anything wrong with the National Theatre and the Royal Shakespeare Company....

If theater sends you to sleep, London's got plenty of music, from opera to jazz and all points in between; dance, ballet to aforementioned experiments; and comedy (this is the home of *Monty Python* and *Absolutely Fabulous*) to keep you amused. There are even sports.

Sources

At the risk of sounding like an infomercial, we have to give the estimable *Time Out* another plug here. If you bought only one "what's on" guide, this would be it—the nearest thing to having a clued-in Londoner on your team (which, naturally, is an even better way into the mysteries of town). The second-best source of entertainment information is the *Evening Standard;* more especially its weekly *ES* magazine. Both those publications give plenty of background to their listings, so you'll get a feel for what's hot at this moment.

Getting Tickets

The best way to get theater tickets is to go to the box office of the theater itself, or to call it with your charge card at hand. There's nothing wrong with ticket agents, like **First Call** (0171/240–7941) or **Ticketmaster** (0171/413–3321), unless you hate to pay the reasonable booking fee, and they do come up trumps for major rock gigs or for when you're having a theater orgy and want to book several shows. If that's you, **Keith Prowse** can be called before you leave home, at the New York office (212/398–1430 or 800/669–8687). If you're planning a theaterfest, are a control freak, and want to do it all yourself, send for the *Complete Guide to London's West End Theatres* (£9.95 + p&h from the Society of London Theatre, Bedford Chambers, The Piazza, Covent Garden, WC2E 8HQ, tel 0171/836–3193), which has seating plans and booking information for all the West End houses. If you're cheap, broke, or smart, wait till you're in London and line up at the indispensable **Half Price Ticket Booth** (no phone) on the southwest corner of Leicester Square, which has tickets for later the same day at about 25 theaters (Mon–Sat 2:30–6:30; from noon for matinees. Cash only; £1.50 service charge). Traditionally, theaters have been dark on Sundays, but there has been a recent smattering of Sunday performances, so check the listings. Hotels—including those with a dedicated theater desk—charge a bigger fee than the phone bookers and are only worth using if you're lazy, loaded, or longing to see Lloyd Webber's latest, in which case the best of them (the **Savoy**, the **Athenaeum**, the **Dorchester**...) may come up with the impossible, pricey, ticket. Those shows, predictably, are the most likely to harbor a crop of **scalpers** outside (known as ticket touts here). Just say no. Never buy from a guy furtively brandishing a fistful of tickets—common sense will tell you when there's someone with a legitimate extra one. If you feel that you must deal with a scalper, you should know that by law the tout must tell you the face value of the ticket at the time of sale so you can see how much he's marking it up, and be warned that it will be more than generous. Know the top prices of the show you want to see and remember that very few are regularly sold out. Every single theater keeps at least one row of **house seats** back till the last possible moment (for emergency oversales and unexpected situations) plus a dozen or two **returns**. Policies on how these are dispensed vary, but be prepared to stand in line, possibly in the morning, probably an hour before curtain, with no guarantee of success. On the other hand, you may find yourself in the stalls (orchestra) at the Royal Opera House for a song (an £85+ seat for about £22). Failing that, if it's a big new show, you don't want to spend your vacation in line, and money's no object, check out the **classified ads** in the *Standard* for sort-of-legitimate scalpers who bought blocks of tickets and are unloading them at a premium. This is also your only hope for major sporting events, like the FA Cup Final (Football Association), or the late rounds of the men's singles, center court, Wimbledon. Apart from those, the toughest London ticket to acquire is the season's hottest fringe production (often called **"Off–West End"** in imitation of New York's "off-Broadway" appellation).

The Lowdown

The West End and the Nationals... "West End" refers to the 50-odd mainstream houses, most of which are in that neighborhood, with a few exceptions. The weird thing about West End is its ever-closer resemblance to New York's Broadway, with productions transferring back and forth across the Atlantic like so much stock from The Gap. To be fair, though, downright West End disappointment usually arises from a combo of overinflated expectations, a large dent in the pocketbook, and a bad pick. The London Les Miserables (nicknamed by some "The Glums") or any of the fifty-three Lloyd Webber monstrosities—sorry, monster hits—will please you as much as a high school production of Fiddler on the Roof, if you hate musicals. Look for the houses that pitch their brow higher—like the Haymarket, the Aldwych, the Arts, the Cambridge, the Comedy, the Garrick, and more. The easiest, safest way to go is to select from the current season at the Royal National Theatre or the Barbican. The latter is where the Royal Shakespeare Company (RSC) has made its home. Many screen stars—from Ralph Fiennes to Patrick Stewart (Captain Picard!) earned their stripes on this legitimate stage, and an RSC production practically comes with a warranty. The other guaranteed ticket is to the South Bank Centre's Olivier or Lyttelton. Less so the South Bank's "theatre-in-the-round" studio, the Cottesloe, where embarrassing juvenilia alternates with exciting edge-of-the-seat new talent.

On the fringe... The fringe denotes all the other theaters—about the same number again. It's where the exciting stuff is—where the much-vaunted British reverence for the stage is still at large. The best of the ones known nowadays as "Off–West End" do theater as it might have been in its premovie heyday—with passion, conviction, infectious adoration of the medium. Those with the best track record for supplying chills of awe are the **Almeida**, the **Bush**, the little **Gate**, the **Riverside**, the **Donmar Warehouse** (actually West End, but nobody remembers), and the increasingly yummy **Young Vic**. The Almeida demands a trek north, but this place hardly ever misses—it's worth it. Others often worth traveling for include the **Theatre**

Royal Stratford East, the **Battersea Arts Centre**, that beauteous old music hall, the **Hackney Empire**, and the Kilburn **Tricycle**. Don't overlook the **Royal Court Theatre Upstairs** or the **Lyric Studio**, which are the factory outlets of their West End selves, mounting works experimental, debut, or in-the-round, while the theater at the redoubtable **Institute of Contemporary Arts** is exactly as it sounds—avant-garde, yet slightly worthy. Many is the show we've endured here in the name of art.

Way out on the fringe... With little fringe places, usually secreted above pubs, behind cafés or way out in the sticks, you're on your own. Quality, degree of professionalism, amount of scenery, size of audience—everything is so utterly variable that generalization would be foolish and misleading. If they're good enough for long enough, they get sucked into the "Off–West End" list, like the Gate, the Bush, and the Almeida's neighbor, the original pub theater, the **King's Head**. However, there are a few pub joints that enjoy a good reputation: the Battersea **Latchmere,** the Chelsea **Man in the Moon**, the Islington **Old Red Lion**, for instance, are long-standing. We've also cried real tears and/or laughed till we were sick at the **Canal Café Theatre** (in lovely Little Venice—a plus) and the **DOC** (for Duke of Cambridge) **Theatre Club**, though this may have been serendipitous, and can in theory happen in any London fringe theater.

Verdi to Schnittke... As it seems to be everywhere these days, opera is big in London. A first night at the **Royal Opera House** is one hot ticket, but every bit as good as the Royal Opera is the **English National Opera**, which lives at the Coliseum, off Trafalgar Square. The main differences are that the ENO costs less to see and performers sing in English. The Royal Opera gets more of the ultimate stars, and projects "surtitles" over the stage. The ENO is far more likely to mount Philip Glass or Schnittke or Janáček, while the House will be first with your Wagner. Another theater with an opera program is the Islington **Sadler's Wells**, which is where to find the D'Oyly Carte, founded by the Englishissimo Gilbert and Sullivan, and still churning out *The Yeomen of the Guard, The Pirates of Penzance,* et al, plus other people's operettas. If the music is not your top priority, then don't pass up the **Holland Park Open Air Theatre**, wherein little companies stage full-scale productions of *Traviata* and *Tosca*—and *The Yeomen of the Guard*—accompanied by the bedtime screeches of peacocks and a Technicolor sunset.

Mozart to Martinu... Indigenous world-famous orchestras and ensembles include the Royal Philharmonic Orchestra—which plays at home in the **Royal Festival Hall**—and the less glamorous London Symphony Orchestra, which lives at the **Barbican** with the English Chamber Orchestra. You'll find a lot of Henry Purcell and Thomas Tallis around—not just because they're English, but because Baroque is in vogue. As for venues...a lot goes on in a few places. Between them, the **South Bank Centre** and the **Barbican** have most of the major recitals and concerts sewn up, the former with its set of three halls of diminishing size—the **Royal Festival Hall**, the **Queen Elizabeth Hall**, and the **Purcell Room**. Other than these there's the glorious **Wigmore Hall** behind Oxford Street, and the aforementioned (in Diversions) **Albert Hall**, which is most remarkable for the wonderful summer series of Henry Wood Promenade Concerts, or Proms. Good for a gentle evening is a recital at one of these two historic houses: Holland Park's **Leighton House** and Hampstead's **Burgh House**.

Pew music... Some of the major classical music venues, and certainly the most numerous, are churches. A few, like the leader of the pack, **St. John's Smith Square**, are deconsecrated; others, including the other big cheese, **St. Martin-in-the-Fields**, retain their pasture, and operate a double life as house of entertainment/house of God. (The latter spawned the famous Baroque ensemble, the Academy of St. Martin-in-the-Fields, by the way.) Others of the genre include several churches in the city, like **St. Giles in the Barbican** and Wren's **St. James's Garlickhythe**, plus the Piccadilly Wren with the plastic spire (OK, fiberglass), **St. James's**. **Southwark Cathedral** is a major venue, and look out for the program at Nicholas Hawksmoor's **Christ Church, Spitalfields,** because the building's as glorious as the music. There's a very good festival there in June. Concerts in churches, by the way, are big bargains—and often they're entirely free, especially at lunchtime.

The dance... This city's up there with the best, in both the classical and young choreographer departments. The ballet is biggest and glossiest when given by The Royal Ballet at the **Royal Opera House**. Stars they own include Irek Mikhamedov and Darcey Bussell, but visiting feet dance here, too, as they do at the other big ballet place, **Sadler's Wells**, where there's also flamenco and tango and whichever specialty dancers are dropping by. If you prefer newer stuff, look out for dance festivals, like the summer Dance Umbrella and the springtime Spring Loaded and the Islington Dance Festival; get the program from **The Place**, which is the center of new dance.

Ha ha ha ha... There are tons of places to catch the funny folks, including the one that kicked off the thing called "alternative comedy," which became the mainstream in the eighties (and still is), the **Comedy Store**. Since way before *Monty Python*, Britain has had a special affinity for comedy, but we will attempt no explanation of the scene, nor of the British sense of humor. You'll have to figure it all out yourself using *Time Out*'s exhaustive comedy listings.

Jolly good sports... On the whole, Londoners like watching other people do sports more than they like exerting themselves. One of the best sports to watch is football (soccer). London has three clubs in the elite Premier League. Catch **Spurs** (Tottenham Hotspurs) at **White Hart Lane**, or **Arsenal** or **Chelsea** at their respective grounds. Rumors about football hooliganism have been greatly exaggerated, although it is true that Chelsea fans like to chant "you're going home in a London ambulance" to the opposing side's fans. By comparison, cricket is as genteel as the afternoon tea that stops play at 4pm. See the quintessential English game at **Lord's** or **The Oval**. On the violence scale, rugby falls somewhere in between. The game's like gridiron without padding; the players are known for singing ditties with filthy lyrics ("rugby songs") in the showers and for their large quadriceps. It's an upperclass sport played at public (read exclusive, private) school, and also the passion of the entire Welsh nation. The 13-a-side professional game's Rugby League Final is played at **Wembley Stadium**; the purists' preferred (it's a bit like American League/National League favoritism) 15-a-side amateur Rugby Union, a.k.a. rugger, is played at **Twickenham**. What everybody wants during the last week of June and first week of July is **Wimbledon** tickets. Well, sorry, but those are allocated on a lottery system in January.

However, during the first week, it's a cinch to see grand slam, big-shot players up close on the outer courts.

The Index

Albert Hall. See Diversions.

Aldwych. A West End theater.... *Tel 0171/416–6003. The Aldwych WC2, Covent Garden tube stop.*

Almeida. Possibly London's best Off–West End theater; it's always exciting, once you've tracked it down.... *Tel 0171/ 359–4404. Almeida St. N1, Angel tube stop.*

Arsenal Football Club. Emotions run high for all the soccer teams, but Arsenal fans may be the most fanatical of all.... *Tel 0171/359–0131. Avenell Rd. Highbury N5, Highbury and Islington tube stop. Season runs August–May.*

Arts Theatre. A West End theater.... *Tel 0171/836–2132. 6–7 Great Newport St. WC2, Leicester Square tube stop.*

Barbican Arts Centre. This major arts center's two theaters are home to the Royal Shakespeare Company, its auditorium to the London Symphony Orchestra and English Chamber Orchestra.... *Tel 0171/638–8891; 24-hr info: music 0171/638–4141, RSC 0171/628–2295. Silk St. EC2, Barbican/ Moorgate tube stop.*

Battersea Arts Centre. A.k.a. the BAC—a long way out, but often worth it.... *Tel 0171/223–2223. 176 Lavender Hill SW11, Clapham Junction BR.*

Burgh House. An elegant Hampstead chamber music venue.... *Tel 0171/431–0144. New End Square NW3, Hampstead tube stop.*

Bush. Off–West End venue with sometimes controversial tastes.... *Tel 0181/743–3388. Shepherds Bush Green W12, Goldhawk Rd. tube stop.*

Christ Church Spitalfields. Nicholas Hawksmoor's church is being renovated, but it still gives concerts.... *Tel 0171/377–0287. Commercial St. E1, Old Gate East tube stop.*

Coliseum. Home of the English National Opera.... *Tel 0171/632–8300, 0171/240–5258 (credit card reservations). St. Martin's Lane WC2, Charing Cross tube stop.*

Cambridge. A West End theater.... *Tel 0171/494–5080. Earlham St. WC2, Covent Garden tube stop.*

Chelsea Football Club. Wear dark blue to see a match at the most geographically accessible London soccer ground.... *Tel 0171/385–5545. Stamford Bridge, Fulham Rd. SW6, Fulham Broadway tube stop.*

Comedy Store. The first—and if not the best, at least one of the most reliable—of the funny clubs.... *Tel 0142/691–4433 (info), 0171/344–4444 (credit card reservations). Haymarket House, Oxendon St. SW1, Piccadilly Circus tube stop.*

Comedy Theatre. A West End theater.... *Tel 0171/369–1731. Panton St. SW1, Piccadilly Circus tube stop.*

Canal Café Theatre. Its Little Venice waterside location is a bonus; there's a late cabaret after the play.... *Tel 0171/289–6054. Bridge House, Delamere Terrace W2, Warwick Ave. tube stop.*

Cottesloe. See National Theatre.

DOC Theatre Club. This sometimes great fringe group plays—often Ibsen—above a north London pub.... *Tel 0171/485–4303. Duke of Cambridge, 64 Lawford Rd. NW5, Kentish Town tube stop.*

Donmar Warehouse. Is it West End? Is it Off? Is it fringe? Cabaret? Who cares—this central place nearly always has something good on.... *Tel 0171/369–1732. Thomas Neal's, Earlham St. WC2, Covent Garden tube stop.*

Garrick. A West End theater.... *Tel 0171/494–5085. Charing Cross Rd. WC2, Leicester Square tube stop.*

Gate. This tiny, ambitious, and well-known theater has been around forever.... *Tel 0171/229–0706. 11 Pembridge Rd. W11, Notting Hill Gate tube stop.*

The Grace Theater at Latchmere Pub. Above the Latchmere pub in Battersea is this very good fringe theater.... *Tel 0171/228–2620. 503 Battersea Park Rd. SW11, Clapham Junction BR.*

Greenwich Theatre. A West End theater, far from the West End.... *Tel 0181/858–7755. Crooms Hill SE10, Greenwich BR.*

Hackney Empire. A loverly old theater in the East End, where a lot of comedy happens—also plays and music.... *Tel 0181/985–2424. 291 Mare St. E8, Hackney Central BR.*

Haymarket Theatre Royal. A West End theater.... *Tel 0171/ 930–8800. Haymarket SW1, Piccadilly Circus tube stop.*

Holland Park Open Air Theatre. The cutest stage in town is in the ruins of a Jacobean mansion.... *Tel 0171/602– 7856. Holland Park W8, Holland Park tube stop. Apr–Sept.*

Institute of Contemporary Art (ICA). The theater at the Institute of Contemporary Arts stages performance pieces, lectures, dance and bizarre hybrids of same.... *Tel 0171/930–3647. The Mall SW1, Charing Cross tube stop.*

Jackson's Lane. A place in the north for dance, usually non-indigenous, with a community feel.... *Tel 0181/340–5226. Jackson's Lane N6, Highgate tube stop.*

King's Head. A very long-standing pub theater; at this one you can drink during the play.... *Tel 0171/226–1916. 115 Upper St. N1, Highbury & Islington/Angel tube stops.*

Leighton House. Hear chamber music in Victorian splendor.... *Tel 0171/602–3316. 12 Holland Park Rd. W14, Kensington High St. tube stop.*

Lilian Baylis Theatre. A dance specialist in Islington.... *Tel 0171/713–6000. Arlington Way EC1, Angel tube stop.*

Lords. The hallowed turf of British cricket since 1811.... *Tel 0171/289–1611. St. John's Wood NW8, St. John's Wood tube stop.*

Lyric. It's a West End theater, though it's in Hammersmith.... *Tel 0181/741–2311, 0171/836–3464 (ticket agency). King St. W6, Hammersmith tube stop.*

Lyric Studio. The experimental version of the above.... *Tel 0181/741–8701.*

Lyttelton. See National Theatre.

Man in the Moon. Another pub fringe theater, this one in Chelsea.... *Tel 0171/351–2876. 392 Kings Rd. SW3, Sloane Square tube stop, then 11 or 22 bus.*

National Theatre. The South Bank Centre's trio of theaters (Olivier, Lyttelton, Cottesloe) are the playgrounds for the occasionally star-flecked, ever-changing, nearly always brilliant Royal National Theatre Company.... *Tel 0171/928–2252. South Bank SE1, Waterloo tube stop.*

Old Red Lion. Here's yet another pub theater in Islington, this one conveniently close to the tube stop.... *Tel 0171/837–7816. St. John's St. N1, Angel tube stop.*

Old Vic. West End, but off the path, this theater stages consistent crowd-pleasers.... *Tel 0171/928–7616. Waterloo Rd. SE1, Waterloo tube stop.*

Olivier. See National Theatre.

Oval. The not-quite-as-hallowed-as-Lords turf of British cricket.... *Tel 0171/582–6660. Kennington Oval SE11, Oval tube stop.*

The Place. This is the place for contemporary dance—practically the center of the world for it.... *Tel 0171/387–0031. 17 Duke's Rd. WC1, Euston tube stop.*

Purcell Room. See South Bank Centre.

Queen Elizabeth Hall. See South Bank Centre.

The Riverside. Hidden by the Thames near Hammersmith Bridge is this happening arts complex.... *Tel 0181/748–3354. Crisp Rd. W6, Hammersmith tube stop.*

Royal Court. This West End theater made its name on ground-breaking programming (e.g., Osborne's *Look Back in Anger*).... *Tel 0171/730–1745. Sloane Square SW1, Sloane Square tube stop.*

Royal Court Theatre Upstairs. The still-groundbreaking studio version of the above stages all new plays.... *Tel 0171/730–2554.*

Royal Festival Hall. See South Bank Centre.

Royal Opera House. Where the Royal Opera Company and Royal Ballet both live. Expensive, world-class.... *Tel 0171/304–4000. Bow St. WC2, Covent Garden tube stop.*

Sadler's Wells. This Islington theater is best known for dance but also transfers European theater and music productions.... *Tel 0171/278–8916. Rosebery Ave. EC1, Angel tube stop.*

St. Giles in the Barbican. A City church with a classical concert program.... *No phone. Fore St., EC2, Barbican tube stop.*

St. James's Garlickhythe. See Diversions.

St. James's Piccadilly. See Diversions.

St. John's Smith Square. BBC Radio often broadcasts concerts from this deconsecrated church, the major minor concert hall.... *Tel 0171/222–1061. Smith Square SW1, Westminster tube stop.*

St. Martin-in-the-Fields. Beautiful church, beautiful music. See if you can catch the Academy of St. Martin-in-the-Fields on their home turf.... *Tel 0171/839–8362. Trafalgar Square WC2, Charing Cross tube stop.*

South Bank Centre. The center of mainstream-but-still-good—often really good—theater (see National Theatre, above), and classical music at the three concert halls (Royal Festival and Queen Elizabeth Halls, Purcell Room).... *Tel 0171/928–8800. South Bank SE1, Waterloo tube stop.*

Southwark Cathedral. London's oldest church after Westminster Abbey has a concert program...See Diversions.

Theatre Royal Stratford East. This Off–West End theater is hit-or-miss, since it stages a lot of brand-new work and young playwrights' stuff. When it hits, it's great.... *Tel 0181/534–0310. Gerry Raffles Square E15. Stratford tube stop.*

Tricycle. This well-loved Off–West End theater almost closed due to lack of funds but now thrives again.... *Tel 0171/328–1000. 269 Kilburn High Rd. NW6, Kilburn tube stop.*

Twickenham. The Rugby Union valhalla where the Pilkington Cup is fought in early May.... *Tel 0181/892–8161. Whitton Rd., Twickenham Middx. Season runs Sept–Apr.*

Wembley Stadium. The FA (Football Association) Cup Final is fought here, as is the Rugby League (as opposed to the Union) Silk Cut Trophy. Since you'll never get tickets to either, go see another match at this 70,000-seater.... *Tel 0181/902–8833. Wembley Middx. HA9.*

White Hart Lane. Home of the Spurs—the Tottenham Hotspur footy team.... *Tel 0181/808–3030. 748 High Rd. N17, Turnpike Lane tube stop.*

Wigmore Hall. This lovely, recently restored concert hall behind Oxford Street has a really accessible program.... *Tel 0171/935–2141. 36 Wigmore St. W1, Bond Street tube stop.*

Wimbledon. For a chance at tickets to the tennis tournament, write with a SASE from Oct. to Dec., or call the info line during the fortnight (last week of June, first week of July).... *Tel 0181/946–2244; 0183/912–3417 (info line, 48p charged per minute prime; 38p off hours. See Hotlines chapter for rates). All England Lawn Tennis & Croquet Club, Box 98, Church Rd., Wimbledon SW19 5AE, Southfields tube stop.*

Young Vic. An excellent Off–West End theater with two auditoria.... *Tel 0171/928–6363. 66 The Cut SE1, Waterloo tube stop.*

hotlines & other basics

Airports... The one you'll almost definitely land at is **Heathrow**, from which central London is a 40–60 minute journey by tube. Take the Piccadilly Line for just over £3 to central London. By changing lines, you can get virtually anywhere without rising above ground, but if you have heavy bags, the sometimes endless walks between lines (see **Tube** below) could be a drag. The other cheap way into town is the **Airbus**. Both routes, A1 (to Victoria) and A2 (to Russell Square) depart all four terminals every 15–30 minutes, take about an hour, and cost £6 one-way. The buses run 6:30am–8pm; the tube about 5am–midnight; after that you'll have to take a **taxi**, for around £35, plus tip. There is one more option that not many people know about: tell the information desk you want a **minicab** into London. They keep a secret list of local firms, with whom a trip into central London is more like £20–25.

There's a slim chance your flight will land at the other main London airport, **Gatwick**, or even at the newest facility, **Stansted**. The **train** is the best way into town from either: the **Gatwick Express** leaves for Victoria Station every 15–30 minutes (every 60 minutes between midnight and 5am), for around £9 one-way, and takes 30–40 mins.

There is also the **Thameslink** train to Kings Cross (north London), Farringdon, Blackfriars and London Bridge (City) every 15–30 minutes (Mon–Sat 4am–11pm, Sun 7am–11pm, for around £10 one-way). The **Stansted Express** leaves for Liverpool Street every half hour, also for £10 one-way.

Whichever airport you leave from, you'll pay a **Departure Tax** of £10 per person on your airline ticket.

The main airlines that fly to London are: **American Airlines** *(tel 800/433–7300)*, **British Airways** *(tel 800/247–9297)*, **Continental** *(tel 800/231–0856)*, **Delta** *(tel 800/241–4141)*, **United** *(tel 800/241–6522)*, **USAir** *(tel 800/428–4322)*, and **Virgin Atlantic** *(tel 800/862–8621)*.

Babysitters... Ask whether your hotel has a preferred local service. Otherwise the **Nanny Service** *(tel 0171/935–3515, 9 Paddington St. W1)* and **Universal Aunts** *(tel 0171/738–8937, 19 The Chase SW4)* are tried and trusted.

Buses... Those red double-deckers, synonymous with London, are the cheapest tourist attraction in town, plus they get you where you want to go... slo-o-wly. During rush hour (approximately 8–9:30am and 4:30–6pm) it's best not to hop on a bus if you're in a hurry; otherwise it's a scenic, if roundabout, way to travel. By no means are all buses double-deckers, but all are hailed the same way—by waiting at the concrete post with a flag-like sign on its top. If the sign is red, it's a "request stop," and you stick out your arm; otherwise the bus stops automatically (unless there isn't room on it). An oblong sign lower down the post illustrates the routes of the buses that stop there, but also check the destination sign in front of the bus, since many fail to run the whole route. Fares are assessed on the same system as for the tube (see below), and **Travelcards** are valid for both modes of transportation. Show your card or pay your coins to the conductor—who often doubles as the driver—and get free bus maps from **Travel Information Centres** at main tube stations.

Car Rental... We strongly advise you not to drive in London. You have to do it on the left, use a stick shift, and park. If you must rent a car, though, your own driver's license is all you'll need (though you could also get an International Driver's Permit from AAA). You'll find **Alamo** *(tel 800/327–9633)*, **Avis** *(tel 800/331–1212)*, **Budget** *(tel 800/527–0700)*, and **Hertz** *(tel 800/654–3131)* at the airports and at other locations in London, charging somewhat higher rates than you may be used to, with unlimited-mileage at around £60–80 per day for a midsize, plus tax, insurance, and extras like collision damage waiver. It's not necessary to make arrangements before you arrive.

Cash... Traveler's checks are worth considering for their safety, best bought in pounds sterling from American Express, Diners Club, or Thomas Cook. If you brought dollars to exchange, do it at banks, which offer the best rates. By far the most convenient method of cash transferral, however, is the ATM, most of which are now tied to international networks—usually **Cirrus** and **Plus**. Make sure your PIN will work, and check your daily withdrawal limit before you leave home. Learn your PIN number as numbers, not a word, since British ATMs show no letters.

Climate... The infamous climate is as unpredictable as you've heard. Summer 1995 (like 1975) saw a long 90-degree-plus heatwave, for instance, and snow is available during an occasional February, but then absent for three straight years. Unless you hit those extremes, you can pretty much count on **rain**—often a soaking, dark-sky drizzle that can go on for days—and mild temperatures, on the cool side (40–50 degrees F) from November through March; hovering around 70 degrees from June to September. For the official London weather forecast, dial 0839/500–951*.

Consulates and Embassies... The **U.S. Embassy** is at 24 Grosvenor Square W1A 1AE, tel 0171/499–9000; the **Canadian High Commission** is nearby at 1 Grosvenor Square, W1, tel 0171/258–6600.

Currency... Pounds sterling and pence are the money here, with notes in denominations of £5, £10, £20, £50 and £100; coins in 1p, 2p, 5p, 10p, 20p, 50p and £1 sizes. The exchange rate hovers around the £1=$1.50 mark.

Dentists... Round-the-clock referral service for dental saviors: tel 0181/677–8383.

Doctors... Doctors on 24-hour call: tel 0181/900–1000. Central London hospitals with 24-hour emergency rooms are: **Charing Cross** *(tel 0181/846–1234, Fulham Palace Rd., Hammersmith W6)*; **Guys** *(tel 0171/407–7600, St. Thomas St. SE1)* and **St. Thomas's** *(tel 0171/928–9292, Lambeth Palace Rd. SE1)*, plus the north **London Royal Free** *(tel 0171/794–0500, Pond St. Hampstead, NW3)*.

Electricity... Different from home, it's 220-volt, 50-cycle AC (alternating current), instead of 110-volt, 60-cycle AC, and the wall outlets accept three-prong plugs. Adapters or transformers are necessary.

Emergencies... Dial 999 (it's a free call) from any phone for police, fire department, or ambulance.

Events Hot Line... Dial 01839/2–3400* for what's on in London this week.

Festivals and Special Events...

January: **1,** The **London Parade**—cheerleaders, floats, marching bands, and the Lord Mayor of Westminster. 12:30–3pm Westminster Bridge—Berkeley Square. **Early–mid-month London International Boat Show** *(Earl's Court, Warwick Rd, SW5; tel 0148/341–8798).* Europe's largest.

February–March: **London Arts Season** packages the arts, with bargain-priced tickets and special events. British Travel Centre *(12 Regent St., SW1; tel 0171/839–6181— number works for Arts Season only).*

March: **Camden Jazz Festival,** for 10 days in north London *(tel 0171/860–5866).*

April: **Oxford & Cambridge Boat Race On the Thames** and the **Nutrasweet London Marathon** *(Box 1234, London SE1 8RZ; tel 0171/620–4117),* see **Diversions** for both.

May: **British Antique Dealers' Association Fair** *(Duke of York's Headquarters, King's Rd., Chelsea SW3; tel 0171/ 589–6108).* **Chelsea Flower Show** *(Chelsea Royal Hospital, Swan Walk, 66 Royal Hospital Rd., SW3; tel 0171/630–7422).* **Football Association FA Cup Final** *(Wembley Stadium; tel 0181/900–1234).*

June: **Trooping the Colour**—the queen's birthday parade on the 4th *(Horse Guards, Whitehall. Ticket Office, Headquarters, Household Division, Chelsea Barracks, London SW1H 8RF; tel 0171/414–2497, or 01839/12—3413*. Send SASE Jan 1–Feb 28 for tickets).*

June–July: **LIFT (London International Festival of Theatre);** tel 0171/490–9964. **Wimbledon Lawn Tennis Championships** *(Church Rd, Wimbledon SW19 5AE; tel 0181/946–2244).*

July: **Hampton Court Palace Flower Show** *(East Molesey, Surrey; tel 0171/630–7422).*

August: **Notting Hill Carnival** *(Portobello Rd., Ladbroke Grove, All Saints Rd.).* Bank Holiday weekend—the big Caribbean extravaganza.

July–September: **Henry Wood Promenade Concerts** (the Proms) *(Royal Albert Hall, Kensington Gore SW7 2AP; tel 0171/589–8212)*.

November: **5, Guy Fawkes Day.** The day when the lack of success of a 1605 attempt to blow up the Houses of Parliament is commemmorated with fireworks and bonfires on which effigies of Mr. Fawkes are incinerated.

Lord Mayor's Show. Band, floats, razzmatazz (Guildhall to the Royal Courts of Justice), a fair in Paternoster Square, fireworks on the Thames. *(tel 0171/606–3030, or 01839/12–3413*)*.

December: Christmas tree in Trafalgar Square, many carol-singing sessions; lighting ceremony.

Gay & Lesbian Hot Lines... London Lesbian & Gay Switchboard *(tel 0171/837–7324)*, 24-hour info and advice; **London Lesbian Line** *(tel 0171/251–6911; Tue–Thu 7–10pm, Mon, Fri 2–10pm)*.

Holidays... New Year's Day (Jan 1), Easter (Good Friday, Easter Monday), May Day Bank Holiday (first Mon in May), Spring Bank Holiday (last Mon in May), August Bank Holiday (last Mon in August), Christmas Day & Boxing Day (Dec 25–26).

Hotel Hotline... London Tourist Board's credit-card accommodation booking service *(tel 0171/824–8844)*.

Kids' Hotlines... Kidsline *(tel 0171/222–8070)*.

Newspapers... London drowns in newsprint. The daily broadsheets, or "Qualities," are: the *Times*, the *Guardian*,

Guy Fawkes

Mr. Fawkes and his cronies failed to detonate the Houses of Parliament in the days of James I, and this minor event is still marked with fireworks displays and ritual incinerations of Guy Fawkes effigies, usually made by children, who use discarded teddy bears for their material. Also known as "Bonfire Night," you'll know the fifth of November is imminent when you start seeing said kids out on the streets begging for change ("penny for the Guy," is the traditional line), ostensibly for buying fireworks, though they will probably go to one of the big public displays (see Index). On the night itself, you're meant to recite this ditty:

Remember, remember the fifth of November,
The gunpowder treason and plot.
There isn't a reason why gunpowder treason
Should ever be forgot.

And it hasn't been.

The Independent, *The Daily Telegraph*, and the *Financial Times*, while the awful, but entertaining, tabloids are the *Mirror*, the *Mail*, the egregious *Sun* and even worse *Star*. There is also the valuable evening paper, the *Standard*, out weekdays around lunchtime. Sundays offer a mountain that keeps you occupied all day: the broadsheet *Sunday Times*, *Observer*, *Independent on Sunday*, and *Sunday Telegraph*, and the tabs, the *Sunday Mirror*, *Mail on Sunday*, the *People*, the *News of the World* and—the father of American *Enquirer*-type trash—the unbelievable *Sunday Sport*. Don't be surprised by its high nipple count.

Opening & Closing Times... Banks, Mon–Fri 9:30–3:30, plus Sat morning in some cases. **Shops**, typically Mon–Sat 9–6, with many now open Sun. **Pubs**, Mon–Sat 11am–11pm (some shut 3–5:30pm), Sun noon–3pm, 7–10:30pm (afternoon opening may be allowed by the time you read this). **Museums**, average opening hours are Mon–Sat 10–6, Sun 2–5, but always check, especially during holiday periods. **Post offices**, Mon–Fri 9–5:30, Sat 9–1.

Parking... You've already been warned not to drive, but if you insist, know that parking is hell, thanks to the usual meters and restrictions, and also the dread "Denver Boot," or wheel clamp—an immobilizing device administered by assiduous independent operators, that costs about £120 to get removed. **NCP (National Car Parks)** lots are open throughout London, but they fill up quickly and they're very expensive–£10 for three hours in most places, and up to £15 in others. Parking **on the street** is no less expensive, nor easy. Meters take varying amounts, anywhere from 20p to £1, it must be in coin, and it will usually buy about 20 minutes of time.

Passports & Visas... U.S. and Canadian citizens need a valid passport to enter the U.K. for stays of up to six months.

Pharmacy... Get late-night drugs from **Bliss** *(5 Marble Arch W1; tel 0171/723–6116; open daily 9am–midnight)*.

Postal Service... Mailboxes are rather attractive scarlet cylinders with the times of collection posted on the front. Get stamps from post offices, many newsagents, and shops. Rates at presstime are: 41p for airmail letters (up to 10g) to the U.S.; postcards 35p; within Britain 25p for letters, 19p for second class and postcards. The post office at **Trafalgar Square** *(tel 0171/930–*

9580; 24–28 William IV St. WC2) keeps long hours: Mon–Sat 8–8.

Radio Stations... There are five national radio stations: **1FM**, 98.8FM (mainstream pop music, with some more interesting stuff after 10pm, including John Peel's great indie and alternative show Mon–Thur 10–12); **Radio 2**, 89.1FM (easy listening); **Radio 3**, 91.3FM (classical, some talk); **Radio 4**, 93.5FM, 1500m AM (talk, news, game shows, drama. A beloved national institution, especially *The Archers*—a 30-year-old radio soap about country folk); **Radio 5**, 433m AM (the new one—sports, talk), plus the **World Service**, 463m AM. The principal London stations are: **Capital FM**, 95.8 (pop), **Kiss FM**, 100 (dance/club music; probably the hippest station in town), **JFM**, 102.2 (jazz), **Classics FM**, 100.9 (AOR classical), **GLR**, 94.9 (talk, music), **Capital Gold**, 194m AM (oldies), **Virgin**, 247m AM (pop and rock music), and **London News**, 97.3FM.

Smoking... It's not outlawed, and many more Londoners still smoke than Americans, but smoking is banned on all public transportation.

Standards of Measure... England is supposed to be metric, like the rest of Europe, but you'll see as many feet and inches, pounds and ounces, as meters and centimeters, kilos and grams. Human weight is given in stones and pounds; one stone=14lbs. Clothes sizes: for women, the rule of thumb is to increase one size for English wear across the board; men's suit and shirt sizes are the same. Clothing sizes tend to vary wildly anywhere, however. Shoes are often sold in European sizes. For men: European 41=U.K. 7=U.S. 8. For women: European 41=U.K. 7=U.S. 10.

Subways... See **Tubes.**

Taxes... **Value Added Tax (VAT)** adds 17.5% to many purchases, and is often refundable. See **Shopping** chapter for details. U.K. departure tax is £10 per person (see **Airports**, above).

Taxis... Hail one when the orange "For Hire" light on the roof is lit. An empty one may stop even if its light is off, since drivers sometimes use this method to screen passengers at night. London cabbies are among the best in the world, since they all have an encyclopedic grasp of London's geography, having passed an exhaustive exam called "The Knowledge." Of this they are justly proud;

don't insult your driver by offering directions. Metered fares are £1 for the first 582 yards, rising by 20p per 291 yards or 60 seconds, plus surcharges as follow: after 8pm, 40p; after 12am, 60p; £1 on national holidays. There are also charges for dogs, and if the driver must put a passenger's bag next to him (there are no front passenger seats in London taxis, so most baggage goes there).

Unlicensed taxis, called minicabs, can't be hailed on the street, but must instead be booked by phone or in person at the office. Most hotels and restaurants keep numbers of local services, and will call one for you. Fares are about 25% lower than for black cabs.

When you get that billionaire feeling and a taxi's not enough, step into an **Autofleet** *(tel 0181/941–5288)* Rolls-Royce, Jag, or Mercedes, or a car from **Camelot** *(tel 0171/235–0234)* with a/c and phone; both from about £100/3 hours.

Telephones... Public phones are either those familiar, picturesque scarlet boxes, or else nondescript booths, and accept either coins, or prepaid BT (British Telecommunications) cards, and/or credit cards. **Coin phone boxes** accept 10p as the minimum payment, but will take all coins except 1p pieces. **Cardphones** take BT Cards, which you can buy in units from 10 (£1) to 100 (£10) and more from newsagents and general stores. Slot in the card, and a display shows how much time is left; the card is returned when you replace the receiver. **Credit cards** are used by swiping the magnetic stripe, as at home. The British ring is a double chirrup; repeated short beeps mean the line is busy, and a continuous beep means the number is "unobtainable"—either it's cut off or you dialed the wrong prefix. London numbers are prefixed by 1071 (inner) or 0181 (outer). Leave off the prefix when dialing within the same area. Standard rate is Mon–Fri 8am–6pm; cheap rate 6pm–8am, and weekends. The international access code is 00; for the international operator, credit card, or collect calls, dial 155. For international directory inquiries (information), dial 153; domestic is 192. For the operator, dial 100. Hotels usually whack on a greedy surcharge, so consider using a U.S. calling card. Some access numbers are: **AT&T USA Direct** *(tel 0500/890011)*; **MCI Call USA** *(tel 800/444–4444)*; and **Sprint Express** *(tel 800/877–4646)*.

Tipping... Hotels and restaurants often add a 10%–15% service charge automatically, so think before you pay twice.

Don't tip theater ushers or bartenders. Do tip: washroom attendants (about 20p in the saucer), waiters (15%), taxi and minicab drivers (15%), porters and bellhops (£1 per bag carried), doormen (£1 or two for hailing cabs, etc.), concierges (at your discretion, for exceptional services like procuring difficult theater tickets or dinner reservations), hairdressers, beauty parlor technicians, etc. (15%).

Tours... Sightsee on an open-topped double-decker bus with **London Transport**'s **London Plus** *(tel 0171/828–7395, Apr–Oct daily every half hour 9:30–5:30; Nov–Mar hourly 10–4, from Haymarket, Baker Street, Embankment, Marble Arch, and Victoria)*. Buses make about 21 stops, at which you can get on and off at will; £10 adults, £5 kids. Some of the best walking tours are led by **The Original London Walks** *(tel 0171/624–3978)*. **City Walks** *(tel 0171/700–6931)* and **Streets of London** *(tel 0181/346–9255)* are also reliable. In addition, there are customized tours given by cabbies with "The Knowledge," in **Black Taxi Tours of London** *(tel 0171/224–2833)*, or, if you want to leave London, by **British Tours** *(tel 0171/629–5267)*.

Travelers With Disabilities... Hot lines include the **Artsline** *(tel 0171/388–2227)*, for advice on accessibility of arts events, and the **Holiday Care Service** *(tel 0129/377–4535)* for help with accommodations questions. **London Transport** has a **Unit for Disabled Passengers** *(tel 0171/222–5600)*, which includes the **Stationlink** service, a wheelchair-accessible "midibus" between nine BritRail stations and Victoria Coach Station. **RADAR** (the Royal Association for Disability and Rehabilitation) *(tel 0171/251–3222; 12 City Forum, 250 City Rd., London EC14 8AF)*, publishes travel information for the disabled in Britain.

Tubes... The London subway is the fastest way to get around—usually. There are 11 lines, plus the Docklands Light Railway, and the future Metro Express (Haringey to Wimbledon via Soho and Fulham), which may be on maps already (in pale green). They all run Mon–Sat 5am–12:30am, Sun 7am–11:30pm approx., and the average waiting time is 5–10 minutes. **Tube fares** are assessed in zones, with the price rising according to how many of the six you pass through. The most expensive way to travel is by single ticket (£1–£3.10). It's a far better idea to get a **Travelcard** (from £2.80/day, £1.50 for children), valid all day from 9:30am for tube and bus, or an **LT Card**

(from £3.90\ children £1.90), without time restrictions. For Weekly and Monthly Travelcards, you need a photo, as you do for a **Visitor's Travelcard**, which you get in the U.S. from BritRail Travel International (tel 212/382–3737; 1500 Broadway, New York, NY 10036) (3, 4, or 7 days for $25, $32, or $49; $11, $13, or $21 for children), which includes discount vouchers to London sights. Leaflets explaining ticket types and fare zones, plus tube maps are all available free from tube station ticket windows. You can be fined on the spot for traveling without a valid ticket.

Visitor Information... Before you leave home, contact the **British Tourist Authority**. New York: tel 212/986–2200 or 800/462–2748; 551 5th Ave., Suite 701, New York, NY 10176. Chicago: tel 312/787–0490; Suite 1510, 625 N. Michigan Av, Chicago, IL 60611. Los Angeles: tel 213/628–3525; World Trade Center, 350 S. Figueroa St., Suite 450, Los Angeles, CA 90071. Atlanta: tel 404/432–9635; 2580 Cumberland Pkwy., Suite 470, Atlanta, GA 30339. Toronto: tel 416/925–6326; 111 Avenue Rd., 4th Floor, Toronto, Ontario M5R 3J8 Canada.

When you get to London, the main **Tourist Information Centre** is at Victoria Station Forecourt, Mon–Sat 8–7, Sun 8–5, and there are others at Heathrow Airport (Terminals 1, 2, and 3), and department stores Harrods and Selfridges, all open to personal callers only. For phone information, you have to pay premium rates (49p/min or 39p/min cheap rate) for the **LTB's Visitorcall** phone guide. Get the menu on tel 01839/12–3456*.

While you're in London, round-the-clock information on bus and tube times, routes fares, etc. can be had by calling 0171/222–1234. Also, **Travel Information Centres** are at: Heathrow, Victoria, Piccadilly Circus, Oxford Circus, Euston, and King's Cross stations.

*... All calls with the 01839 prefix are charged at the premium rate of 39p/min; 49p/min during peak time.

FROMMER'S COMPLETE TRAVEL GUIDES

(Comprehensive guides to sightseeing, dining and accommodations,
with selections in all price ranges—from deluxe to budget)

FROMMER'S $-A-DAY GUIDES

(Dream Vacations at Down-to-Earth Prices)

FROMMER'S COMPLETE CITY GUIDES

(Comprehensive guides to sightseeing, dining, and accommodations in all price ranges)

FROMMER'S FAMILY GUIDES

(Guides to family-friendly hotels, restaurants, activities, and attractions)

FROMMER'S WALKING TOURS

(Memorable strolls through colorful and historic neighborhoods, accompanied by detailed directions and maps)

FROMMER'S AMERICA ON WHEELS

(Guides for travelers who are exploring the U.S.A. by car, featuring a brand-new rating system for accommodations and full-color road maps)

FROMMER'S SPECIAL-INTEREST TITLES

Arthur Frommer's Branson!	P107	Frommer's Where to	
Arthur Frommer's New World		Stay U.S.A., 11th Ed.	P102
of Travel (avail. 11/95)	P112	National Park Guide, 29th Ed.	P106
Frommer's Caribbean		USA Today Golf	
Hideaways (avail. 9/95)	P110	Tournament Guide	P113
Frommer's America's 100		USA Today Minor League	
Best-Loved State Parks	P109	Baseball Book	P111

FROMMER'S BEST BEACH VACATIONS

(The top places to sun, stroll, shop, stay, play, party, and swim—with each beach rated for beauty, swimming, sand, and amenities)

California (avail. 10/95)	G100	Hawaii (avail. 10/95)	G102
Florida (avail. 10/95)	G101		

FROMMER'S BED & BREAKFAST GUIDES

(Selective guides with four-color photos and full descriptions of the best inns in each region)

California	B100	Hawaii	B105
Caribbean	B101	Pacific Northwest	B106
East Coast	B102	Rockies	B107
Eastern United States	B103	Southwest	B108
Great American Cities	B104		

FROMMER'S IRREVERENT GUIDES

(Wickedly honest guides for sophisticated travelers and those who want to be)

Chicago (avail. 11/95)	I100	New Orleans (avail. 11/95)	I103
London (avail. 11/95)	I101	San Francisco (avail. 11/95)	I104
Manhattan (avail. 11/95)	I102	Virgin Islands (avail. 11/95)	I105

FROMMER'S DRIVING TOURS

(Four-color photos and detailed maps outlining spectacular scenic driving routes)

Australia	Y100	Italy	Y108
Austria	Y101	Mexico	Y109
Britain	Y102	Scandinavia	Y110
Canada	Y103	Scotland	Y111
Florida	Y104	Spain	Y112
France	Y105	Switzerland	Y113
Germany	Y106	U.S.A.	Y114
Ireland	Y107		

FROMMER'S BORN TO SHOP

(The ultimate travel guides for discriminating shoppers—from cut-rate to couture)

Hong Kong (avail. 11/95)	Z100	London (avail. 11/95)	Z101

irreverent notes

irreverent notes

irreverent notes

irreverent notes

irreverent notes